<u>How To</u>

HERO

The Teenager's Toolkit for Building Self-Esteem

Alyson Reid-Larade

2

Published by Alyson Larade, B.H.K, B.Ed, through CreateSpace Independent Publishing Platform.

Cover design by Scott Fair

Website: www.byoh.ca

I believe this book found its way to you for a reason.

You might not agree with everything you read—that is OK—but

you should stay open to all the possibilities.

I want to challenge your tendency toward habitual thinking.

If you are down, you can't get out of your hole

using the same thought patterns that put you there.

Habitual thinking won't get you very far.

Maybe it's time to shake things up.

Dedicated to every student I've ever taught.
The learning has been mutual.
Thank you.

Thank You

Writing this book has been an incredible journey. It is the culmination of 20 years working with wonderful teenagers, all of them amazing and challenging in their own way. I have learned something new every single day. I've taught many things too. I have received incredible support and gratitude from my students for treating them with dignity and for talking about topics that many teachers didn't talk about. They've thanked me for explaining things in a way they could understand and connect with. They've thanked me for listening to them.

To all my students, each and every one of you, thank you for the opportunity you have given me to be a part of your lives.

I am incredibly grateful to my family, especially to my phenomenal husband, Andre, without whom this book would not have reached the light of day. He has been the number one staff on this project and a constant support for me. To my amazing children, Keogan and Hazel, who have given up too much mom time so I could write. Your support has been incredibly important to me and I was inspired to keep writing so that a book like this would be available to you when you reached your teenage years.

To my co-workers, I have always loved being around all of my fellow educators. I have loved when we could share ideas with each other, whether it was about curriculum or how to handle a challenging situation. I do love that teachers are not in competition with each other. When we understand our main goal is to help create responsible, contributing members of society, we know we are all on the same team. It is wonderful to see how our different strengths and interests help us to reach the wide variety of students we face everyday. No single teaching style could work for every student, but usually every student can find someone they can connect with within our schools.

I would like to thank my best friend Sue, who has been with me through it all. She is my rock, my sounding board and my idol in the classroom.

I would also like to thank Dr. Gordon Neufeld for sharing his insight and wisdom with so many through his courses at the Neufeld Institute, his videos and his book *Hold On To Your Kids.*

Thank you of course to my own parents and to my sisters. You have been so supportive through all of this. Mom and Dad, I am truly sorry for all the crap I put you through when I was a teenager. I cannot thank you enough for helping me see how important it was to Be My Own Hero.

Learning how to lift yourself up is the greatest lesson of all.

Special Thanks to:
All of my students, friends and family, specifically,
Andre Larade, Keogan and Hazel, Glenys Reid, Don Reid,
Andrea Reid, Marci Reid, Susan Ragaisis, Randy Peyser,
Nadine Millet, Jill Lublin, Wayne Logan, Scott Fair, Dr. Gordon
Neufeld, Darlene Swanson, Sheila Kerwin, Angela DiGiacomo,
Cyndi Edwards, Carol Bergeron, Michael Curry, Michael Scott,
Samantha Paquin, Michael Baine, Kathy Soule, Kim Schreider,
Jan Bentham, Thomas Pakenham, Corina Jarret, Olivia Giroux,
Mike Prusakowski, Gavin Cullain, Tracey Major, Jason Major,
Sandra Konji, Michael Moreau, Dominique Dauost, Melissa
Creede, Camelia Touzany and Mathilde Levasseur.
Thanks to all the students who bravely shared their experiences.
And thanks to all the Student Artists who submitted art work.

Chapters

Introduction

Table of Contents

INTRODUCTION

Artist: Joy Doonan

I have one question for you:
Do you want life to get better?
If your answer is yes, then read on.

The Truth

This is what I know about you:

- You are amazing
- There is incredible resilience in you
- There is inner peace and true happiness inside of you
- There are incredible skills, talents and strengths inside you
- These skills, talents, and strengths you possess are a gift to the world

You may not feel any of this yet, but it is all there, waiting for you to discover.

Uncovering all of these qualities involves a journey. Should you choose to take it, it will be the most worthwhile journey of your life.

Some people live their whole lives and never take this journey – that is sad. It's sad because it means they never reach their full potential and never have any lasting success, peace or joy in their lives. You probably know some of them. They are the constant naysayers.

It's time for you to make a decision. Join them or move forward. Going on this journey is your choice.

If you want to move forward, this book will help you do that. Many tips and tools are here. Consider it to be one of the many helpers that will accompany you on your journey.

What you must supply is the perseverance, the determination, the grit. Moving forward is not the same as moving on, getting older or simply allowing time to pass. Moving forward is taking action to make your life better.

No one else can do it for you.

You will be tempted to give up when the going gets tough. When that temptation arises, ask yourself these questions:

Do I want my life to get better?

Do I want the lives of others to get better?

If you can continue to answer these questions with a firm YES, then move forward.

Step one is to realize your starting point. To do that you need to take a hard look at where you are now.

Look Within

Do you sometimes feel frustrated or sad?

Good. That is an important starting point. Seriously. These negative feelings are normal, they are life's way of telling you that you are in transition.

The teenage years are full of change. You enter as a child and you leave as an adult. This is one of life's biggest transition times. New experiences, new awareness, can be exciting, or disappointing, frustrating, or even scary. As a teen, you are having new experiences regularly. And you will also make many mistakes navigating through these new experiences. No one is perfect.

Don't be afraid of your sadness or your frustration. Feelings are meant to be felt. Don't make the all too common mistake of trying to avoid these feelings. In Chapter 8, we'll discuss people who actually can't feel feelings as a result of experiencing extreme pain. They become hard and numb. The problem with being numb is that happiness is also a feeling they become numb to.

Your feelings are important and can help guide you. Note: If you feel negatively most or all of the time, or if you already feel numb, these are messages to you that you are off track. You will find helpful information in Chapter 8 on Vice Grips.

Feelings help to wake us up, to allow us to feel alive, they are motivating. If everything was perfect in your life, then you would have no desire to make one single change. This would also take away your resilience, your ability to *adapt* to change. Everyone needs motivation to adapt to changes, to take action. If you want life to get better, then let these negative feelings motivate you to make positive changes.

Maybe you don't have negative feelings every day. Maybe it's just once in a while. You don't have to be unhappy about *everything* in your life; maybe you're unhappy just in one area. Maybe it's your school, friends, romantic partner or lack of one, pressure about your future, issues with drugs or alcohol, body image, social media image, and/or so many more. Don't hide from your sadness and anger or try to suppress it. Feel it. Learn from it. Then release it.

Unhappiness, even in a small area of your life, can give you the motivation to evolve, to learn and adapt in this transition stage of life. It helps you to move onto a better path. Yes, I'm talking about your life.

One could stay here of course, in this sad or angry place. So many people do. Complaining, but not really taking any action to change their situation. They get into a habit of either 1) identifying with their pain, attaching to it, or 2) ignoring the feelings, not releasing them and not learning from them. Either way, they are doomed to repeat the same mistakes over and over.

Another option is to view this sad or angry place you are in as a temporary stage of internal adjustment. Viewing it as your *starting* point on your path to a better life.

Stop Chasing Happy and Just Be

You are supposed to be happy (but not 100% of the time.) Consider it your default setting. Look at a child playing, and you'll see our natural state. Unfortunately, it is easy to condition yourself to focus on pain and sadness and anger, and move farther away from your happy setting.

Do you find yourself getting upset because things aren't working out perfectly? If you focus on perfection, you will always get the pain and sadness, you will always see the shortcomings that are not perfection. But you are missing the point. There is no perfect life.

None of us can be great all of the time. It is from the not-so-great times that we learn about ourselves and how we can improve.

Happiness is in your face everywhere you go. It's in ads, posters, commercials, videos, movies, but that happiness is fake. It's manufactured, and it leaves us longing, comparing ourselves to this happy mirage, chasing it – chasing happiness.

It's time to stop chasing happy. That just makes us unhappy.

Life gets better as you age, but that isn't always the case for everyone.

Take charge. You have a choice to make every day: You can choose to complain, lay blame on others for what's going on in your life, and feel sorry for yourself, OR, you can accept your current situation *as a starting point* and decide to make positive changes so your life is set on a new path.

The actions you take or don't take are up to you, but, remember, the only winner – or loser – in this game is you. Many people go through life angry. They aim their anger at other people. But, the anger they carry is really hurting one person more than any other – themselves.

The anger begins as frustration. Frustration is meant to move to sadness and then be released. If it isn't recognized and released, frustration can get sealed up in anger and then directed at others and/or internalized, where it festers inside and builds on itself, and then, either way, that person winds up hating themselves.

Even worse is the reality that so many teens contemplate suicide. Have you ever perceived life to be so hard that you can't go on?

***

| 0 | 50 | 100 |

Consider the timeline above. If zero is birth and one hundred represents the end of a long life, consider how few years you spend as a teenager (***). This rollercoaster of fabulous times and horrible times are just a handful of years. There is so much more to life than what you have experienced so far, as a teenager.

Don't get me wrong – some people do live very tough lives. It is true that many adults are very unhappy, often angry. This is probably because of a deep unresolved pain. When feelings are left unresolved, especially if it's because of a situation that you think is out of your control, you may begin to feel that you are a victim of circumstance. If you never deal with your pain, you cannot change your mindset. If you always believe you are the victim of circumstance, then the events in your life will often be perceived as negative. And so, you find yourself in a downward spiral.

You are not a victim of circumstance. You are in control of how you perceive your life, and once you have a broad perspective, you can make better decisions for improving your life.

You are the creator of your life story.

Many teens tell me, "But the high school years are the best years of your life!" Look at the timeline again. How can a teenager, possibly know that? If an adult has told you this little "pearl of wisdom," in my opinion, that's a pretty sad adult.

I have met many teenagers who follow in the tracks of those sad adults, turning to extremes to enjoy a "fast life" of overindulging in drinking, sex, drugs, crime, etc., because, they think, "Hell, life is over once you hit twenty, anyway, so I may as well live it up now." In other words, they wholeheartedly believe that their teen years will be the best years of their life, and any other years after will never come close.

Unfortunately, this way of thinking about their youth creates situations that can lead to a very hard life in their future, filled with addictions, criminal records, teenage pregnancies, and/or disconnection from their family. All of these come with *lifelong* complications and these teens end up creating the crappy future that they had imagined. It does not have to be this way.

With a shift in thinking, you can learn to make good decisions. Any wise decisions you make will bring the best outcomes for you so that you can enjoy every stage that life has to offer.

Life is not only a road of heartaches and pain, but also of joy, excitement, and fulfillment. Sure, there will be ups and downs, but the lows are not the toilet-bowl-downward-spirals you might have been feeling.

There is one point of focus. It might seem small, but once you see it in action, you'll understand why it's the most important card in your deck. It's the biggest factor in your smooth transitions through the teenage years and beyond. This point of focus is called Self-Esteem. This single aspect of you is the underlying source for every decision you make now and every decision you will ever make in your life.

I suppose it's time I introduce myself. I am a high school teacher.

If you had told me, back when I was in high school, that I would become a teacher, I would have laughed my ass off. I figured I'd be a sports doctor, and, on route to that goal, I started my first career as a kinesiologist (a specialist in exercise science and injury rehabilitation), before shocking myself with having an interest in teaching. Entering this next career was the best decision I ever made.

As a Physical Education/Health & Science teacher, I have been discussing the topic of self-esteem with teenagers for more than twenty years. It has always amazed me how the concepts we discuss seem so surprising to them. Over the years, I have had the opportunity to watch, talk with, and listen to many teenagers. I have seen far too many teenagers who are caught in a self-defeating spiral caused by their low self-esteem.

Fortunately, I have also met many teenagers who, despite many hardships, have managed to keep their heads on straight. Their healthy outlook has prevented them from getting caught up in poor decisions that would have caused them pain, and, therefore, they have been going through life a little easier than others. It is obvious to me that they have a strong sense of who they are, and they carry that with them wherever they go. They are not cocky or full of themselves. They routinely connect with healthy supportive adults, put challenges into perspective, think positively, and make better decisions. Not all of the time, but most of the time.

At first glance, there is no way of categorizing teens into one group or the other. Both groups are found in all social circles. I am fascinated by both mentalities, and I want to show the first group how the second group makes decisions. It really comes down to who they seek as guides and how they view their own worth – which is their self-esteem.

As a teacher, I am constantly reminded that there is always a lot more going on in students' lives than just their education. I am not a psychologist, but I am a passionate teacher who has been fortunate enough to really reach a lot of students (not all, but most). I have been very real with my students and always treated them as the adults they are becoming. I don't candy coat anything, and for my efforts and caring, I receive the most wonderful reward: trust. I have had so many students come talk to me about their personal lives. They come in to talk about their parents divorcing, how they want to quit school, about how they are afraid to tell their parents they got their girlfriend pregnant. They want to talk about how they got an STD after having sex for the first time. They talk about their fears of being gay, frequent fights with their parents, having an eating disorder, their drug and alcohol problems, and fears of being pregnant. They drop in to tell me they won't be in class tomorrow because they'll be getting an abortion.

I don't teach in a strange, underprivileged school. I teach in an average school, with average teens.

The lives of teenagers are tough. But, not all students get into trouble, and as you've read, the ticket to an easier ride comes down to one thing: self-esteem. Now, I know what you are thinking: "Well, of course I have poor self-esteem. My grades are never good enough, my family life sucks, I can't trust my friends, and every movie or video I watch makes me feel dumb, ugly, fat or scrawny. I don't have a clue what career I want when I grow up, I feel like everyone is judging me, social comments online can ruin my day, I'm getting "spontaneous erections" in class or "surprise periods," and I have pimples. So, how the hell am I supposed to feel good about myself?"

It is possible; believe it. It's true, and I'll show you how you can see your world in a whole new way. In fact, I'll help you see that if you *don't* fix up how you feel on the inside, then you can't expect good things to happen on the outside and an improvement in your everyday life. The good news is, with the right guides and tools, a positive transition is completely within your grasp.

Now, some of you will have a lot more work ahead of you than others. If you've come from a positive, caring family and have experienced few traumatic events, you may have still learned to feel crappy about yourself, but changing that will be easier than if you are a teen who comes from a family of neglect and negativity, or if you have experienced multiple traumatic events. If you are from the second group, your journey will be longer, but more amazing and rewarding than you could possibly imagine, as you select positive guides and heal yourself from the inside, like a caterpillar transforming into a butterfly.

Let's start the journey with one phrase. Feel free to dog-ear this page or highlight this next line and revisit it when you feel the need to be reminded. Here we go:

You are in control of your own happiness.

This is lesson number one. I'll say it again.

You are in control of your own happiness.

Now that statement might be hard to swallow. Sometimes happiness is found on a more mindful path, through the profound act of changing your mindset. But Sometimes the path to happiness is to move through the thick of deep frustration and sadness, moving to tears to come out on the other side, more joyful and calm. You are about to begin an exploration of self and self-improvement, because, well, no one else can improve you. You *are* your own hero, but you don't have to do it alone. Life was never meant to be lived alone. Helpful people are all around you. If you are far from where you want to be, then getting help will be necessary. The further you are from your goal, the more support you will need. Once you are open to the possibility of being happy again, you will see that support is available. But, remember, *you* are in control of *your* happiness. It is up to you to make the necessary changes. It is up to you to seek the support and accept the help. It is up to you to shift paths. It is all up to you. People close to you, like your family and friends, want you to feel happy, but if you are not willing or ready, the changes will not happen. No matter what anyone else wants for you, the happiness is a state of mind that only *you* can invite.

We are creatures of habit if we don't actively make changes. The faulty self-defeating thoughts and actions I observe in many teens are not limited to teens alone. So many adults, many of them parents, also have the same self-defeating habits, but they truly are *habits* in the adult years. Many of the worst problems in our societies stem from these habits. I am offering you an invitation to change your thinking while you are still young. I want to show you that you can make a huge, positive difference in your own life and the lives of those around you, and then you can make *this* your lifelong habit.

There are many things in this book that will frustrate you, even anger you. At some passages, you'll quickly respond defensively and may feel insulted. Remember, this book is here to challenge you. As Einstein said, "We cannot solve our problems with the same thinking we used when we created them." Now, you may not have been the one that created your problems, but the point is, allow yourself to be open-minded. Change is necessary. You'll have to step outside of your comfort zone. In order to better your life, you must better your beliefs, better your thoughts, and better your actions.

A Decide-For-Yourself Book

Not *everything* in this book applies to *every* teen, but there is *something* here for *every* teen. Whether you are a guy or girl, straight or gay, single or dating, A+ student or on the verge of dropping out of school, happy-go-lucky or suicidal, this book is packed with tips that can strengthen you and help you steer yourself clear of self-destructive decisions. It is set up as a decide-for-yourself kind of a book. You can choose your path by deciding which chapters apply to you. You should definitely read the first three chapters plus the last three chapters. Those are critical and apply to everyone. As for the middle chapters, you can choose the ones that deal with the issues that are specific to your life. Keep in mind that the chapters are connected and are best read in order, but it's not necessary to read every one, if the issues do not apply to you, right now.

A Guide to the Chapters

Chapters 1, 2, 3, and 8, 9, 10 are for *every reader*.

Chapters 4, 5, 6 and 7 are optional (**) as they deal with specific areas in your life.

I hope you read them all!

Chapter 1 explains how important self-esteem really is. It also uncovers the reality of false esteem. Once you understand false esteem, you'll be able to recognize it in others wherever you go. You'll also be able to recognize true esteem and to understand the value of healthy self-esteem. This chapter begins your journey and helps you to recognize when you are on the right track. This chapter will get deep inside your developing brain. We'll look at the neuroscience that explains what has been changing in your teenage brain, which will give you a new perspective on your decisions and responses.

Chapter 2 shows you the many faces of low self-esteem. It outlines the ways that people fill their inner void. You see how constant distraction, attention and/or power-seeking behaviors become a habit for those who do not have true esteem. This chapter helps you let go of comparing yourself to others. It will remind you that everyone has struggles, and they show up in many different ways. As you gain understanding, not only will you perceive yourself differently, but you will perceive everyone around you differently, which will help you walk with your head held higher.

Chapter 3 is one of the most important chapters. It deals with stress and coping strategies. It takes you inside the Emotional Trio called ASA (Anxiety, Sadness, and Anger). It will get into the physiology of stress and where these emotions come from. This chapter helps you to take a look at your current coping strategies when times get tough and will help you figure out if these strategies help to improve your situation or keep you down. It will show you the bird's-eye, big-picture view of the coping strategies you use and how they become lifelong habits. You will also learn what it means to externalize or internalize your stress, and how to deal with it so you stop taking your problems out on others and/or punishing yourself. This chapter shows you healthy, positive strategies to try out and use to deal with your ASA.

** Chapter 4 is for those of you who are having a tough time with friends, family issues, school, and/or figuring out what career path to follow. This chapter helps you to understand the importance of healing your relationships and standing up for yourself. It will give you tools to deal with toxic friends. It will uncover ways to stand up to toxic friends who bully you as much as they hang out with you. It deals with the bully circle, namely, who is involved in the bullying and how to understand them, so you can help stop the cycle.

This chapter also gives you a glimpse into the minds of your parents, so you can start to understand why they do the things they do. You may be able to appreciate rules. I'm not saying you will start to like them, but you will understand the value of them, which will make them easier to follow and decrease the conflicts at home and at school.

You will read tips on how to win arguments and earn some much-needed freedom. Yes, it's possible – not all the time, but some of the time.

This chapter also attempts to uncover the sometimes elusive "relevance of school." You'll read some tips on doing better in school and on using classroom topics to help you find some potential career paths. You'll even get some tips for using your career path – whatever you may choose – to make the world a better place.

** Chapter 5 is for those of you who are in, or want to be in, a relationship. This chapter, on sex, love and relationships, helps you recognize the two magic ingredients that lead to a healthy, lasting relationship. You will read about what to do if you are in a love triangle, or if you are tempted to cheat and how to know if breaking up is the right move. Then, if breaking up is what you need to do, how to do it respectfully. You will read about sex and what it does and does *not do* to a relationship. You learn how not to be a fence-sitter and how to decide when you are ready to have sex. There is advice about dating and relationships that shows you how to respect yourself and respect who you date. This chapter discusses how to be happy in love, and how to be happy and single. So, for those of you who are longing to be in a relationship but aren't in one yet, this is a great chapter to help you get happy on your own. This way you can enter into a relationship confident and secure, not clingy and desperate.

** **Chapter 6** is dedicated to your body. It is for any of you struggling with body image. It deals with food and why you eat what you eat. You will confront the love/hate relationship you have with your body. You'll be given tools to approach food and exercise with a healthy respect for your body and why you should not diet or try fad weight-loss or muscle-gain products. You will learn how to begin the healing process and move away from eating disorders, over exercising, or, the opposite, the couch-potato lifestyle. In addition to discussing food, this chapter also focuses on exercise and sleep, as well.

** **Chapter 7** is dedicated to those of you who are slipping past the socially acceptable level of drinking and using/over-using recreational drugs. It unravels the big picture of how these substances begin to control your life. If you are considering experimenting, you'll learn about alcohol and marijuana – and what they really do to you. For those of you considering going past T.A.P. (Tobacco, Alcohol, and Pot), you'll see that you don't have to go looking for hard drugs because they are looking for you. And, for any of you using *any* amount of drugs or alcohol, you'll read some tips for safer partying and for improving your chances that you can laugh with friends on Monday, and not be afraid to go to school out of embarrassment.

Chapter 8 deals with being really low or at risk of falling into a vice-grip. You'll learn what a vice is, how it may have taken over your life and may be keeping you down. This chapter explains, through neuroscience, how our brain changes when it is in pain. It explains how people make subconscious efforts to distract or numb their pain. This Chapter deals with the "Why?" as in, "Why do you continually turn to vices when you know you are hurting yourself?" This chapter will challenge you to figure out the root cause(s) of your decision(s) and then take a path of healing and being in control of your life. It will help you decide if you are really ready to quit by asking you for honest answers to some "reality checks." It will give you some tips on getting the help you need to get better.

Chapter 9, Hero Training 101 focuses on healing. Read this chapter after you have confronted your specific challenge areas in chapters 3 through 8. This chapter contains a self-healing starter kit and practical tools and strategies you can use every day to feel better and feel strong. It will also remind you of the many mentors and guides you have in your life that you can turn to for help and support. This chapter is closely connected to the vices uncovered in Chapter 8 and the root causes of your pain. Having a pen and paper handy will be helpful here.

Chapter 10 guides you to finding your greatness, continuing the focus of healing from Chapter 9. This chapter guides you on how to change your habitual thought patterns from negative to positive. You'll uncover the power of your thoughts and how to surround yourself with positivity. It reveals concrete tools to help you be courageous in the face of challenges, to be wise when faced with difficult decisions, to believe in yourself when doubt overwhelms you, and to begin the path toward healing yourself from the pain you've been carrying around. This chapter puts you on the path to finding inner peace, true happiness and finding your greatness. This chapter will set you up to watch amazing things unfold in your life.

So, there you have the chapter summaries. For chapters 4 to 7, feel free to choose your own path with these topics that deal with the specific areas you may struggle with or want to know more about. Again, chapters 1, 2, 3, and 8, 9, 10 are for everyone. But, remember that all the chapters are designed to show you why, and how, to boost your self-esteem so you can make the best decisions to have a long, happier and healthier life.

I will finish this introduction on one last note: Why I chose to write this book.

There is only one answer: because my students told me to. Over and over, in the classes where I discussed these self-esteem concepts, they kept saying, "Every teenager should take this course. Every teenager should know this. Ms., you should write a book."

Umm, well, OK.

Thank you to every student I have ever taught. The learning has been mutual.

Thank you to you the readers. I am inviting you on a journey to change your path, your life.

So, are you ready? Let's get started.

Big-Picture Points

- *In order to better your life, you must better your beliefs, better your thoughts, and better your actions.*
- *A sad or angry place is a starting point.*
- *You can't solve your problems using the same negative thoughts and beliefs that you used to create them. You must allow yourself to be open-minded. Change is necessary. You'll have to step outside of your comfort zone.*
- *Unhappiness, even in a small area of your life, sets you up to question where you are now and move toward a better path. It gives you the motivation to evolve, to learn and adapt and make yourself better. Emotions & Feelings are important.*
- *There are some things in this book that will frustrate you. You may even feel insulted and want to quickly respond defensively. Understand that this book is designed to challenge you.*
- *Life gets better as you age. Start living in a way that will make this true for you.*
- *With your new independence that will come with age, you must remember that you are not a victim of circumstance.*
- *You are the creator of your life story.*
- *The biggest factor in smooth transitions through the teenage years, and beyond, is Self-Esteem. This single aspect of you is the underlying source for every decision you make now and for every decision you will ever make.*
- *If you don't change how you feel on the inside, you can't expect good things to happen on the outside.*
- *You are in control of your own happiness. Sometimes you have to move from frustration through to sadness, in order to access happiness.*

CHAPTER 1
Self-Esteem: Sink Or Sail

Art by Sarah Knowles

You have Incredible Strength inside of you.
Your self-esteem is the faith you have in that inner strength.

Your Greatest Ally or Your Worst Enemy ...

Self-esteem is a sense of your own worth, a sense of who you truly are, and it is the single most important item you carry on your journey through life. How you view yourself and your worth in the world will affect every decision you ever make. Low self-esteem sets you up for disasters while good self-esteem protects you from them.

Life is full of choices. Up to this point, most of the critical decisions were made for you, but as a teenager, you are making more decisions for yourself. There are strong links between self-esteem and the major aspects of your teenage life: relationships, sex, alcohol and drugs, food, your body, your education and career path, your family, and your friends. The goal of this book is to point out the importance of having a strong, healthy sense of self and give you concrete strategies to change your thinking, so you can build up your self-esteem and start living a wonderful, strong, purposeful life. I believe achieving healthy self-esteem is *the* most important thing you can do. It will improve your life in every area.

I am not here to judge you on how you live or have lived, or the things you do or have done. What you do with your life is entirely up to you. My goal with you is the same goal I've had with every student I have ever taught. I want you to be informed so that when you make the decisions you do, you know why you are making them and where they are likely to lead. Awareness is critical. The opposite of awareness is ignorance. Far too many decisions are made in a state of ignorance and impulsiveness, and they are followed by regret or a victim mentality of blaming others for the consequences that come. Instead, choose awareness. Become informed, then make your decisions with eyes wide open and move through life with purpose and appreciation of all the good that comes to you.

Shades of Gray

We often talk about high and low self-esteem, but these labels are not exactly accurate. These "high versus low" terms lead us to believe that there are only two types of self-esteem – good versus bad. The reality is that self-esteem exists in shades of gray.

Healthy self-esteem is faith in your inner strength. It is not boastful of personal strength, it simply knows strength is there, like a card in your pocket. Healthy self-esteem also allows you to admit that you have areas of relative weakness without putting yourself down.

Healthy self-esteem is also reliant on knowing who and where safety is. Who can you turn to when you need support? Who can you trust to make good decisions for you when you can't yet make them yourself? Who knows the real you? Who knows your goals and dreams? Who can forgive your mistakes and help you learn and grow from them? Where are you safe? Deep down you need to know these things.

Once this security basecamp is established, healthy self-esteem strives to grow and expand itself through new, healthy life experiences. Identifying emotionally safe people and safe places is critical for ensuring healthy experiences.

Choosing new life experiences is also key to discovering your potential. Some examples of new experiences might be trying a new sport or entering a community running event, entering an academic contest, joining a field trip opportunity, volunteering in your community, shooting for a great mark in a class, or cooking a healthy meal for your family. Be open to learning new life skills that will improve your future. If you never test your inner strength by trying new things, then you'll never know your true potential. You may begin to fear things that are outside of your comfort zone. If Fear is high, then Faith is low.

False Esteem

Everyone has self-esteem. It can be high or low or anywhere in between. It can be high in certain situations or circumstances, but low in others. One thing we need to clarify is that healthy self-esteem should not be confused with "being full of yourself." We have all met people who are arrogant, tough, conceited – full of themselves. This is not a desirable trait. Do not confuse this with high self-esteem. They have 'false esteem'. Their self-esteem appears high, but it is really the opposite. The reality is, those individuals are trying so hard to cover up their weaknesses that they overcompensate and must constantly paint a persona or compare themselves to others in order to make themselves look or sound better. False esteem can come in many forms: arrogance, bullying, being overly flirty, etc. There are many masks you could wear. If this sounds like you, you are aware that most people won't take the time to look past your facade. They will either fear you and run away, be annoyed by you and leave, or swoon over you because they are fooled by your persona, even though that is truly not who you are. Every once in a while, you might meet someone new or have an old friend or family member who knows you, and then you can genuinely show your true colours to them. These relationships are crucial for you because they are the beginning of the realization that you are deeper than the image you show to the world.

True Esteem

True esteem comes when you understand your own value. You understand what an incredible miracle you are. Do not interpret this as being perfect. True self-esteem does not compare. With false esteem, one must constantly compare themselves with others, one must be better than everyone else. The beauty in knowing you've reached the point of true self-esteem is when you see the value in everyone around you. As you learn to respect yourself, you also learn to respect others deeply. As a bonus, all relationships in your life improve.

Many people wait until they are much older to seek out their true worth. They wait until they have destroyed their marriages, friendships, connections with their children, their jobs, their finances. Only then do they realize they need to look deep inside and ask, "What really matters here?" Then, they see that the persona they have created and lived with all those years is actually very far from who they truly are. Spare yourself years of torment by developing true self-esteem now.

As already mentioned, your sense of self also determines the value you give to others. Do the lives of other people, or other living things, have worth? Do only your family and closest friends have value? Do others outside of this group annoy you to the point that you cannot see their value? Do you find you have less patience with some people and more with others? When you can find the value/love in yourself, then, and only then, can you open up to the true value/love of the lives and life around you. When you can say, "I am worth loving, worth caring for, worth protecting, worth compassion," and learn to fulfill each of those for yourself, then you can learn to truly apply this to other people and to the living things around you. At that point, others will reinforce these truths about your life by reflecting them back to you.

Think of love as filling up a cup. Dr. John Gray, author and relationship expert, says that "when you fill yourself up first, the love that overflows is what you give to others." It has to start with you.

Every day, I see teenagers lost in the early turns of this downward spiral, where they want love, but they cannot find it because they do not love themselves. When we discuss ways to recognize where they are and relate it back to a level of self-esteem, they begin to see how it permeates every aspect of their lives and the decisions they make along the way.

You can take this opportunity to reset your course onto a path that is more in line with your true value.

One evening, I was walking down a city street, and I saw a prostitute who was obviously high. My first reaction was, "Whoa, I'm in the wrong place at the wrong time." And I walked on – quickly. But the farther I got, the more I thought about her, and my mind kept coming back to the same question. I wanted to ask her, "What have you been through in your life that has led you to this point, this place?" Once you are wounded, it is easy to fall deeper and deeper into your own personal hell. But, what if numbing your pain isn't enough? What if you really don't want to fall any deeper? Is there a way out?

Every one of us, without exception, has the power to heal ourselves. Regardless of what you have been through, the power to heal comes from within. You don't, however, have to do this alone. Once you decide you want to better your life, you will be opened up to many people and circumstances, that will guide you along your journey. The catch is it has to start with you. You have to *really* want it! It is hard work, but it is more rewarding than I can describe. To take purposeful, positive action is life-altering. Well, actually, to *not* take these actions will also alter your life, but in a direction that will bring only more trauma and pain.

Help is Around You

Help is all around you, but it comes in two main forms. And one of them is more effective for the long term. It all comes down to who you turn to when times are really tough. Should you turn to others who are themselves tottering along their own path of similar challenges? Or, should you turn to people who've made it through really tough times themselves and are now standing on solid ground?

Tendency and Mastery

The tendency is to turn to same age friends when times are tough. The mastery is to *also* turn to healthy adult mentors for input. If you put your faith in the healthy mentors in your life, they will show you your strength when you cannot see it for yourself. If you put your faith only in your same-age friends, this creates a problem.

Friends are great when times are good, but they are not equipped to care for each other and help each other grow, when times are tough. First, they may offer advice, but they may have no experience with the problem you are facing. Friends can support you, but the bigger the problem, the less likely it is that they can actually help you. Second, some friends are not mature enough to handle your deepest issues with the discretion you need. What you tell these friends today, may be something they throw in your face when you are no longer friends. Friends change, and so your deepest fears, mistakes, your dreams and goals are vulnerable. This is the reason family is so important. If you cannot rely on healthy family members, turn to other healthy adults when times are really tough.

There is a difference between the way that healthy adults will help you through a tough time and how same aged peers will help. Hopefully first they will listen. If they won't, sit them down and say, "I need to talk about something and I need you to just hear me, please." Sometimes we just need ears and shoulders. The wisest people around you will not try to remove your obstacles for you, they will gently help you to recognize your part in all of it, so you can learn from the situation. They will help you to see your inner strength to help you face the challenge or steer away from it next time. They believe in your inner strength. They believe in the good in you. They truly know you can get through this. Their belief in you is critical, because it will help you to believe in yourself. That is the first step to being your own hero.

Your friends are good at hearing you out, which is wonderful, but often their next move, which comes from a place of truly wanting to make you feel better, is often to tell you that you are totally innocent and that the circumstance could not have been prevented, that the other person is completely wrong and you are right, that you truly are a victim. Sure, this will make you feel better in that moment, but it also deep down makes you feel vulnerable.

You are left wondering, "If this mess couldn't be prevented, what terrible mess is coming up next that I cannot prevent? Why is life so hard?" Often the same situation will come up repeatedly and you are left with a feeling of falling victim to circumstance. In reality, problems are just challenges and they don't really go away until you face them constructively, which includes admitting your role in the situation.

The teens I see who are secure with healthy family members and/or healthy adult mentors, learn from their mistakes, and feel more secure in their day to day lives. The teens who rely on same age friends alone for support are less secure and more vulnerable.

The Storms That Are the Teenage Years

What does it mean to be a teenager? It's an amazing, wonderful, horrible, traumatic, exciting, tumultuous time between a heavily controlled and directed childhood and the responsibilities and freedom of adulthood. It is a time of high highs and low lows. It is also a time of newly claimed independence, and of self-discovery. Obviously, you could describe it in your words, but then, once you exit this era of your life and look back on it, you might describe it in a different way. It is important that you do not limit yourself by thinking you know more about life than others at different stages of life. Whatever stage of life we are in, when we are living that age, we are limited by our age and/or experiences, or lack thereof. Be open to new ways of looking at your life.

The most common way that adults describe teenagers is, "They think they know it all." Teenagers love to act that way, but it is rare to meet one who truly thinks that way. You know it is a changing world, and although you are scared about not having all the answers, you are pretty convinced that no one else does either. I mean, really, adults are wrapped up in war, dirty politics, choosing work over families, and destroying the earth. So, really, why would you want to listen to them? It is easy to shut down the adults in your life when they try to help. Adults, in general, seem too distracted and don't see the world the way you do, and they don't care about the things that you do. To add to that, no one has been though your life the way you have, so how can anyone else have the answers for you? Maybe you are right, but maybe not. It might be accurate to say that no one has all the right answers, but the reality is that some guidance along the way, through troubled times, is helpful. It might be in your best interest to let your guard down a little and search inside *and out* for what really matters in life.

There are some key differences going on in your life now compared to your first decade of life. One of which is that you are questioning your parents. They don't seem to have the answers to everything anymore.

What a let down!

Let's put this one in perspective. Many parents can easily and accurately answer questions that children under the age of eleven ask. But then you get older and start to ask much more complex questions. When you can't get a definitive or correct answer from them, it is disappointing, and you may begin to question everything they ever told you. It's important for you to understand that *every* adult is an expert at *something,* but no adult is an expert at *everything.* You may have gotten used to Google being the source of all information, but the reason Google "knows" everything is because billions of adults from all around the globe have contributed their expertise to the world wide web. In the adult world we rely on each other to fill in information gaps. Just because someone doesn't know something that we know, doesn't mean we think they don't have value. We work on the basis of information sharing. Most adults know we all thrive because of our collective knowledge.

We all have areas of expertise that we were trained in, but no adult knows everything. You are among the first generation of teens to have access, at your fingertips, to experts from around the world. It doesn't mean you should stop looking up to your parents. They still have incredible wisdom to share with you throughout your entire life. Their wisdom will be incredibly valuable because they know you so well and care for you so deeply. You can never say that about anyone the internet.

Another huge change in your life is that you have, as renowned Psychologist, Dr. Gordon Neufeld, calls it, a "boom of awareness." You gain a much wider perspective of what's out there in the world. You are more aware of the crap that goes on in the world, which is very upsetting. On the flip side, you are also more aware of the ridiculous abundance that some people have. Suddenly, you are exposed to the world of endless material items and what you have and where you live, seems like it's not good enough. This can be deeply troubling. The spiral of constant comparisons is a big component in creating high highs and low lows in the world of teenage angst.

Take it from those who have lived through adolescence and survived, we all know that it is a time of sad and annoying ironies.

- You are desperately striving for independence and want your parents to have some faith in your own ability to make the right decisions, yet your emotions and hormones control your actions more than your conscious mind does.
- Your body goes through big changes. You can become gangly, or overweight, and/or pimply, and develop new body features you are not comfortable with, yet you place physical appearance above all else in the judgment of yourself and others.
- You disconnect from family moving towards friends and media, but social circles and social media are not emotionally safe places.
- You experiment with new and, sometimes, dangerous aspects of your social life, yet, at the same time, you are avoiding parental guidance and input.

What a confusing time.

Times have changed. There is no doubt, as a group, your generation has been exposed to more issues and more information, with less guidance than any generation before you. I am not suggesting that your parents are not giving you guidance (OK, for some of you, that is the case), it's just that, with the Internet, you are exposed to more trauma and world troubles than teens ever were before. Of course, your parents, and every generation before them, had incredible struggles to overcome, some of which you could not possibly imagine having to endure. Nonetheless the issues facing teens now are very different. The main difference is the amount of freedom and information that your generation has at your disposal. Where, in the past you may have been more protected, now that comfort is removed. In this communication age, most *adults* have a hard time digesting everything that they are exposed to on a daily basis from the Internet, TV, social media, music, and so on. And yet, here you are with your young impressionable minds out in the battlefields, becoming numb to what you see. You may not be aware, but it still seeps in.

Your Amazing Brain is also Changing

Another huge change is how your brain is functioning. When the human brain is developing there is one part that develops last. It is so complex, and it can only function well once it has gathered a lot of information from all of the other parts of the brain. It is called your prefrontal cortex (PFC).

The PFC is located at the front of your brain and it handles many complex tasks such as long-term planning and decision making. One of its jobs is to store your goals and dreams and keep them in sight. It helps you make tough decisions by weighing pros and cons.

When you see something you want or think you need, other developing areas of your brain are stimulated, and they scream, "I want it now!" Your PFC is slower to respond and helps you consider your options, keeping your long-term goals in mind. In a way, this is where maturity lives.

Your PFC does something else that can really bother you. It gives you many different thoughts at once. When you are a kid, your brain focuses on one thing at a time. "I want that cookie and I want it now!" When your PFC is developing, your brain starts to weigh decisions with incredible amounts of information. "I want those cookies - but I know that dad will be upset if I don't eat my dinner like last time - but I really want those cookies - but I know I should wait," and back and forth. Your PFC rolls many ideas around in your head all at once and sometimes it seems overwhelming.

The PFC also contributes to complex concepts like guilt, remorse and regret, but also forgiveness, patience and perseverance. It also helps you to steer away from trouble, no matter how tempting it may be. Unfortunately, it takes a long time to develop. Luckily, while you wait for your PFC to mature, nature has a plan to keep you safe. Nature provides you with a family. Older family members will help by making tough decisions with/for you to keep you on track, until you can keep yourself on track.

Retrain Your Mind

Before the Prefrontal Cortex (PFC) is fully developed, we can be quite impulsive. We also tend to rely on only those with whom we have a deep and direct connection. When the ideas of other people outside of this group oppose ours, we may dismiss them quickly. This spirals us into repeating thoughts. Instead of expanding our thoughts and ideas by opening ourselves up to different views, we put up defences and stay stuck in our ways.

The way we think is a learned behavior. Our conditioned reactions and thoughts cover us like a fog. Because they are automatic and there all the time, we don't bother to search for anything deeper inside. In order to change your life for the better, you have to retrain your mind to think in a new way. Be open to new information, take time to process it.

If you always do what you've always done, you'll always get what you've always got.

-Henry Ford

Everyone thinks in a different way because of where they come from. You can't change your past, but the amazing thing about life is that you can choose the path you take from here. If you are in, or have experienced, considerable pain and you feel like you are stuck, professional counselors are amazing resources. They can help you move through whatever experience has you stuck. They can help you to clear your emotional baggage and shift your thinking. Once free, you can change your thoughts. You can change your Future.

"A victim mentality tells you that your past dictates who you are today."

-Eckhart Tolle

Stop struggling. Let go of things you can't change. You can't change the past, so let go of the past. Eckhart Tolle beautifully states that a victim mentality tells you that your past dictates who you are today. If you look at it differently, *the present dictates who you are tomorrow*. You are the creator of your life. Look at that again. It's very important.

The present dictates who you are tomorrow.

You can control how you think and how you react to situations in your life. By retraining yourself to look at life with a brighter perspective, you can change the emotions you experience from negative to positive throughout the entire day, every day.

Another way to retrain our brain is to shift our habitual focus. It's hard to admit it, but we carry pain from our past with us voluntarily. You have a choice. You can train your mind to let go of the past through emotional release and move freely through life without resentment. Everyone has a responsibility to move themselves forward through life. It's true we don't always need tears to move forward, sometimes we just need to shift our focus. Instead of letting your past keep you trapped, aim high and let your goals for the future guide you. Next time you find yourself spinning negative thoughts, stop and ask yourself, "Is the way I'm thinking or reacting actually improving the situation?"

Let's relate this to school.

It is quiz day and Dan and Malcolm are not prepared. They both bomb the quiz – failing it. To his friends, Dan starts ranting about how stupid the quiz was and how he thinks the subject sucks and who cares about failing it anyway. He might fall into an old belief pattern about himself as a kid who gets crappy marks. He might lay blame on the quiz, the subject, or the teacher. He focuses on "poor me." Are Dan's thoughts and actions doing anything to improve his situation? No.

Malcolm could easily take that stance as well. But Malcolm realizes that negative thinking will not help the situation. So Malcolm swallows his pride and goes in to talk to the teacher and gets extra help. When he is there he finds out that getting help boosts his confidence because now he understands the information. He becomes motivated to try harder on the rest of the tests and quizzes and in the end, not only improves his grades, but improves his perspective on his own potential.

It's just a shift in thinking.

Reminder: Laying blame and giving excuses is completely useless.

Tip: At all times, avoid giving excuses and laying blame on others when things go wrong.

Mistakes are not weaknesses, they are a vital part of life and of learning. Being aware of our mistakes allows us room for self-improvement. Instead of excuses and blaming, accept responsibility for the actions you took, or did not take, and take steps to learn from your mistakes.

You may find this hard at first and that's OK. When you feel negative emotions, try to break the cycle. Pause and become aware of what you are thinking and why. At the beginning, you may find that your automatic reactions are too strong to break through. If that happens, later, perhaps when you calm down or the situation has changed, take time to look back at your emotions and reactions in a more objective way. In your mind, replay the situation that has caused you to feel negative. Evaluate your decisions and reactions. If you don't like something you did, or you think you could have done something differently, OWN IT. Take responsibility. Make a prevention plan for next time. Mentally plan it. Play the scenario back in your head again, but this time, imagine yourself making the right choice or reacting in a different way that has a positive outcome. If you think your actions affected someone else in a negative way, own that too. Apologize. You will feel better. And they may thank you for your apology, which will make you feel even better still. Apologies are not a sign of weakness. They are a sign of strength, of maturity.

Healthy Self-Esteem - The Ultimate Goal

Every decision you ever make will first be viewed through the veil of your self-esteem. If you are insecure, and your sense of self-worth is *low*, then the decisions you make and the way you portray yourself to the world will reflect that feeling. If you are secure, and your sense of self-worth is *healthy*, then the decisions you make and the way you portray yourself will reflect that *healthy* feeling.

Security is so vital. Where are your safe spaces? Who are your safe people? Where can you go where you don't have to be "on" all the time? Where no one is teasing you? Where you can really be yourself and be relaxed? We need these safe spaces daily. Then we can thoughtfully connect with our mentors and ourselves. We can learn who we are and appreciate our own skills and interests and strengths. This personal growth can allow us to have faith in our inner strength.

Your life unfolds in essentially a positive direction or a negative direction based on your inner feelings about yourself. Many people blame others for the way they feel about themselves. Of course, your relationships with others has a huge impact on how you see yourself. If you are low, you need to take a hard look at who you are influenced by, who are you following? Protect yourself by choosing to spend time with safe people. Once your feel stronger, eventually you will understand that no one else can actually add to or take away from your self-esteem – only *you* can do that.

Changing your thinking and habitual patterns will be challenging. But do not interpret this as impossible. Challenges present themselves to you throughout life. As you face each one, see it as an opportunity for you to find inner strength. Here are my two favourite mantras.

"Life does not put things in front of you that you are unable to handle." - Author unknown

And,

"I Can Do This."

The second one I sometimes repeat over and over as I am trying to get through whatever physical, mental or emotional event I am having difficulty with. It helps me to work harder and achieve great results.

When it comes to improving your life and the lives of others, set positive goals, and repeat out loud,

"I Can Do This."

Big Picture Points

- *Do not confuse the concepts of self-esteem and false esteem. People who are arrogant, conceited, and full of themselves have false esteem. It appears to be high self-esteem, but it is really the opposite.*
- *True self-esteem is when you see the value in yourself and everyone and every living thing around you. As you learn to respect yourself, you also learn to respect others deeply. You will begin to notice all relationships in your life improving.*
- *Next time you find yourself spinning negative thoughts, stop and ask yourself, "Is the way I am thinking/reacting actually improving my situation?"*
- *Your opinion of yourself is not created by others. No one else can actually add to or take away from your self-esteem – only you can do that.*
- *Laying blame on others and giving excuses is completely useless.*
- *Accept responsibility for the actions you took, or did not take, and take steps to learn from your mistakes.*
- *You can't change your past.*
- *Stop struggling. Let go of things you can't change. You can't change the past, so let go of the past. A victim mentality tells you that your past dictates who you are today. Spin that around: The present dictates who you are tomorrow. You are the creator of your life.*
- *Tears are an important way to release emotions*
- *You can change your Future.*
- *Believe in yourself and the positive changes you want for your life. Repeat to yourself, "I Can Do This."*

CHAPTER 2
The Faces of False Esteem

Art by Danielle Nolan

"Shine a little light where you need it the most."
- Jeremy Fisher from his song 'Shine A Little Light'

When you are down, and you look around, it doesn't help that it looks as though everyone else has got their shit together and you don't. Everyone else seems happier than you, more confident than you, more attractive than you, smarter than you, and so on. Let's take a closer look and maybe, just maybe, you'll see that you're not alone. Maybe this lack of self-esteem has many faces. In this chapter, you will open your eyes to what I call "D.A.P" and you will see the underlying motives for the actions and behaviors of others around you. Hopefully, once you recognize the struggle in others, you won't be so hard on yourself.

A friend of mine was listening to her four-year-old son playing with a neighbor's toy gun, a toy she was hoping he'd never play with. He was talking about shooting the "bad guys." In a spectacular and wise response, she said, "There are no "bad" people, only people without enough love in their hearts." I love this lesson for children, but it also rings true for people of all ages. We are all good people; we just have a tendency to make bad decisions when we don't have enough love in our hearts.

To finish the story, later on, her four–year-old ran up to her and told her he was using the gun to shoot love into the bad guys' hearts.

Remember, just as a lack of light creates darkness, a lack of love creates the many forms of darkness in humanity.

Let's get inside your head for a minute. We have some very powerful instincts to attach to others for safety and security. Dr. Gordon Neufeld is a renowned Psychologist who has worked with children and teens in challenging scenarios at critical points in their lives. We can't ignore the neuroscience of attachment when we think about self-esteem. According to Dr. Neufeld, attachment is our number one survival instinct, and the foundation of self-esteem. Primarily, the family should remain the primary attachment and therefore the guiding force, but eventually we start looking outside of the home for security in the outside world.

When we turn to peers as our primary source of validation, depending on the friend group, we may fall into a deep trap. Every young person is trying to find their own way in the world. Their footing is not solid enough to support the needs of other young people consistently, and so you will inevitably let each other down. If you want to eventually become a healthy adult, then you need the support of healthy adults in your life.

The peer centered world is full of constant comparisons and is very emotionally wounding. Peer culture needs constant validation and relies heavily on media, following shows, musicians, social media, etc. These are all fun and exciting as long as you can understand you are only getting the final product. What do I mean by that?

This is a time of life when you cling to the concept of perfection. But please remember that when you watch a show or listen to a song, you are seeing/hearing the "perfect" version. You are not seeing/hearing the hundreds of "takes" that are essentially *mistakes,* that it took before they got the final one.

There is no perfect person. They were not born this good! The talents you are admiring, they had to struggle to achieve. This is important to acknowledge because so often when you are struggling in your own life, you may believe you are worthless, or you are not talented, that your unique interests are not interesting enough. But, really, you are just comparing yourself to perfection, which is unrealistic and unfair to you. Remember, everyone is a work in progress, and you haven't been at it that long, so give yourself a break.

Similarly, you will start to look at the adults in your life with the "perfection lens." When you were younger you looked up to them. You did not seek many comparisons. You were in full acceptance that these were your safe people, they protected you, and you did not really notice their imperfections. Now that you are older you can recognize their struggles.

Unfortunately, if you view them through the *perfection lens*, then you may lose respect for them because they are not perfect. No one is perfect.

The teenage years are a rough stage of life when we cling to perfection. Until you can fully accept mistakes and individual differences as valuable, this stage of life will be full of disappointment.

The Quest for Security

Everyone needs love and security. We receive that from only three areas:

1- From family
2- From friends
3- From ourselves

Now, this seems simple enough, but it isn't. The first issue is that teens and young adults inevitably will experience insecurity. You have to face a lot of unknowns as you grow up. This can be emotionally scary and wounding. Especially if you don't use the assistance of healthy adult mentors.

The second issue is that so many people don't even consider the concept of self-love at all. If you have avoided the support of healthy adults, this leaves you dependent on the love you receive from peers. But, this leads to your third issue: You cannot control the other people in your life. They may or may not give you what you want every time you want it, and so, a possible lack of consistent love and attention from others in your life generates a feeling of insecurity and perceived lack of self-worth. This lack of self-worth eventually becomes low self-esteem. How do people respond to this? Generally, people subconsciously move in one of three directions, although the directions can be intertwined:

1. Falling into <u>Distraction-Seeking</u> behavior, using material possessions or constant entertainment to mask inner unrest.

2. Falling into <u>Attention-Seeking</u> behavior, which will provide temporary validation, in order to feel more secure.

3. Falling into <u>Power-Seeking</u> behavior, which is based on comparisons with others (push others down to raise yourself up) in order to feel stronger.

I call these "DAP" which stands for:

- <u>D</u>istraction-Seeking Behavior
- <u>A</u>ttention-Seeking Behavior
- <u>P</u>ower-Seeking Behavior

Let's get to know the forms that insecurity can take. And, for each example, see if you can recognize it in yourself, or someone in your life.

Distraction-Seeking

Distraction-seekers, similar to everyone else, desire completeness on the inside. They don't realize what is missing in their lives, and they do not realize how this insecurity is affecting them. Lack of emotional security creates a sensation of general unrest in the body. Feelings of agitation and anxiousness are common. Distraction is, by design, an attempt to avoid these feelings of unrest. Seeking distraction is mainly sub-conscious, meaning, people usually do not Distraction-Seek on purpose.

The distraction-seekers make a habit of trying to fill the void with something on the outside that makes them feel good on the inside. Unfortunately, whatever substitute they choose and the good feeling it creates will always be temporary. So temporary that it brings about more negative feelings when it's finished. "What? That was *it*? OK, well on to the next substitute." Distraction-seekers satisfy needs with food, games, downloads, music, movies, TV shows, shopping, relationships, and also with sex, drugs, fights, crime – you name it – one right after another. It's an insatiable appetite. They can never get enough. They want excitement, the fast life and quick fixes.

This self-generated affliction is so common in our society that it is considered normal. Once you are aware of this constant need for distraction, you can easily recognize it in others. They are the ones who simply have to *have* everything, want to *do* everything, they are always up on the latest this or latest that. If you observe them closely, it looks like they will do anything to keep from being alone and quiet with their own thoughts. They use outer *things* in their lives to distract themselves from connecting with the inner peace that they are disconnected from.

Don't get me wrong, entertainment is a wonderful thing. Everyone loves to be entertained. It's not a bad thing. Movies, videos, music, gaming … entertainment in so many forms can be great ways to escape. Distraction can be great when you are going through a hard time. For example, let's say you haven't been invited to a party or an event, and most of your other friends were. Setting yourself up with a movie and turning off your phone, so you don't have to be tempted by constant social updates, is a great way to get through the night. Distraction is really good for us, sometimes. But, you should seek it in moderation. For way too many people, it is a constant activity. Do you count on it to keep you from boredom? Do you jump from one form of entertainment to the next? Are you bored easily? Are you uncomfortable being alone, quiet with your own inner thoughts and ideas? If so you could be a distraction-seeker.

Many distraction-seekers constantly have music in their ears, are constantly watching on-screen entertainment, checking social media, or are always reading up on celebrities or fashion. Do you live vicariously through on-screen adventures, the actions and music of others, the lives of others, instead of getting out there and creating your own life adventures?

Distraction is very easy in our society. You can fill every waking moment with entertainment and tasks to the point where you don't know how to truly relax anymore.

Do you seek distractions when you are feeling overwhelmed and tired?

Do you use distractions to get away from the problems in your life?
Do you rely on these forms of entertainment to relax you?

If you are at home and want a break, do you turn on a screen somewhere to block out the world around you and call this *relaxing*?

You are not alone. As a society, we've lost track of how to bring peace into our lives on many levels. It's actually even worse than that. We are so off track that, when the opportunity presents itself to have a peaceful, quiet moment, people often say, "This is so boring." So, essentially, we've taken a time to calm the mind and be at peace, and we've turned it into something so negative that we don't want anything to do with it. Many children and teens often say, "I'm bored," or "This is boring." This is the result of an addiction to distraction, using *things* to distract away from the perceived-emptiness inside. Many teens and adults feel the need to fill every moment with outer excitement to avoid the perceived "boredom" of their day-to-day lives. But, each high is followed by a low and, when the thrill is over, they are left with the need for the next high.

BUY **THIS to feel good:** The excitement of shopping and buying something new is always followed by a time when the new item doesn't bring you happiness any longer, and you feel the need to go out and buy more temporary happiness and excitement. Advertisers love this notion of buying happiness. I remember an incredibly obvious magazine article that gave the reader 50 ways to kick the winter blues. The article outlined 50 products that you can buy. The huge title read "Get Happy."

TRY **THIS to feel good:** This is the "This Will Work For You" approach to protein products and energy products, diets, and recreational drugs to change how you look and feel. They bring a temporary fix, if at all, and then, when the benefit dissolves, you are left wondering, "What else can I try?" You can be invited to try things by word of mouth. Often, it is someone who is using a product and feels very knowledgeable, and they are still on the upslope of their own inner roller coaster ride of distraction, and they are feeling good. This person can be very convincing. I hear this talk all the time in gyms, but it also happens with drugs at a party. Chat with them in six months to a year's time and see if they think it's still working out the way they want. Chances are, they have experienced a downturn and are seeking something new.

Is it bad to want to have and do things? Of course not. It is a way of experiencing our lives. What is problematic is if you use these things to fill a void in your life, to depend on them for your happiness.

It's time to ask yourself, "How would I feel if all of these things and experiences were taken away?" If you did not keep up with the latest items or events or people, would that change your perception of who you are? Do you think it would change how others perceive you? Have the things in your life become your identity? Who are you without them?

The truth is you are so much more than you realize right now. It seems that consumerism and, to some extent, our society at large, is dependent on people's lack of esteem and their needs to fill their voids with lots of stuff, events and excitement. The good news for the economy is that all of these things require money and so we dish it out to feel fulfilled. Remember, this is only a distraction from the thoughts within that seem to scare us so much. Peace is a good thing. If you spent even half as much time searching for yourself as you do in searching for your next partner, the next clothing item, the next gift, the next electronic gadget, you would soon realize that you do not need a constant bombardment of these substitutes because when you discover *you*, this discovery is so much more rewarding. The truth is that, once you start searching for yourself, you will soon see that you don't have to search very far. You already are good enough. You just need to be at peace with yourself. Be at peace. Be quiet. Just *Be*.

- If I could describe distraction-seeking behavior in one word, it would be "MORE."
- Do you have a habit of falling into Distraction-Seeking behavior?
- Can you think of anyone that you know who exhibits distraction-seeking behavior?
- Have you ever felt jealous of them and all of their possessions? Look closely, why do they need all of those things in the first place?

So, if distractions are everywhere, how do you stop? The truth is that you don't have to stop completely, just try to use them in moderation. Here is my tip: Seek 30-60 minutes a day, you can split it up throughout the day if necessary, to be alone in peace. Now, you might be asking, "Why would I want to do that?"

The answer to that has three parts:

Experiment with Solutions

1. The solutions to your problems are *within* you. Try asking a question:

- "How am I going to get through [insert problem here]?"
- "What are some solutions that will improve my situation?"

Then, be still, quiet and let your mind uncover solutions and strategies for you – focus on the positive, healthy ones. Focus on life getting better. The truth is that we carry problems with us all the time, but we rarely take the time to be peaceful and see the wonderful solutions all around us that are waiting to be discovered. Call it positive, purposeful thinking.

2. Identify your safe spaces and safe people. Where can you go where you can calm down completely, where you don't have to be "on"? Who are your safe people, who you can truly be yourself with, who do not tease or taunt or bug or seek to be impressed by you? Who can you be around to just be at rest with? Seek out these places and people for small periods of time each day.

I've already mentioned that high schools are crazy places. It is rare to see a student who is emotionally at rest. Many students use music to calm down. Is there a place you can go to relax? Maybe a favourite teacher's classroom at lunch? Or going outside for a walk? Can you rest at home at the end of the school day?

Keep in mind that being on your electronic device can be part of the solution but can also be part of the problem. For example, listening to non-alarming (calming) music in a busy part of a school day can help to block out the craziness and help keep you calm. But when you are in a quiet space, surfing the internet and social media, listening to alarming music, is not going to provide emotional rest - it has quite the opposite effect.

3. Don't fear your thoughts, more past them. Strive for a state where you are not thinking at all – true peace. By being truly peaceful, you enter a mental and emotional state of calm. This is one of the goals of Meditation. In addition, being aware of how it feels to be calm will help you recognize those times when you are stressed out. If you can recognize those stressed-out feelings early, then you can gain control through relaxation before the overwhelming feelings take over.

4. Get in the Zone. Inner Peace can be found in experiences where you are incredibly focused. Think of yourself on a sports field. You have a specific task or role to play, and it requires all of your attention and focus. You don't have time to think about the 10 different things that were bugging you earlier, you can only focus on action in this single moment. That is a beautiful state to be in. Sports is a phenomenal access point to 'The Zone'. Playing an instrument or doing some form a of Art can bring you there as well.

The key is Doing, not observing or listening or watching – If you are observing then you are simply distracted by others who are in the zone. Yes, that is neat to see as amazing skills are revealed, but it's a totally different experience when it is YOU in the zone. Try it, you'll see.

How will these help a distraction-seeker? Being in a state of focus and peace teaches you that feeling good comes from the inside. You don't have to seek outside things to make you happy, and that you can achieve inner peace and true happiness all on your own. The truth is you never needed any of those distractions to find happiness.

How should you spend your 30-60 minutes or six 10-minute segments? Well, you can sit quietly, lie on your bed in a quiet house, or go for a walk, run, skateboard, or bike ride, play a sport, draw, paint, play an instrument, or go for a drive. My most peaceful moments are always in nature, which I will discuss further in Chapter 9. If you are interested in diving in, try yoga or mediation. If the single word description for Distraction-seeking is MORE, then the solution should be LESS. Surround yourself with Less. Then you'll discover the abundance of life within you.

Attention-Seeking

We have an innate drive to attach to others for security. When we are lacking that secure attachment, we seek attention to fill the void and try to replace the missing security, so we don't feel *insecure*. We can easily misinterpret attention as a substitute for someone giving us love. If someone gives you attention, that means they care about you, which means they like or love you. Yes, there is truth in this, but if you are really insecure, you may need constant proof of attention to feel cared for, to feel safe. You may especially seek the attention of others when you are feeling down. If you know an attention seeker, or you realize that you are an attention seeker, you will recognize a repeated pattern of complaining about something but not moving forward towards improvement. There is a difference between seeking *Attention* and seeking *Help*. Seeking help is extremely important. If you are struggling and want to stop, asking for help from others is absolutely key. Those who are seeking help are ready to take action to better their situation. Attention seekers will often receive good advice from others, but will readily come up with excuses as to why the solution does not, or will not, work for them. Subconsciously, they are so attached to their issues, and the attention they receive because of them, that they are scared to let them go.

Complaining

As a teenager and young adult, I tried to help everyone who complained about anything. I would offer suggestions to try to solve their problems for them. After a while, I started to observe a pattern in some people and it was that they didn't really want help, they just wanted to complain. After hearing so many people in my life do this repeatedly, I came up with a strategy to protect myself from their negativity. I started saying, "Don't complain unless you are willing to do something about it."

"Poor Me" Attitude

In some cases, people will use food or body image to bring attention to themselves. For example, one student of mine described a friend this way: "She never eats and, yet, always tells me she's hungry. So, every time she comes over to my house, I always make sure I have her favorite food." How about when people ask, "Do I look fat?" This is often asked by individuals who are anything but fat, but they are seeking the attention of others and reassurance.

Another example is when students say, "Oh, I know I failed that test," right after they have taken a test. I hear this so often from very good students, who are, nowhere near failing, but they subconsciously enjoy the reassurance they receive from their friends: "No, you didn't. You probably did great on that test!"

Negative Attention

Breaking rules at home or at school is another way to seek attention. Sure, they get in trouble, but for some people negative attention is better than no attention at all. This is related to the "Nobody cares about me" problem.

If someone is insecure, they are probably lacking attachment and seeking attention. If you are desperately seeking safety, you will do what you are told by the person you perceive to have your best chance of social survival – this is a social group leader. If that person is breaking the rules, you may follow what they are doing without really thinking. Then you will share in the negative attention (consequences) and feel like there are many events going on that seem out of your control.

If you feel that you are lacking attention and you wish you were getting more, generally the desired attention is from peers. Once you have peers mattering much more than adults mattering, this opens you up to a whole range of behaviours that are going to dismiss rules. Rules are from the adult world and teens who heavily associate with friends often see adults as enemies, so why would you follow the rules that are made by people you are not connected with? Social rules are far more important, and the consequences of breaking social rules can be more wounding.

This is really destructive because you probably will get into more and deeper trouble, following troubled peers, making more and more mistakes. If you are unable to realize that you are hurting yourself, or are unable to break out of the cycle, you will end up making yourself feel worse and worse. If you are at that point, the solution comes down to you. People will help you, if you genuinely want it and ask for it. But, same as before, you have to own up to your mistakes. You have to want to feel better than you do. The good news is you can get the love and attention from inside, so you don't have to be dependent on others. You will find the next chapter on coping strategies as well as chapter nine on hero training very helpful.

We also must acknowledge that rule-breaking can happen spontaneously, and so many people respond with, "I wasn't thinking," when it comes time to face the consequences. Many times, poor judgment and no judgment turn out the same way.

Sexual Attention

Some people will seek the sexual attention of others around them. If they are lacking attachment, they again seek attention, and confuse attention with attraction, confuse lust with love. They are often seeking someone to fill the attachment void, and to keep them safe. They have a very difficult time being single and are extremely flirtatious. This concept will be covered in greater detail in Chapter 5.

- If I could describe attention-seeking behavior in two words, it would be "NOTICE ME."
- Do you have a habit of falling into attention-seeking behavior?
- Can you think of anyone that you know, or have been jealous of, who exhibits attention-seeking behavior?

Does this sound familiar?

- Do you have a habit of attention seeking?
- When given a suggestion in response to your complaints, do you come up with excuses easily? Do you come up with reasons why it won't help before you've even tried it?
- Is this strategy working out for you or do you find yourself swirling in a cycle of complaining?
- Are you satisfied with the love you are receiving, or do you always need more from others in order to feel good?

Experiment with Solutions

If you want life to get better, you will have to change your actions, try new things. When you are complaining, but you don't really have any intention of helping yourself, it is frustrating for the others. People want to help you, but they will get tired of this cycle and you will feel hurt over and over. Everyone around you wants to see you succeed. They want you to feel better. They want you to try and not give up. Set those same goals for yourself.

1. The first step for an Attention Seeker is to self identify. Are you someone who is willing to take action in order for life to get better? I refer to these people as being *On The Launch Pad*.

Or, are you someone who doesn't want to bother putting in the effort. You've tried before, it didn't work. If you are here, you may find that complaining is strangely satisfying for you. I refer to this group as being in the *Habitual Spiral*.

If you are part of the second group in the *Habitual Spiral*, you might want to put this book down now, stop reading. Pick it back up when you are tired of life sucking for you. If you are already tired of life sucking, read on.

2. The second step is to figure out who you are surrounding yourself with, who you are seeking attention from? Can you connect with your family? They should be the safest ones to fill the void. Parents are an obvious choice, but it could be grandparents too, mentally healthy aunts, uncles, or older cousins.

Healthy adult mentors can also be found outside of the family unit and they are key people too. Close friends of your parents, maybe your own friends' parents, or teachers, coaches, etc. These healthy adults will act as a bridge between you and your parents.

They will help you to learn life skills, to show you your value as a citizen. They will help you to see the good in yourself. Healthy friends can do this too. Healthy friends together with healthy adults are a solid support for you. Just remember no one can give you attention all of the time. Don't take it personally. Every person has their own life to live. That's why it's important to have a whole range of healthy people and your own healthy strategies that you can turn to. We are going to get to these in the next chapter on stress and coping strategies.

3. Write out your goals and your current situation. what actions make the situation better, what actions make it worse? Listen to your words, observe your actions. Become self-aware of how often you are complaining or taking actions that set you back. Ask yourself "Is this making my life better?" Let this simple phrase become your mantra, "I will use good judgement to improve my life."

4. Really seeking help is another way. How about paying for a counselor or life coach who makes you accountable for your actions. When you have to pay for help, it forces you to avoid the *Habitual Spiral* as it becomes too expensive.

5. Keep Reading. The issues you are complaining about are bound to come up in the coming chapters. Read with an open mind. Seeing things through a new perspective will be helpful. And once you are done reading this book, read or watch biographies of amazing people who have survived through incredible challenges – make them your role models. Their true stories will help you to put your own struggles into perspective and give you strength to push through.

On the Receiving End

How do you *respond* to attention-seeking behavior of others in your life? Are you on the receiving end of all of this? If so, if you repeatedly respond to the attention-seeking behaviors of others, then you may risk becoming an *enabler* – meaning you are actually encouraging and reinforcing their behavior by providing the response they seek. Many parents, particularly mothers, can become enablers. Close friends can do it, too. Followers are definitely enablers. Be careful – you are not helping the individual. Be aware of people around you who repeat the same mistakes or repeat the same complaints. Help them to be aware of their patterns. Do not give them the sympathy or attention they are seeking. Do not become an enabler.

Power-Seeking

The third way we see people substituting self-esteem is by power-seeking. Everyone wants to feel good about themselves. It is completely natural. But, sometimes when people are unable to feel good from the inside, they seek power to make themselves feel good. They feel powerful when they deflate others. The problem with power is that it is, essentially, a tool that requires people to *compare themselves to others*. One has to be higher than the other for this to work. "I don't feel good here, but if I push you down, then it raises me up." It is the classic bully scenario. The bully feels so low about his or her life situation, that the only way to elevate his or her status is to put others down. "My life might suck, but at least I'm not lying face down in the mud like you are."

Power-seeking is actually everywhere you look. It is crucial for you while on this journey to be able to see through the false ideals of shallow people in our society. This struggle, this desire for higher ground, permeates every level of society. It is so common that it is actually considered normal, and our entire society suffers from it and because of it. The relationship between power and self-esteem is an incredibly important one to examine. The confusion between esteem and power has caused most of the pain around the world. If you can differentiate between the two, you can prevent a great deal of pain in your own life and the lives of those around you. Power, as a substitute for healthy self-esteem, is, in my opinion, the greatest human flaw. Those who seek it do so because it feels good. They are not even aware that they are doing it. As a society, we talk of the desire for peace, but this cannot truly happen until we recognize and dissolve the desire for power within us.

*The essence of **power** is based on the **differences** between you and others around you.*

*The essence of **peace** is based on the **similarities** between you and others around you.*

There are many ways that the power goal surfaces in everyday interactions. Let's take a look at a few of them.

Creating a False Identity

Many people, including teens, create a false identity to feel they are good enough. They want others to think they are more than they are. There is nothing wrong with wanting to put your best foot forward – that is not the problem. The problem happens when you are putting others down in order to feel good. We have already spoken about false esteem which relates to people who are full of themselves. You may know them as being conceited. They are sometimes tough, obnoxious, overly flirtatious, overly charismatic, overly competitive, trying to seem perfect. But, they may be empty inside. They survive on the acceptance of others, on the attention of others to make themselves feel good, feel worthy. They have to make it up. They cannot simply be themselves. They might believe that being the best is important because it means they are "better" than the rest. If they are not the best, they will portray themselves in a way to seem as if they are the best – in the way they talk, the way they dress, the people they hang out with. They are very critical of themselves and of others. It is easy to see this with close friends. You might see them acting one way with you, but then completely different in a crowd of people. They are striving for social status as power to validate their worth. If only they understood their inner worth, they would realize they don't have to compare themselves to others.

Competition

There is nothing wrong with competition and being competitive. Whether you are competing in sports or for school grades or for a job, competition is a part of life. How we use competition stems from our self-esteem. If you develop a strong sense of self, you will use competition simply to strive to be the best that you can be. Instead of focusing on taking others down, you focus on climbing to the top. Instead of fearing, or hating, your opponents, you can use the wonderful talents of other people to push you to your limits, to challenge you. Appreciate the talents of others instead of resenting them for what they can do. Focus on your own capabilities, on what you do, what you achieve. If you fail and lose, ask yourself, "What did I learn? "What could I do differently?" "What are my strengths?" "What are my weaknesses?" "How can I train harder to improve?" "What can I do to become mentally, emotionally or physically healthier to compete better?" Most importantly, do not place your personal value, your self-worth, on the win or the loss. This competition is simply an experience on your journey through life. What will you take away from it?

Power Plays

The following examples are ways that people commonly seek out power to fill a void.

Power and Relationships

Many children grow up in families with an obvious power difference between their parents. As teens, they grow up with the assumption that this is normal. They seek out relationships that will satisfy their desire to overpower, or to be overpowered. In this book, you will find Chapter 5 is devoted to healthy and unhealthy relationships.

Violence as Power

Violence, and threats of violence, is the lowest-of-the-low form of power seeking. Violence can be learned behavior from witnessing the violence of parents or siblings, but it can also be learned from the media. In fact, you, as a generation, are exposed to so much violence that you are numb to the horrible realities of it. From what I have observed, boys are swept up in this much more easily than girls. In the hallways at school, I see boys pretend-beating their friends. It gives them a little rush. Mostly it is just for fun as they wouldn't really hurt each other. But for some, it becomes more real. Sometimes the violence is aimed at animals, a younger sibling, or a smaller student at school, or maybe a girlfriend. The act of trying to dominate another living thing to the point of causing harm or pain screams out, "I am more powerful than you!" Oh sure, he's tough or she's tough – he just tortured a two-pound frog, or, along with three other friends, she beat someone up. While you might think it makes you tough, it's your sadness that I see. I feel sorry for you. You must feel so empty inside that you sink to the most primal, subconscious, lowest form of power, harming others, generating fear to elevate yourself. Many teens will join gangs. They feel a benefit that comes with joining any group. They can feel a sense of belonging, of safety in numbers, which serves to distract them from the emptiness they feel, but does not cure it. In fact, it does the opposite by creating a situation that only encourages violence. Each negative act creates more negative feelings on the inside, and a greater impulse to try to fill the growing emptiness. And, so, it can lead to a downward spiral. The toughness associated with violence is built on the premise that building yourself up on the outside will build you up on the inside. That is false. You have to build yourself on the inside first. That is when you will truly rise up.

Crime as Power

Anyone who is carrying a type of illegal weapon does so to instill fear in others. This makes them feel powerful; it hides their weaknesses. This form of power is a poor substitute as it traps the individual in a life of crime. They are trapped because they need others to fear them to boost themselves up. They most likely have experienced extreme fear in their own lives, maybe as a child, and their defense is to say, "Never again." So, they become the one who creates fear in, or inflicts pain on, others. It is very sad that our society glorifies weapons. So many boys, in particular, seek that fantasy world of violence. They obsess over violent games and play them for hours. They get a rush from the power they feel. They do not understand that members of real gangs or people in possession of real weapons have deep pain and emptiness inside. All forms of physical violence and crime rely on the need to instill fear in someone else, to overpower someone else. This is the lie that someone with low self-esteem tells themselves because they have confused having power with having value. Respect cannot be taken or demanded. It must be earned and given freely. Crime and aggression as power is an incredibly common and sad misconception in today's world. On a smaller scale, vandalism and tagging stem from power, too. The individuals who destroy other peoples' property do so to feel powerful and instill fear. Taggers use their secret identities to feel powerful as they damage city or town property. If only these individuals knew that the emptiness they are trying to fill is their own lack of self-esteem. In some municipalities, certain areas are designated for murals. In those cases and places, people can channel their creative energy in a positive way and earn the respect of their friends and community for their artwork.

Objects as Power

Does keeping up with the latest gadgets or fashions make you feel good? This is extremely common in our society. Being in style and up to date makes you feel included in an exclusive "with it" crowd. You may often find yourself judging others who are not "with it." Somehow, you believe your possessions have become an important part of who you are, as they separate you from others who cannot keep up or afford to have what you have. In reality, your objects have nothing to do with who you really are. You have created this false belief about yourself. Conversely, does it bother you to not have these possessions? Does it make you feel like you are worth less than another person? Actually, you are in a better position because you have fewer possessions to attach yourself to. Possessions do not make you a better person. The power they seemingly bring about is completely false. The joy that possessions bring is fleeting. Isn't that why people always want to buy more? Media tells you that possessions matter, but, if you can see through the hype, you can save yourself a lifetime of brainwashing.

Sexy as Power

I have observed many girls who dress in extremely sexy clothes, clothes that are revealing, tight and suggestive, not only for parties or clubs but to go to school or work. The attention they attract from the guys makes them feel powerful, as if to say, "You can look, but you can't touch – I am in control," or, "I have what you want and you can't get it [right now]." They feed off the attention. The media is a huge contributor to this one. Girls are so often portrayed in sexy clothes that it is considered normal and acceptable. Why? Because the media and advertisers love power. Self-esteem is not going to sell you anything. But, power is so appealing to the empty viewers. And so, ladies, according to the media, being sexy will get you power. To confuse the matter even more, the sexy clothing actually makes you appear *vulnerable*. So, it attracts the guys for the exact opposite reason you're trying to project. If she is viewed as vulnerable, then *he* feels powerful, regardless of whether it is to overpower her or to protect her. It is a strange power struggle. I see that the happiest teens can cut through the bullshit and dress for comfort and simplicity. Be yourself and strive for self-esteem. Once you get started and dress and act in a way that reflects your inner confidence, you will quickly see how shallow it all was.

Fame as Power

Most teens idolize celebrities. Most amazing athletes, musicians, and actors have overcome incredible challenges and adversity to make it to where they are. They didn't lose faith in their dreams and quit. They held on and tried harder. These are wonderful attributes. Perhaps, we should support them for the journey they made and not for how they look, or a single song, or a single movie. Find information about your favorite stars and learn about their journey.

Value them for their perseverance and talents and how they use them. There are wonderful, amazing celebrities out there, changing the world for the better, using their talents, success and status to raise important issues and being great role models. Through their talents, they enlighten us and get us to think in positive, inspiring and empowering ways using their music, movies, books, or personal actions to reach out. You can see their true self-esteem as they are trying to improve the lives of others. They recognize the value of everyone. That is impressive and is very much worth supporting.

Unfortunately, there are also a huge number of celebrities who are leading famous but miserable lives. If you listen to their stories, you will know so many of them were unhappy before they were famous. They were running away from misery or chasing after happy and that pushed them to make the many sacrifices they made to get to where they are. Ok, they made it, now they are rich and famous and unhappy. We read about their drug addictions, arrests, violence, using people, break-ups, divorces, and media scandals, you name it. It is important to realize that these celebrities don't put themselves on a pedestal. It takes the general public to play the game. You have to ask yourself, who made the "rich and famous" rich and famous? You did! Along with millions of others, that's who. Next time you pay to catch a glimpse of your favorite star, to see a movie or a game or go to a concert or download an offensive song, ask yourself, "What am I supporting? What am I paying for? To support their lifestyles? To support their drug dealers and their prostitutes? To support their addictions? To support more of their failed relationships?"

See through their misery and see the power-seeker inside. The money they make is a quick fix for them. They feel powerful as others bend to their wishes. And bend they do – money talks in the power game. They are not gods and should not be treated as such. Fame and fortune do not create happiness. Until they find that inside themselves, it is still missing. And the pain inside, and the pain they cause others, will continue. It is common for many spotlight-seekers to lack self-esteem, believing that, when they make it big, they will finally feel good. But, happiness comes from inside of you, not outside of you.

If you have a wonderful talent and you have a goal of fame in sharing your talent with the world, then go for it! But, don't mistakenly think that is where you will find your happiness. Get happy first, then let that shine out to the world, as you share your talent.

Status as Power

So many people are caught up with the fame complex. You have the ability to instantly broadcast yourself to the world on YouTube and post your every thought on social media networks. Add in the obsession with reality TV shows, and it is easy to imagine your own 15 minutes of fame. What is all the fuss really about? If you meet someone who has been on TV, are they better human beings than you? Are they more valuable than you? Maybe in monetary standards, but is that the only "value" we consider to be of worth? Is your Number One goal to be a star, to be rich and famous? Is that how you will judge your personal worth?

You need to realize that power does not give you self-esteem. No situation can give you that. No career can give you that. No other person can give you that. And, without it, no matter how big you become, you are still empty inside. Imagine if the goal to be famous became a goal to become a better, kinder, more generous human being? Imagine the world we would live in if everyone's goal was to make the world a better place. I have high hopes for humanity.

Power as Status

People of all ages are hurting themselves and others in an attempt to achieve or hold a certain social position in society. For adults, you will hear about people striving for a particular position at their work. They are rewarded financially for having the most clients, highest sales. As the saying goes, they are climbing the ladder of success. They gain a special status in the company or social circle. Is it wrong to try to achieve a high level? No. Everybody should try their very best to believe in themselves and strive to be the best they can be. As we discussed in the section on competition, this is part of healthy self-esteem. What is not healthy is the backstabbing, the stepping on others to get to the top. Many people reach the top this way and look around at everything they have. They look at the relationships in their lives they had to sacrifice to get to where they are, and they say, "Was this all worth it? Am I truly happy?" The answer is an overwhelming, "No." Teenagers are not exempt from status goals. In fact, some would say that it is more common in the teenage years than in any other time of life.

Fitting in is probably the number one goal of most teens. I think that is a healthy goal. Everyone should have a circle of friends whom they can trust and around whom they can be themselves. What is not so healthy is the disaster called the popularity contest. Consider online popularity, 600, 800, 1,200 Facebook friends??? Come on, really? Do you think you have that many friends? Online friends are not really your friends, and, yet, how many people update their status comments as if they are chatting with their five closest friends? It is very strange and, at no point, is it smart. If fitting in is your goal, that's fine, but don't fall into a delusion of popularity because of the number of Facebook friends you have or the number of people who "like" your posts. Popularity is a wicked game to play whether it's online or in reality.

Think of your school and the social circles there. I am sure you can think of some superficial people who think status is everything and others who don't think that. I can think of four specific groups or branches. Not everyone fits neatly into these four groups, but, perhaps, you will be able to recognize them.

- The Climbers
- The Defenders
- The Rebels

- The Awakened

The "Climbers" are people trying to climb the ladder of popularity and will sacrifice their pride and many true friends along the way. They are living with thoughts of, "I'm not good enough yet." The "Defenders" on the other hand, are individuals at the top of the popularity ladder who are constantly thinking about doing everything perfectly. They are careful of who they are seen with, who they are friends with, what they look like and who they date. They believe this is how they are valued. They live in fear of losing their higher ground.

Defenders and Climbers are very judgmental of others and themselves. They are constantly comparing the differences between themselves and others. If the differences a newcomer possesses are beneficial to them, they may be offered a spot in the social circle because it will elevate the defender's or climber's status. If the newcomer's differences offer no status value, the individual will be snubbed. Girls are more likely to judge others on appearance. Boys will judge more on talents (for example, athletic ability) or money and possessions, than on looks, but they still judge. In addition, I have observed that boys have a tendency to follow the snubbing actions of their female friends against other females. Girls at the top of this game can be downright mean. They are cruel to other girls, acting as if they are constantly in competition. Boys at the top of this game tend to seem overly confident and tough. They are often making jokes about others and leading conversations that tease or taunt someone in the circle. With their words, their humor, they seem to constantly compete with their friends and, of course, the climbers.

Both defenders and climbers place incredible importance on looks. They are the most likely to diet, regardless of how slim they are, or – at least, the guys – exercise mainly for the maintenance of their body, their looks. They want the coolest clothes, the latest electronic gadgets, and the coolest music. They party hard because they believe that is the way to be cool, the way to impress. In addition to looks, they might place importance on their own or other's money, skin color, religious differences and ethnic backgrounds. Inside, they may have extremely low self-esteem. They can be their own worst enemy. Their thoughts are on autopilot and are constantly judgmental, whether they are directed at themselves or others.

Are they bad people? Of course not. Saying they are "bad" or "wrong" is simply more judgmental thoughts. These people are good people who are suffering. They are trapped in a self-defeating spiral of comparison, living high highs and low lows. But their underlying negative thoughts turn to actions, and, of course, to consequences that constantly affect their happiness. The worst part is that most of them don't even know they are suffering.

In these first two groups, we have been describing people who place a great deal of importance on social status. We've discussed only two of the four branches. There are, of course, those people who do not place a great deal of importance on social status. There are generally two groups here as well. First, we have those who feel that they don't stand a chance at achieving the top of the ladder and so they have given up completely and hate or rebel against the status ranking altogether. Let's call these people "the Rebels."

The rebels have a different set of issues, and, on the bright side, they are much more accepting of others and their imperfections. They will band together and are a close group with loyal ties. They don't have much to lose, so you don't see the backstabbing behaviors that surface in the climbers and the defenders. But, where the climbers live with thoughts of not being good enough, and the defenders live in fear, the rebels live in anger and resentment of the other two groups. Their tolerance for conformity is low. They might be quiet but will express themselves physically through clothes, hair color, tattoos, piercings, etc. in a way that reveals to others how they feel.

When Rebels Become Defenders

Sometimes, unfortunately rebels can be just as shallow as the other groups. Let's say, for example, that you cannot possibly rise up the status ladder in your community or school because you have differences that set you apart. Sadly, sometimes it comes down to being from a different culture than the defenders. In this situation, if you are not alone, then you might simply start your own social circle and put yourself, and your new circle, at the top of a new ladder. Great. Now, we have Cliques, or worse, Gangs.

The final group is a group of people who have a very strong sense of who they are, and they respect themselves and all others, as well. They can see through the vanity in the first two groups and simply do not see any value in belittling others or the self-defeating thoughts of doubt. Let's call this group "The Awakened."

There are, of course, varying degrees of commitment to each of these groups. That is why I like to call them branches. People can find themselves anywhere along the branches. It is important, however, to understand that in each of the three groups – the Defenders, Climbers and sometimes the Rebels – their thoughts and actions are, unfortunately, focused on the same flawed thinking. They are each focusing on the **differences** between themselves and others.

Now, let's bring in the Awakened. These people form quite a fascinating group. I am amazed by the students I know who think in this way. In some cases, they might have suffered in the past – emotionally, physically, and/or socially – or, maybe, they have caused suffering for others. Perhaps, at one time, they found themselves in one of the other three groups, but, at some point, they recognized the unease within themselves, the emptiness, the spiral of unhappiness, and they said to themselves, "This is not the way I want to live."

In other cases, they might not have experienced trauma, but may have been raised differently, in their families, from the way the others were raised. Their parents planted the seeds of true self-esteem from an early age.

This Awakened group are calm in situations that others would find upsetting. Their priorities seem more in check. They live more by their own values and morals and are not easily swayed by trends. One of the most amazing qualities in people who fall into this group is how they treat others. They have amazing self-respect, but also amazing unconditional respect for others, for everyone. The Awakened can look at the Defenders, the Climbers and the Rebels and won't judge or resent them. They will get along with everyone. They simply recognize that, quite often, other people are unaware of their own behavior. They can sense that the others are kind of sleepwalking, just going through the motions. They are more emotionally connected, alert, awake … conscious. One could even say more alive.

How do they get to that point of consciousness? Instead of focusing on the differences between themselves and all others, they focus on the **similarities**, what we all have in common.

The good news is the world is seeing more and more conscious people. It's like we are waking up and becoming more conscious.

- If I could describe power-seeking behavior in one term, it would be "PUT-DOWN."
- Do you have a habit of falling into power-seeking behavior?
- Can you think of anyone that you know, or you have feared, or have been jealous of, who exhibits power-seeking behavior?

Leadership

Often power-seekers move into positions of leadership. Do not confuse Power-seeking leaders with good leaders. There are distinct differences between the two. Good Leaders recognize their own skills and strengths and they see how they can help to improve a system for others. They have climbed up to that position with hard work and dedication to improving that system. They help others below them to see their own personal value. They use the teamwork approach because they know that many different skill sets are required to achieve big goals, and that no one can do it alone. People who are working hard under them feel valued and appreciated.

Power-seeking leaders abuse their power and put others down. They push others down in order to feel higher up. They often do not recognize the value of others around them. They focus on people's errors and inadequacies, not their specific skills and strengths. People who are working hard under them do not feel valued or appreciated.

Power-seeking leaders demonstrate false esteem. They are generally trying to make things better for themselves. Good leaders demonstrate true esteem and they are trying to use the skills of many team members to make things better for everyone.

As you go through life, you may have leadership opportunities open up for you. I hope you take your special skills and talents and rise up to become a good leader full of expertise and wisdom.

True Self-Esteem

In the beginning of this chapter we discussed two sources of love – love from others and from oneself. True self-esteem comes from unconditional self-love. True self-esteem comes when you can let go of pain and begin to understand how truly incredible you are. It's when you become conscious of the inner life and love inside of you that has been there all along, but just covered up by pain. You realize that you are connected with everyone and everything around you. Anyone can be powerful or feel powerful, but what does that bring them? Go back and read the "power" examples again. This time, consider the feelings of the other people in their lives. There is a pathway of destruction following them everywhere. You see, one of the most amazing things that comes along with true self-esteem is that you also begin to understand the *incredible value of everyone else around you.* You have no desire to put others down or bend them to your will in order to elevate yourself. You have no desire to upset people by damaging property or threatening them. You no longer feel the need to make up stories about yourself because you finally understand that the real you *is* good enough.

Another incredible side benefit of self-esteem is how your perception of others changes. It was mentioned earlier that the essence of Power is based on the *differences* between you and others around you. It is important to understand that, when you achieve true self-esteem, your connection with others grows because you focus on the *similarities* you share. Once you understand the DAP (Distraction, Attention and Power-Seeking behavior) struggles when esteem is low, you can recognize them in others. Except instead of the negative reactions you would normally respond with, you can respond with understanding and peace because you now know where they come from. You won't feel angry and resentful at the power-seekers in your life, you won't feel jealous and try to keep up with the distraction-seekers, and you won't be annoyed or feel the need to rescue the attention-seekers. Life becomes calmer when you can stop judging others. When you understand why other people behave the way they do, you can respond with understanding and kindness to all. You know the incredible potential inside of them, even if they are not yet aware of it.

- Instead of distraction, seek inner peace and true happiness.
- Instead of attention from others, seek self-love and spend more time with healthy adult mentors.
- Instead of power, seek empowerment, and tap into the strength within you to bring *yourself* up.

Once you make it to this glorious place, you will want to *help* others, not hurt them. In your transformation you are elevated and, when you see the view from up here, you will only want to bring others up here, too. It is an incredible feeling – one worth sharing.

Big-Picture Points

- *Everyone needs love. We can receive love from only two sources. One source is others - family, friends, and partners. The second source is ourselves.*

- *Unfortunately, we often don't even consider the self-love concept at all. So, this leaves us dependent on the love we receive from others. This leads to a big problem because we cannot control the other people in our lives.*

- *A lack of love and attention from others causes a lack of self-worth. Generally, we move in three directions. We revert to D.A.P (Distraction, Attention and/or Power-Seeking) behavior.*

- *Distraction-seeking behavior is the attempt to fill the void inside with something that feels good – even if the good feeling is temporary. Any Distraction seems like a good distraction. These people have a very hard time being alone, being quiet. They are easily bored.*

- *Attention-seeking behavior confuses attention with Love. Any attention, good or bad, will create a temporary fix. It includes the "poor me" attitude, constant complaining, or causing trouble to gain attention.*

- *Power-seeking behavior works on the premise that putting others beneath you raises you up. Power-seekers must always involve comparisons between yourself and others. The positive feelings generated here are always temporary.*

- *There are many ways that people use power to make themselves feel better: Power in status, in sex and relationships, in material possessions, in crime, in violence.*

- *True self-esteem comes from self-love. With self-love, there is no need for any comparisons with others.*

- *You have the strength within you to bring yourself up. Once you are able to bring yourself up, you will stop searching for external sources of power, and deflating others to inflate yourself. Once you make it to this glorious place, and you see the view from up here, you will only want to bring others up here with you. This is why this incredible feeling is one worth sharing.*

CHAPTER 3
Stress and Coping Strategies

Photograph by Olivia Giroux

"Success is determined, not by whether or not you face obstacles, but by your reactions to them. And, if you look at these obstacles as a containing fence, they become your excuse for failure. If you look at them as a hurdle, each one strengthens you for the next."
— Ben Carson (Gifted Hands: The Ben Carson Story)

Freedom. That is one of the greatest benefits of becoming a teenager. You are now making your own decisions and being independent. This continues on into your adult years. But freedom comes with a catch. Along with freedom, come responsibilities. Responsibilities to friends and family, to events, to school work, jobs, teams, clubs, safety, etc., come with every decision you make. Growing up means that you have to carry your own responsibilities – the more we have, the heavier the load. It's like rocks in a backpack. Each rock represents a specific responsibility. For example, you may have a responsibility to a team, or for each of your classes, or to help out at home. We all carry a backpack of rocks around with us and for the most part we can manage quite well with the load we have. But sometimes added rocks are piled on. A fight with a friend or family member, a test or project, added work shifts, an illness in the family, money issues. Then the added load becomes too hard to carry. This is what we call stress. Stress is the Overload.

As teenagers and adults, every one of us carries around these backpacks of responsibilities and we all develop coping strategies when life feels heavy. The more overloaded/stressed we feel, the more often we turn to these coping strategies. The strategies we choose are either healthy/positive or unhealthy/negative. There are no neutral coping strategies. The healthy positive strategies help us to feel mentally, physically and emotionally stronger and help us carry our load. They also help to constructively deal with each individual rock and, therefore, lighten the load. When you use positive coping strategies life gets easier. Negative coping strategies do something very different. They add rocks. At the time they feel right, but in the long run, they make the load heavier and more difficult to carry. Then life gets harder and more frustrating.

I call the healthy, positive coping strategies *Toward Strategies* because they move you towards your better life and bring out the best in you. I call the unhealthy, negative ones *Away Strategies* because they move you away from your better life. It is very difficult to use the *toward* strategies one hundred percent of the time, but if you think of them as steps toward your better future, you can motivate yourself to experiment with some healthier ways to cope with life. Three steps forward, one step back is a great deal better than ten steps away. Once we take a closer look at the *away* strategies in this chapter, you will see that they have a sneaky way of keeping you low, keeping you down.

I think of stress as a boxing ring. In one corner is your self-esteem, your faith in your inner strength. In the other corner are the challenges you are facing. When your self-esteem is strong you can take on any challenge and make it through. When your self-esteem is low, you feel beaten up and deflated. In that state, sometimes you take one look at your opponent and give up before the fight even starts.

The ultimate goal with this book is for you to improve your self-esteem. Once you get there, you will be amazed at how strong you feel and how capable you are to face new challenges.

Life presents challenges. It's unavoidable. It is important that you learn to embrace the challenges you face. When we meet a challenge, we have a choice to work harder to get through it or run away and hide in a corner. Do not be afraid of working harder. Every time you rise up to face challenges, you reveal the amazing skills, gifts and strengths inside you. People who habitually shy away from challenges do not give themselves a chance to grow. They choose to stay low.

Let's break stress down into three main questions:
1. How does your brain and body handle stress?
2. How many challenges are you facing?
3. What are your coping strategies for dealing with stress?

Let's consider the first question.

Stress, by definition, is a change in something external or internal that your body has to respond to. We really do enjoy the feeling of predictability, so changes are often perceived negatively. But let's take look at what is really going on inside.

The Physiology of Stress and Anxiety

To fully understand what's going on in your body when you are dealing with stress, we need to look at the plan that nature has in mind for our survival. Biologically, humans are animals and our bodies have predictable, natural responses to sudden changes and threats to our safety and security.

To grasp this concept, let's head back in history, *way back* to caveman days. Imagine yourself as a caveman (or caveperson) and you are joining the hunt for a mammoth to supply food for your clan. While you are out on your quest for food, your hunting group is surrounded by a pack of sabre tooth tigers. What happens to your body in this terrifying situation? It goes into an Alarm response – your survival is at stake! In this instant, your body is making rapid preparations to generate incredible speed and strength for you to race to the safety of your family/clan if you are young, or to fight to save loved ones if you are a provider/caregiver/leader. This alarm response maximizes your chances of survival. If you can not identify a path to safety and fighting is futile, then freeze mode may take over.

Although many refer to this as the Fight, Flight, Freeze response to stress, Gordon Neufeld, PhD and Gabor Maté, MD in their 2013 book *Hold On To Your Kids*, call this an Alarm response. "Anxiety is an emotional alarm that warns us of danger, whether from attack or the threat of being separated from those who matter to us."

Lets adds context to these terms when discussing this Alarm Response. Flight (running) is a powerful instinct during times of high stress, but the direction is specifically towards our parents/caregivers/partners. Dr. Neufeld refers to this as Pursuit energy (for us to pursue our protectors.) The Fight is for our own survival and the safety of those we care for, and provide for, if they are threatened. Think of a parent fighting for their child's safety.

When faced with danger or a threat, the Freeze instinct kicks in as we take in as much sensory information as possible (there is no thinking involved, it is all subconscious.) The Freeze instinct might be helpful to make us invisible to predators if we can stay still long enough. All of these actions are completely innate – subconscious – there is no thinking going on. These are our survival instincts.

As we delve into the "alarm" state, it's important to mention the opposite state our body can be in. Envision an ON/OFF switch in our brain. If the switch is "on," we are in our alarm state called the Sympathetic Nervous System (SNS). If the switch is "off," we are in the Parasympathetic Nervous System state (PNS). This is our resting state. Here we are relaxed and calm, we sleep well in this state and can be very introspective and creative in our thinking. This Parasympathetic state is also the digestion state. In the PNS, blood flow can be diverted away from the muscles and sent to the digestive system. The nickname for the Parasympathetic System is "Rest and Digest." *(Remember this, we will come back to it a few times in this book.)*

Let's get back to the SNS, your alarm state. Once the Alarm is triggered, it is your Sympathetic Nervous System (*sympathetic* to your dangerous situation) that controls the changes. Specific internal adjustments unfold as the hormone commonly known as adrenaline races through your bloodstream. Adrenaline acts as a signal communicating to all of your body systems that it's time to kick into survival mode. Your senses become heightened, so you can detect vital information in your surroundings. Your breathing becomes rapid to gather more oxygen for your muscle cells. Your heart beats faster to deliver blood to the muscles. And your body, which has a fixed amount of blood, has to direct blood flow to the muscles, which means it has to divert blood flow away from other body systems. Some of the systems that are sacrificed, and will only receive the bare minimum blood flow, are your digestive system and your reproductive system. Your muscles will tighten and twitch as all systems fire up and sweating will increase to cool the body.

These changes happen almost instantaneously, and we gain the strength to run with incredible speed and fight with incredible power. When you do make it out alive, if the threat is still nearby, sleep will be restless as your brain constantly monitors sounds that could translate into danger in the night. Once the threat is over, your Parasympathetic Nervous System takes over and you will sleep incredibly deeply out of shear exhaustion from the physical energy you've exerted. You will also have hunger return and blood will be diverted to your digestive system to help you refuel. Remember this is our "Rest and Digest" state. All of these biological adjustments have served humans throughout history in life or death situations. Our body's response to danger is amazing!

Now, let's fast forward to present day. Our sources of perceived danger (stress) have changed immensely. But our stress response system can't distinguish between a life or death physical threat and a source of mental stress like writing a test or making a presentation. So, we experience the same alarm response. Our body's automatic response induces rapid breathing, racing heartrate, tight and restless muscles, and excessive sweating. Digestive system symptoms include dry mouth, stomach ache, nausea, diarrhea (from reduced blood flow to the digestive system), easily distracted and racing mind, and difficulty sleeping. Sound familiar?

The chart on the following page will help you connect your symptoms of stress and anxiety with your body's natural responses.

System	Reason for the Natural response	Stress/Anxiety Symptoms
Nervous system and senses	Senses heightened to scan surroundings for vital information for survival. Light sleeping, listening for threat.	Easily distracted, mind racing, over-active thoughts "What if…?" Difficulty sleeping, always feeling tired.
Respiratory system	Breathing faster and deeper to supply oxygen to power muscles.	Fast breathing, some may feel like they are hyperventilating.
Circulatory systems	Heart rate increases to send oxygen rich blood to muscles faster. Blood/fluids are diverted to skin to cool body.	Heartbeat racing, sweating, cool clammy skin.
Digestive system	Receives less blood flow so muscles can receive more. Digestive Organs will temporarily shut down until the threat is over.	Dry mouth, Abdominal pain and discomfort, Lack of appetite, Nausea, Diarrhea. *(Note: large intestines normally turn liquid waste into solid waste by absorbing water, when they are given time to do their job properly.)*
Muscular system	Primed for intense speed and power.	Feeling restless, fidgety, tense, stiff neck and back.

So many students report anxiety and think something is really wrong with their bodies. They believe that when they experience symptoms of anxiety, when they have to face a specific challenge, that physical harm is unfolding inside of them and these symptoms freak them out. In many cases, their fear of these symptoms creates further stress and the situation snowballs. It is important that people understand that these symptoms are completely natural.

Our alarm center in our brain that controls all of this is the Amygdala. It's a tiny part of our brain, but it can override many other brain functions, particularly the developing Prefrontal Cortex mentioned in Chapter one. If we are alarmed, our brain goes into survival mode. It is preparing for rapid responses, quick actions, so it actually decreases activity in the PFC, as that area weighs decisions over longer periods of time. Keep this in mind. We are going to come back to this soon.

Although the Alarm response is natural, there is a significant problem with the design of this historically successful physiological reaction when used to respond to present day stressors. The biggest issue comes down to the length of time that we are exposed to the stressors.

We are not designed to be dealing with stressors that remain for days/weeks/months. Usually we get a short-term release of adrenaline and we respond with physical exertion. (This is why exercise is so important to decrease the stress/alarm response.) When the stressors do not go away the longer-term hormone Cortisol is called in. The build up of stress hormones like adrenaline (the gas pedal of stress response) or Cortisol (the cruise control of stress response) can exhaust the body's systems and cause long term (but *reversible*) damage.

Since challenges will always present themselves in life, it is critical that we all find ways to recognize the natural alarm/stress response and that we choose helpful coping strategies to strengthen ourselves to better manage it. Positive coping strategies can be used to calm ourselves in the moment to help us get through the challenge. They can also help us to release the adrenalin that has been building up. The goal is to use a variety of healthy strategies in your day to day life to keep your baseline experience set to "calm" instead of a baseline set to "racing." Choosing helpful coping strategies can significantly improve your response to challenges and will make life a lot easier for you.

Additionally, at some point when the alarm state has really been on intensely, it is important to release the emotional build up with nature's design for this - tears. Crying, shedding tears, is our brain's way of releasing emotional build up. This helps us to access our

---

Prefrontal Cortex again for clear thinking after the emotional release (crying in a safe place - alone or with an emotionally safe person.) Releasing the emotion, not stifling it, is what moves us towards resilience.

If you are carrying intense emotional pain, or pain you have been holding for a long time, try turning to nature's most instinctual response to let it out. Cry. Once emotion has been released, we have access to peace and clear thinking again. Afterwards, we can look at our situation, and possible solutions, literally with fresh eyes.

John punched a kid at lunch. He'd had a really crappy morning. He was so pent up about so much happening at home. His parents were fighting again, threatening divorce, he hated school and had just bombed a test. When Miller started teasing John at recess he just snapped.

This wasn't the first time that he'd been sent to the office, but something different happened on this day. Usually, when he goes to the office he gets a lecture. He doesn't really listen, he usually remains silent with his back up. Afterwards, nothing changes for him. This time, the VP sent him into his office and he told him to wait on his own.

While he was sitting there alone, fuming, his frustrations turned to tears. He started to cry and then it turned into sobbing. He couldn't stop it, but in a weird way he didn't want to. When the VP finally came in, John tried to hide the fact that he was crying, but of course he couldn't. When the VP asked him what happened, tears fell again. The VP was patient and kind. John's tears stopped and, without the VP asking him, he apologized on his own. John was able to think very clearly and came up with a calm strategy for next time.

No lecture, just time, tears, release and clear thinking. He walked out of that office feeling lighter then he had in a very long time. It was also one of the last times he was ever sent to the office.

It's kind of sad that for many generations we've been told that tears are a sign of weakness. In fact, once we've released what's been building up, we can unlock the door to our inner wisdom. Let's revisit our original three questions and deal with #2. How many challenges are you facing? This can also be read as, "How much stress do you have?" If your answer is, "Too many challenges, too much stress," then take a look at the sources of your stress. Perhaps it comes more from one area than another. Maybe it's a combination of sources. Is it friends, school, parents, family, career path, work, relationships, or health? I hope, as you read this book, you become more motivated to heal yourself and heal these areas in your life to help reduce the anxiety you feel.

Stress can be caused by a single traumatic or heartbreaking event, or it can be the combination of many smaller events that still feel overwhelming. Issues like breakups, infighting in peer groups, worrying about friends, family separations, school pressure, and increased responsibilities are difficult to handle. Another issue that everyone faces at some point is learning to manage your time. It can be a challenge to juggle part-time work schedules, homework, sports and activities, relationships, friends, family time, and personal time. The frustrations and anxiety you feel are very real. Don't ignore them or push them under the carpet. Deal with them. Deal with the feelings and deal with the causes.

Sometimes when I am feeling stressed about too many things, I find strength in the following quote:

"God grant me the serenity to accept the things I can not change, the courage to change the things I can, and the wisdom to know the difference."
                    -Reinhold Niebuhr

Sometimes stressors are unavoidable. If you can't deal with them by addressing them or making healthy decisions to avoid them, you still need to recognize them and deal with them another way. That's where the positive *Towards Strategies* can help you reduce your stress response and help you get through the stuff you have to deal with. More on that coming up.

Now, let's consider the third question, "How do you handle your stress?" If you are easily stressed out or you usually overreact to challenges, perhaps you need to make some changes to how you react. It is easy for us to respond with what I call, A.S.A. (Anxiety, Sadness and/or Anger.) I will not use the term "depression." Depression is a clinical diagnosis, and I find many teens overuse the term. While I cannot diagnose anyone as depressed, I do know that many teens feel deep sadness and anxiety, and that it is, in many cases, preventable. I find it amazing the number of young people who are overcome by A.S.A. and don't know what to do about it. Life will always present challenges. The trick is learning to deal with these challenges in a healthy, productive way in order to control your stress, and improve your relationships and life.

Coping With A.S.A. (Anxiety, Sadness and/or Anger)

I had a student who confessed to me that she wasn't eating because she hated herself. I replied that it must be horrible to feel the need to punish herself, and I could imagine that, without food, she was feeling physically terrible. I also asked her, point blank, if she wanted to live or die. She was shocked by my blatant question, but then, she replied, "Die." We talked about her sadness and it led her to a really good cry. Something she admitted she'd been avoiding.

Afterwards, I said, "What if you could feel better, mentally and/or physically, three months from now, would you still want to die?"

She shrugged her shoulders because she didn't know. She said she hadn't thought about it before because she figured she'd always feel this pain. I asked her if it was worth a try, and she responded

with something I'd never seen on her face – a smile – followed by,
"OK."

Feeling deep sadness and anger are completely normal and important. Do not feel bad about your emotions. Don't fight it. Feel it. Be.

The Alarmed Brain

Emotions are there for a reason, they are a way that our brain communicates to us that things are not going the way they should be and that we have to adapt. Emotions are tied deeply to the body's natural stress response that we discussed earlier.

When we are on overload (overstress) our brain tries to protect us. Our brain's number one goal is survival and we rely on each other for survival. When we are young, we are not meant to be alone. Our brain actually perceives this as a threat to our survival. So, when we feel alone, or excluded, or different than those around us, we go into a stress response.

This is tricky because our brain works like we are cavemen with solid and continuous clans, but in modern times, we have an ever-changing social environment. On top of that, change and unpredictability are constants for a teenager. You are travelling from childhood to adulthood and there are new things to learn and experience everyday. Your brain feels pretty threatened during this time.

Don't worry, adulthood is much easier. As an adult, our pre-frontal cortex is developed, and we can make really good long-term decisions, even under stress. This allows us, for the most part, to be in control of our daily events (until you have your own children.) For now, let's get back to this alarmed brain thing and figure out what's going on.

Level ONE Threat/Emotional Stress

At this stage, your brain is triggering the sympathetic stress response that we spoke of earlier. The part of the brain that sets this off is the amygdala (emotion central.) It throws the *sympathetic switch* sending nerve messages to stimulate the pituitary gland, which sends a signal to the adrenal glands, which in turn will release adrenaline, our stress hormone.

As mentioned before this hormone will wake up the body and call us to fight/flight action. But it is designed to be short term. This is the biggest problem. Our stresses stay with us too long, or pile on top of one another, and we can't get away from them. In an effort to find safety and security, we use an instinct we've had since childhood. When under threat, our instinct is to follow our protectors, do what they do, and do what they ask us to do.

Generally, this worked for a family unit. This is nature's plan. Parents keep kids safe. But this is complicated now that you are a teen because sometimes you are looking to your friends instead of your parents for direction. And some friends may lead you away from safety, not towards it.

When we are experiencing prolonged alarm, our brain may start seeking other ways to get to the resting state, the *Parasympathetic mode*. Do you remember this from a few pages back? This is the Rest and Digest state of the nervous system, or the stress "OFF" switch. Our brain desperately wants a break from the alarm state. The alarm state is being triggered by external events, so it tries to trick the system internally. It tries to start up the digestive system.

Your brain attempts to kick start the digestive system by telling you to eat or put something in your mouth, so you can fall into the parasympathetic resting state. This is why people stress eat, bite their nails or smoke cigarettes. Weird, isn't it? If you don't turn to healthy mentors to help you release your emotions and help you to problem solve, and if you don't turn to healthy coping strategies, you'll likely wind up at the next level.

Level TWO Threat/Emotional Stress

If kick starting the digestive system doesn't work, there are more things the amygdala will do. If it feels very threatened, from too much pain (usually social pain), it will request a ramp up of stress hormones to wake the body up. It's almost like it's saying, "This is bad. Why can't this person wake up to the situation and get away from all of this pain? I'll just have to wake them up!"

This causes an increase in adrenalin in our blood stream, as well as a second stress hormone called cortisol. This starts as an emotional response, and we are meant to feel these emotions. But if we don't react and adapt, our brain increases the stress response, so we will wake up and seek safety. Unfortunately, if this occurs too often or for too long, and we don't adapt, we become hyper-sensitive to feeling this increased stress response, and now it just feels like anxiety.

If we don't or can't adapt to this increased stress response, neurologically our brain starts ignoring it. The underlying emotions are still there, but we are cut off from the "feelings" to protect us from too much pain. The brain stops registering the feelings altogether, but the stress response continues. The hormones are still circulating to keep the body alert. The result is that we'll just be agitated and restless, short-fused, often on a hairpin trigger. In an agitation state, we are overreactive and angry, easily annoyed by others. If you still don't turn to healthy adults to let you release your emotions and help you to problem solve, if you still don't turn to healthy coping strategies, you may wind up at the next level.

Level THREE Threat/Emotional Stress

For some people emotional pain is really intense. This is particularly true if home life is not a safe place. We all need a place where we can relax and be calm, not feel threatened. (I'm not talking about your parents nagging you to do your chores, I'm talking about harmful or traumatic situations at home, where you are regularly not feeling safe and supported.) If emotional pain is not being released and the stress hormones are continually building, then a feedback mechanism kicks in.

One of our controls in our brain is the hypothalamus. It continually monitors what is in the bloodstream and makes internal adjustments. When it registers too much adrenaline and/or cortisol, it intervenes and stops the signal to the adrenal glands. The result is very little, if any, of the stress hormones entering the bloodstream. Now before you consider this a good thing, I want you to know that Adrenalin is not just a stress hormone. It is also released when we are really excited, happy, laughing, and during times when we are feeling emotionally connected to others, like being in love. So, when this signal is interrupted, people at this level of emotional pain are left feeling numb. They can do very alarming things without having much of an emotional response. Sometimes they seek out risky activities just so they can feel something/anything. Some may describe them as being emotionally cold.

Let's go back to levels one and two for a moment. Emotions are meant to be felt, they are important. If you didn't know deep sadness, you could not appreciate great joy. If you cannot experience intense anger, you could not appreciate peace. Without a deep understanding of struggle and frustration you could not appreciate the excitement of success.

We should not fear our feelings and try to avoid or suppress them. In fact, the fastest way *out of* sadness is to go deeper into it until release comes in the form of tears. All emotions require release, safe release in a safe place, maybe with a safe person or maybe alone. If we suppress our negative emotions, they will stay with us and keep us low as we bottle them up. As a result, sometimes we may erupt, sometimes we may go numb/cold. Releasing emotions, especially through tears, helps us move into the control of the Parasympathetic Nervous System and we can rest deeply.

Tears are nature's design for releasing pent up energy in the amygdala region. After a good cry in a safe place, alone or with an emotionally safe person, we find ourselves in the parasympathetic state, calmer, more level headed and much more able to think of solutions to our problems. (Note: an emotionally safe person is someone who will allow the tears and will not try to hurry them or stop them. They will also not tease you for crying.)

I know this is tricky when, for generations, tears have been perceived as a sign of weakness, especially for boys. But nothing could be farther from the truth. Through unrestrained tears, we can shake off what's bugging us, recover quickly and move on towards true emotional resilience, while maintaining our ability to connect deeply with others.

I heard Dr. Neufeld describe the term "cool" in one of his talks in a most revealing way. Dr. Neufeld has worked with numerous troubled children and teens, many who were incarcerated for serious crimes. As we all know, "Cool" is something that many teens strive to be, or they strive to follow those who are "cool." This may bring to mind someone who exhibits an "I don't care" attitude.

Dr. Neufeld explained that cool means emotionally cold, to suppress emotions. While working with these troubled teens, he was able to make direct links to the use of drugs and alcohol to suppress their sadness and anger. Sadly these "cool" or emotionally cold individuals sometimes acted out in dangerous or violent ways that made it seem like they had no conscience. Often these individuals had dealt with severe trauma and so the brain set up a defence against extreme pain.

So, how cool does "cool" sound now? Should we really admire this emotionless state?

Sometimes life is tough and all we can do is to get to a safe place and cry. It is a resiliency tool. Remember, it gives you access to clear thinking afterwards. When it comes to coping strategies, there are basically two roads to take. You can choose coping strategies that will help you in the long run and strengthen you, or you can choose strategies that add to your pain.

Teen Stress is Real

Do you want life to get better? Once you decide you want to feel better, there are many ways you can do it. It is of paramount importance for you right now to establish healthy coping strategies in response to overload. Here is the reason.

As a teenager, you are experiencing real stress in your life, hopefully for the first time. For those of you who experienced extreme stress in childhood, I will discuss that in a moment. For now, let's assume that, as a child, your family protected you from most of the big challenges that life has to offer, exposing you only to what was appropriate for you to handle at that age. But, now, here you are in the teenage years, and, for the first time, you are in the full throws of balancing school, jobs, teams, clubs, friends, family, illnesses and any and all effects those issues bring. You have many challenges. You are under stress.

Well, I'd love to tell you that it's just a phase you're going through and it will get better, but challenges will always present themselves. Stressful situations can and will hit at any, and every, stage of your life. Along with the stresses growing, so do the pressures and your responsibility toward others. But just because life has challenges doesn't mean that life sucks. On the contrary, the better you are at handling challenges, the easier life gets and the smoother your ride through life. And so ...

Right now, as you begin this rollercoaster of coping with challenges and stress, it is CRITICAL that you choose some healthy coping strategies, because what you learn to use now are the very same strategies that you will continue to fall back on for the rest of your life. The fights you pick, the alcohol you drink, the joints you smoke now, as a teen, might not seem so bad as coping strategies – relaxing you, getting your mind off things, relieving stress – but they have a very different face when you are a professional, an employee, a caregiver, a spouse, and, most importantly, a parent. In the long run, unhealthy *away* coping strategies will make your life worse and create more stress for you. So, right now, as you are making your first attempts at figuring out various coping strategies, choose wisely. Choose more *toward* strategies and you will come out better, stronger and healthier.

Have a look at the chart on the following page. Make a note of, or circle, the *toward* and *away* strategies you have used.

(The list of Toward and Away Strategies is also provided as a downloadable/printable file on the website www.byoh.ca.)

"Toward" Coping Strategies Move you *toward* your better future	*"Away" Coping Strategies* Move you *away* from your better future
✓ Talk to a close family member or caring adult and ask them to listen ✓ Release your frustration in safe ways ✓ Exercise/work out/play sports ✓ Cry, Bawl, let it out ✓ Ask for Help ✓ Focus on the end goal: success ✓ Problem solve ✓ Create a timeline to get work done ✓ Get outside for fresh air/spend time in nature ✓ Go to bed early and get a good night's sleep ✓ Write down your issues and potential solutions ✓ Draw or paint ✓ Play an instrument/sing/dance ✓ Write a song/poem/letter ✓ Write in a journal; focus on solutions ✓ Pray – for strength, guidance to find solutions ✓ Breath slower/Yoga/Meditation ✓ Run/bike/skateboard ✓ Improve your eating habits/cook a healthy recipe/eat slowly ✓ Walk the dog/play with a Pet ✓ Build something/take on a project/hobby ✓ Tidy up your room/space at home ✓ Have a nap ✓ Take a day off ✓ Connect with healthy friends & laugh ✓ Watch a movie: funny movie to let yourself laugh uncontrollably, or sad movie to let yourself cry, and create an emotional release ✓ Confront the person who is causing you stress (*but in a way that works toward a mutually acceptable solution)* ✓ Listen to Sad music so you can cry and release your sadness and frustration ✓ Listen to positive music that strengthens you ✓ Talk to a counselor or therapist ✓ <u>Focus on positive thinking – focus on the solutions</u>	✕ Negative self-talk ✕ Vent on social media ✕ Watch more Screens/TV ✕ Play more computer games ✕ Eat more ✕ Eat junk food ✕ Don't eat ✕ Go shopping (spend more than you should) ✕ Stay up late ✕ Sleep less ✕ Turn towards friends who themselves use "away" coping strategies ✕ Skip school ✕ Complain continually ✕ Blame others ✕ Avoid responsibility for your actions ✕ Scream/yell at others ✕ Play violent video games ✕ Send mean messages on social media ✕ Direct your anger/sadness at others in your life (such as family) ✕ Bully others, push them down to raise yourself temporarily ✕ Manipulate, insult, try to control others ✕ Avoid other people or situations ✕ Hide at home (or in your room) ✕ Listen to angry music that fuel your thoughts of unsafe actions ✕ When you think you might cry, fight the tears do not allow the release ✕ Suppress your feelings, try to numb your pain ✕ Smoke Cigarettes ✕ Drink Alcohol ✕ Take Drugs ✕ Self-harm ✕ Think of, or plan, revenge ✕ Think of, or plan, suicide ✕ <u>Continue your negative thinking – focus on the problems</u>

How "Away" Coping Strategies Backfire on You

There is a wonderful saying that I fall back on when times are tough:

"This, too, will pass."

It is an amazing way to view life. Enjoy each and every moment, because they soon pass.

And, do not lament about the tough times, because they will pass as well.

The stress you are experiencing will pass, but the *away* coping strategies you choose will make the recovery process much more difficult. For example, if eating is your coping strategy, then know that the trigger will eventually pass, but those extra pounds you've gained while "coping" will just add more stress to your life for a longer time than the trigger, because you will wind up carrying around extra weight. If you unload your frustrations on social media as a way to vent, then long after the trigger has passed, you are stuck with the repercussions of the angry words you typed. If skipping school is your favorite way to wind down, then you can look forward to extra piles of catch up work, disappointed teachers, arguments with your parents, and the added stress of working harder to make up for your coping strategy.

Can you see the snowball effect? You begin with challenges and, as you "cope," you create more problems, more stress for yourself. Remember the rocks in your backpack? In the long run, each *away* coping method puts more rocks into your bag. They make life more challenging, more difficult. Look at the big picture. It's time to jump off the train before it crashes. I don't expect you to use *toward* coping strategies every time, but hopefully you can use *toward* strategies much more often than the *away* ones. I'm sure you can think of adults in your life who have poor coping strategies. Maybe you have witnessed firsthand the snowball that rolls and gets out of control. The teenage years are a great time to experiment. If you can recognize that you are using a lot of the *away* strategies listed in the chart, realize the ways you deal with stress now will be the ways you deal with it in the future. The strategies you repeatedly turn to now will become habits as you get older. Now is the time to experiment with new ways to cope and to develop new, healthy habits. We're talking about the direction of your life. Don't you think it's worth the effort to experiment with some coping strategies that move you *toward* your better future?

I often take classes out to our local nature trails for a day of hiking and fresh air. During one Friday's hike, I overheard a Grade 12 student talking to her friend. She said, "I can't believe how great I feel out here! I've been so stressed lately. I was going to party it off tonight, but it's so nice to know that there is another way to feel better."

As I was walking behind them, I couldn't get the smile off my face.

Try out some *toward* coping strategies. It's worth it! *You* are worth it! Your future is worth it!

Childhood Trauma and Coping Strategies of Young Children

There are a group of you who, unfortunately, have been exposed to a great deal of trauma during childhood. The *toward* coping strategies on the previous page are hard to do, even as a teen. For a child who has grown up witnessing unhealthy ways of coping with life, those healthy *toward* strategies seem way beyond their reach. Children who have experienced trauma will use any means they can in order to adapt to their situation and survive. They will hide, become emotionless, steal, hurt themselves, hurt other kids at school, disconnect from school, avoid certain situations or people, blame themselves, become perfectionists to an extreme, become numb to difficult events, you name it. Children who are exposed to trauma do not have the experience or thought processes to explore positive, healthy coping strategies. Sadly, they are caught in a trap.

These behaviors are symptoms, not problems. These are symptoms of their feelings of anger and sadness that they don't know how to deal with or express. They haven't had the healthy models they need to teach them how. Their behaviors are, literally, cries for help. Unfortunately, often these cries are not heard and go unanswered. As a result, many will carry their extremely unhealthy coping strategies into their teenage and adult years. These strategies further alienate them, which leads to more stress in their lives.

IF YOU HAVE BEEN EXPOSED TO EXTREME STRESS OR TRAUMA AS A CHILD, PLEASE SEEK COUNSELING. Seek assistance as soon as you can. You are not responsible for the stressful events in your early life, and you are not responsible for your childhood coping strategies, but you ARE responsible for your behavior and coping strategies as a teenager and, later on, as an adult. Please GET HELP, especially if you find yourself falling into the trap of unhealthy coping strategies. Choosing to ask for help is a sign of strength. It is a big step toward a better life.

Some stressful, traumatic events that can affect children are:
- Abuse (verbal, physical, emotional, sexual)
- Bullying
- Divorce
- Death of a family member or friend
- Watching parents, family members fight, especially if they are under the influence of drugs and alcohol
- Witnessing severe illness in a family member
- Experiencing a traumatic event (natural disaster, fire, theft, violence)
- Being exposed to Television that is inappropriate for children
- Being exposed to Internet information that is inappropriate for children

The last two are extremely common.

Internalizing and Externalizing Stress

When we have poor coping strategies, we can hurt ourselves, and we can also hurt others.

Internalizing stress means that we take our stress out on ourselves through negative thoughts and vices, as we will discuss in Chapter 8. The majority of teens internalize their stress, although many are capable of externalizing their stress as well.

Externalizing stress means you take your stress out on others. Usually the victims of your pain and anger are the people closest to you, usually in your own family. You will yell at a parent or sibling or maybe at a girlfriend or boyfriend. It happens easily and is far too common. We've all done it. You are upset by something and you, simply, but not necessarily on purpose, redirect your frustrations at someone or something else. Unfortunately, for many people, this becomes the pattern of how they deal with their stress and, quite often, they take it out on the weakest and most vulnerable people in their lives. This is the core of an abusive relationship.

The goal of this book is to help you improve your own self-esteem, for many reasons. One of those reasons is so that you never become a victim of abuse. But I also want you to improve your self-esteem so that you will never be a *Perpetrator* of Abuse. Yes, you read that right. It is critical for you to get a handle on your own issues, so YOU do not harm others.

Whether it is a boss who yells a lot, or a verbally abusive girlfriend or boyfriend, or physically abusive parent, or a gang member who gets in fights, or a rapist, each of these examples are people who externalize their stress. They cannot handle the crap in their own lives and so they take it out on others. Their anger has become their habitual negative coping strategy. Our world is so full of violence that taking your frustrations out on others is actually considered the norm. For example, these days, people can watch the violence in videos, movies, and on TV without so much as batting an eyelash at what they are seeing.

I desperately want you to learn healthy ways to handle your stress before you have children. You might ask, "What does that have to do with me right now?" Well, if you ever want to become a parent, you'd better start retraining your emotional responses now. It might take you years before you get it right. Babies and children are, by far, the most vulnerable group of humans on the planet. If Mom or Dad starts taking out frustrations on them, what are they going to do? Where are they going to go? Nowhere. They take it because they have no other choice.

I am bringing this up because, once you are a parent, on top of every other stress in your life, it is unavoidable that your children will give you more stress even though they don't mean to. They will wake you up four times a night, every night. When you are exhausted, they will cry uncontrollably, they will misbehave, they will poop in their pants when you are in a rush to go somewhere, they will talk back to you, and they won't eat the dinner you've just spent an hour making. They will push your buttons in ways you cannot yet even fathom. And, undoubtedly, you will get pissed off and, if you are not well trained at dealing with your stress in a healthy way, you might scream and yell at them for nothing (*really*), and, if you are really bad at handling your stress, you might just hit them or lock them in a room or totally lose control and beat them. It happens in far too many homes to far too many children. And, of course, they might grow up and think that acting that way is normal and they will do it to their kids because no one has taught them how to handle their own stress except to externalize it and take it out on someone else.

Understand this truth above all others: You have Absolutely NO RIGHT to harm another living being, cause damage to someone's property, or cause an animal to suffer.

Get your shit together. Now! Do it before you hurt the most important people in your life.

Confront your dark secrets now.

If, right now, you have the following thoughts recurring, it is critically important for you to seek help immediately before these dangerous thoughts become actions.

- Serious negative thoughts
- Recurring thoughts of suicide or hurting someone else
- Deviant sexual thoughts
- Thoughts of hurting children or animals or women or people of a particular culture

Once these thoughts become actions, they will take you down a horrific road that leaves a trail of incredible pain for you and others. Some of you are in so much pain now that you want to share the pain. That is what this entire book is for, to show you that you do not have to live in pain. You have a choice. Keep reading. And, be open to getting help. Talk to trustworthy adults or call a teen help hotline and get some counseling. Some helpful organizations are listed at the back of this book. Yes, this is a huge challenge for you, but do it and you will see how much healthier you can be and feel. Then, at the end of this journey, you will look back and know it was the most important decision you ever made.

To Survivors of Abuse

If you are a victim of abuse, whether it is emotional or verbal abuse and, especially, if it is physical or sexual abuse, you must understand that what happened to you or is happening to you, is NOT OK. It is not acceptable, and you do not have to try to live with it or the memory of it. It is not your fault. My heart goes out to all of you, and I want you to be strong and courageous. Ask for help. Tell someone who is in a position to help you. It pains me to know that many victims cannot talk to their own parents about their abuse because either the parents are in denial or the abuse has happened in their home, for example between siblings, or the parents themselves are the perpetrators. In these cases, going to your parents may not be an option right now. Going to a teacher, coach or counselor is critical. Be specific with your words. For example, you can say, "I don't know what to do, I need help." Or, "I need help. I need a safe place to stay." Perhaps you need to get away from home. Running away is not a good idea, as tempting as it may seem. Ending up on the street is not going to make your situation any better. Instead, go to a friend's house, where you know the family and they are not close friends with your parents. Sit down with your friend's parents and tell them everything. Ask for a safe place to stay and say that you need help. Or go to an aunt, uncle, older cousin or grandparent, as long as they will help you and not just try to shut you up and keep "the family secret." Make sure your parents and siblings and extended family all know why you left and that you are not going to take the abuse, or their silence, anymore. Create a support network for yourself by telling as many trustworthy adults as you can. Talk to someone you can trust about going to the police. Youth-counseling services can help. Ask your school guidance counselors for help and information.

People abuse others because they are in pain. They don't do it because they don't like you, they don't do it because you deserve it. They abuse because they are in pain. And, until they learn to deal with their pain, it will continue – *unless* you let them know you won't take it anymore. I have heard people say, "They only abuse when they are drinking/or using *(fill in a drug)*. Their addiction causes them to do it." That is false. People don't abuse others because they are drinking or on drugs. They are on drugs and drinking *because of their pain*. They are abusing others because of their pain. The alcohol and drug abuse is a symptom of this pain. It is not the cause. It is not OK for anyone around you to rationalize abuse. These concepts will be explored in greater detail in Chapters 8 and 9, but, for now, know these truths about you:

- You deserve to be safe from harm.
- No one has any right to abuse you.
- Home is supposed to be a safe environment.

- If home is not safe, then find a safe place to stay, and the street is *not* a safe place.

Getting away from the abuse is step one. After this comes a journey of healing where you must first forgive yourself and truly believe that this came from the abuser's personal pain and was not your fault. If you do leave home and stay with someone as a kind of safe house, please remember that – wherever you go, whoever you stay with – you must abide by their house rules, be helpful and respectful. The last thing you want to do is burn these support bridges due to poor manners and bad behavior.

This next part may scare you, but it is extremely important to be aware of. The fact that you are a victim means you are in pain and if you do not deal with your pain and release it in the right way, there is a possibility that you will take your pain out on someone else. The cycle of externalizing pain continues easily, generation after generation, for people who do not face their experience of abuse and the pain it caused them. You may have already sworn that you would never do this to anyone else, but it can surface as an adult, if you have not developed healthy coping strategies when times are tough.

I will now repeat a critical point from earlier in this chapter: You have no right to harm another living being or their property. This includes the perpetrator. You may defend yourself when they abuse you, and they may be harmed in that process – this is called self-defence – but you cannot initiate an attack or harm anyone. If you do, you have become an abuser and are taking your pain out on them. Make a vow to seek counseling and to learn to deal with your own stress so you NEVER repeat the cycle you have experienced.

Get away.

Get safe.

Get help.

Focus on healing yourself on the inside.

If someone shares with you that they are being abused, or have experienced abuse, do not judge them. Ask how you can help. Tell them you are there for them, to support them and to listen when they need to talk.

If this is <u>abuse from the past</u>, ask them if there is an adult that you can both confide in to get wise advice. For example, you can ask, "Can I talk to my mom about this?"

If the abuse is <u>going on right now</u>, you have a responsibility to talk to a trustworthy adult who can help your friend get to a safe location. Remember, your friend came to you. They reached out to you for help. This is too huge of an issue for you to solve it alone.

If you hear about abuse and you know it is going on, it is your responsibility to tell an adult who can help stop the abuse. These adults would include parents, school administrators, guidance counselors, teachers, coaches, ministers, doctors, kids/teen help hotlines, and of course you can just call the Police.

When it comes to abuse, Silence is a terrible thing.

Important Note: In this book, you will sometimes see the term "Victim Mentality." It does not apply to you, as you are one who *truly* is/was a victim of abuse. A victim mentality is when someone is facing a consequence of their *own actions* and is making up excuses or blaming others for their own poor decisions. For example, if a teen is in trouble at school or at home because of their behavior, they will often complain, "I didn't do anything!" Or, they will say, "He/she is singling me out, getting me in trouble." That is a victim mentality – feeling unfairly treated when you can't face up to the consequences of your own actions. Once again, the term "victim mentality" does not refer to you and your very real story.

Handling Immediate Anger – Arguments and Fights

Let's face it, anger is a part of life. Whether you get angry or not is less important than how you handle your anger.

Here are a few reminders:

- Never try to get your way when you are upset. Calm down and think before you speak.
- Try to keep your cool.
- If an apology is warranted, saying sorry is really powerful.
- Walk away. Wait until the emotional storm passes.
- Stay silent. If the other person demands a response, you can say, "I am not talking to you until you [or, I] calm down."
- If the conversation is getting heated, call for a "timeout." "This is going nowhere. I'm going out to walk this off." Then, actually go and take a walk around the block.
- Talk it out with a very positive friend, who can help you calm down.

Physical Outlets

- Go for a run, or bike ride or skateboard, or walk.
- Punch a pillow or throw a pillow around.
- Go in your room and scream.
- Go to a safe place and Cry.

When the emotions have settled, and your mind is not controlled by the angry or sad emotions, you will be able to sift through the situation and find solutions.

To summarize, being sad or being angry is only one part of the misery. A much bigger role in dictating our ease, or hardships, in life is in the coping strategies we choose.

If you don't use a healthy coping strategy you will not only be sad or mad about X, but now, on top of that, you have:

- Deep sadness because you hide out in your room, inside, with no fresh air or exercise.
- Difficult relationships because you externalize and yell at people.

- Poor marks because you turn to drugs, alcohol, or you simply disconnect.
- Extra weight packed on because you eat when you are stressed.
- Credit card bills because you feel better when you shop.
- Relationship issues because you vent on social media.

I hope you are getting the picture. The A.S.A. (Anxiety, Sadness and/or Anger) is only one small part of the misery when you look at the big picture. It is well worth it to examine your coping strategies and to get into the habit of choosing healthy ones.

Single Thread versus a Net

You may feel that, since you are so deep in the hole that you've dug for yourself, a way out seems impossible. So, you just resign yourself to the belief that this is your reality for always. You cannot dream of what it feels like to be out of the hole – you've forgotten. If getting out of the hole is something that you want, you may be tempted to count on others to get you out. You latch onto someone as if your life depended on that person, and, to you, it does. This is dangerous on a number of levels.

Firstly, what if you put all your eggs in their basket and they let you down? How much farther can you fall? You will soon find out. Consider being that person, trying to live their own life plus yours, too? Wow, that's one hell of a load to carry – even if they offer. At some point, resentment may turn up, followed by disappointment for you, and the cycle begins again. To rely on one person is dangerous. You could think of them as a thread. If you have only one connection, one person, you are holding onto life by a single thread. Instead, surround yourself with a complete net, a support network. Reach out to as many people as you can: family, caring adults, professional help, close friends whom you can trust. Create a network of support so that, if a single thread lets go, you won't fall.

There is one critical person in this process. YOU. All of these people can help, but the real hero is *you*. You are the one shining person in your life who can save you every time, regardless of how deep your hole is or how long you've been in it or what you went through to fall down into it. Your true hero is YOU. To put it another way, if you don't seriously want to get better, you won't. It's plain and simple. It is pointless to ask anyone else for help, unless you are ready to help yourself. Support and help is all around you, but it doesn't work until you are ready to be an active part of the healing process.

You have to *want* to get better.

How do you get to the point of wanting to help yourself?

Step One

Believe that there is a life for you that is not painful to live. Imagine your future self looking back on you now and saying, "Wow, that was a really hard time, but I am so glad it's over, and I'm thankful that I made it out and have the life I do."

Once you can welcome the possibility of a happier outlook on life, move to:

Step Two

Seek help from healthy adult mentors. Ask for help. Additionally, write yourself a little poster. On it write, "I want to feel better, and today I will take actions that will move me towards a better future." Then, hang it up in your room so that you see it all the time, and it will help you every day.

Step Three

Experiment with some Towards Coping Strategies.

Dealing with Loss

Life throws us many challenges. We feel blindsided by events that seem out of our control. Other challenges are consequences of decisions that we made in the past. Every once in a while, you will face challenges that overwhelm you. You may feel like the world is closing in on you, like you are drowning in sorrow and anger and self-pity. This pain and confusion is very real and should not be dismissed as trivial. Sadness, anger and despair are very important. Without these emotions, you would not be able to appreciate joy, peace and hope. By now, you understand the concept of choosing positive coping strategies, so you do not create more stress and pain for yourself. With every challenge that you get through, you will be strengthened to meet future challenges.

Heartache is one of the worst stresses to deal with, whether it is a breakup with a girlfriend or boyfriend, betrayal of a friend, parents separating, or death of a loved one. Loss and heartache can seem almost unbearable. Please consider carefully how you choose to deal with overwhelming emotions. Remember that crying, truly bawling, is nature's design for us to release our emotions. Unfortunately, sometimes we are encouraged to "get over" painful experiences too quickly before we have had a chance to move fully through the long and natural grieving process.

Turning to healthy supports is critical as well. One of the most inspiring young people I know is a former student who went through incredible deep pain and sadness, and the whole time he stayed focused on being good to himself and those around him.

To know Adam in high school, you'd have seen a great athlete, a wonderful, popular, funny, hardworking, and incredibly dependable guy. Every student thought the world of him, and so did every teacher. He was a tell-it-straight kind of guy, honest and compassionate. He cared about everyone. To know him now, he is still all of these things, and he owns his very own successful company, which he started from the ground up right after college. Through an environmental focus, his company is making the world a better place. To know this guy is to love and admire him.

Adam has been through a lot though, more than any teen should have to endure. Many teens dealing with even a fraction of what he has gone through have turned to extremely negative coping strategies. When Adam was 12, his parents divorced. He watched his dad battle alcoholism and saw his dad's life slowly unravel. After the divorce, he lived with his mom, but, when he was 15, his mom moved away to remarry, and Adam chose to stay and live on his own. That same year, he was called to the hospital to find out his dad had died. Adam continued to live on his own throughout high school and into college. When he was 19, he received an early morning phone call that his girlfriend had died in a drunk-driving accident. Alcoholism, divorce, living alone, death of a parent and then the death of a girlfriend ... How does a person get through all of that and still have hope and optimism?

When I was writing this book, I asked Adam to share with me how he made it through. He said, "I depended on a lot of great people. The teachers at my high school were amazing, and they became my family, I owe a lot to them. My friends were a huge support. They always called me to go out and fill my time, and I almost always said yes. Distraction was very good for me. I had to get my mind off things. I turned to the gym. I worked out hard and released a lot of negative energy that way. I also had to cry it out, too. When I really felt bad, I would remind myself that there were so many people around the world that have it way worse than me. I would think about them. I would also think of my girlfriend, who was incredibly positive, and I would think, 'How would she have wanted me to carry on?'"

Adam is a perfect example of someone choosing positive coping strategies in the face of misery. I think he saved his own life, certainly the quality of it. He still falls back on healthy strategies, and he knows he can get through a lot; he's proven it to himself. He wants to help others find their inner strength, too, and he takes every opportunity to do just that.

Adam managed to stay true to himself because he had a strong sense of his own value and the value of others' lives, the value of life itself. He is incredibly wise. That's true Self-Esteem. It's a beautiful thing.

Pain is an important part of life. As I mentioned before, sadness and anger enable us to fully appreciate joy and hope. Without conflict, we could not appreciate peace. Without sickness, we could not appreciate health. Without death, we could not appreciate life. We spend so much time searching for answers to the pain in our lives, when we should be searching for the lessons that pain teaches us. If we have learned nothing, the pain will be all that we have in the end.

There is one strategy that I deal with in more detail in the final chapter, but I will introduce it here. It is called, "A Glimmer of Hope." When you are in your darkest hour, is there a tiny glimmer of hope that can get you through this? Is there a tiny glimmer of hope that life will get better? Hold on to that glimmer, focus on it, and let it grow. Believe in your inner strength.

Aim for life getting better and use *toward* coping strategies to get there. Move toward hope, kindness, peace and health. Focus on Life. Focus on Love.

"The journey of a thousand miles begins with one step."
-Zen saying

Big-Picture Points

- *"Success is determined not by whether or not you face obstacles, but by your reactions to them. And, if you look at these obstacles as a containing fence, they become your excuse for failure. If you look at them as a hurdle, each one strengthens you for the next."* — Ben Carson

- *Life presents challenges. It is a natural part of existence for everyone. How you interpret those challenges will dictate the amount of stress you experience. The big question is how do you handle the challenges in your life?*

- *It is easy for us to respond to stress with A.S.A. (anxiety, sadness and/or anger). It is amazing the number of young people who are overcome by A.S.A. and don't know what to do about it. You need to learn to deal with these challenges in a healthy and productive way in order to control your stress response, improve your relationships and to improve your life.*

- *This is a critical time in your life for you to try out healthy coping strategies when you are faced with challenges and stress.*

- *The coping strategies you learn to fall back on now are what you will continue to fall back on for the rest of your life. The fights you pick, the alcohol you drink or joint you smoke now, as a teen, might not seem so bad as a strategy, but it has a very different face when you are a professional, an employee, a caregiver, a spouse and, most importantly, a parent.*

- *The goal of this book is to help you improve your own self-esteem. Improving your self-esteem is important for many reasons. One of those reasons is so that you will never become a Victim of abuse. But, it may surprise you to know that I also want you to improve your self-esteem so that you will never be a Perpetrator of Abuse. It is critical for you to get a handle on your own issues, so YOU do not harm others.*

- *In the long run, unhealthy coping strategies make your life worse and create more stress in your life. So, right now, as you are figuring out how to deal with life's challenges, choose wisely. Choose healthy strategies so you can make it through the rough times life has to offer and come out a better, stronger and healthier person because of those choices.*

CHAPTER 4
Friends, Family, and School

Art by Taylor McNeely

You are a son, a daughter, a brother, a sister, a friend, a student, an athlete, a musician, an artist, an employee. Each one of these roles comes with relationship expectations, rewards and conflict. This chapter deals with friends, family, school pressures and your career goals.

Friends - The Support They Provide and The Frustration They Cause.

Unlike family, you can choose your friends. Well, OK, you might not feel like you have complete freedom in this department, but it will get better.

Let me ask you some questions about your social circle.

1. *Do you feel like you fit in?*
2. *Do you have friends who do things that cause you to worry about them?*
3. *Are you part of a bully circle either as the bully, or the victim, a friend of a bully or a bystander?*
4. *Is there someone in your social circle that you pretend to like, but, secretly, you don't like?*
5. *Do you hang out with some people because it is better to have them as friends than to have them as enemies? Are you sometimes scared or untrusting of one or more of your "friends"?*
6. *Do you have one or two friends that you can tell anything to and know that you can trust them?*
7. *Do you have friends who you complain to and they sit there and just agree with you over and over?*
8. *Do you have friends who complain all the time?*

Social Torture

Right now, is the most challenging time of your life in terms of fitting in. The good news is that it will get better. Your close circle of friends will change as you age. Right now, in high school, you are all crammed together in one building because you have two things in common: your age and where you live. Your interests and ideas, beliefs and lifestyles could be incredibly different, but you are forced to be around each other daily because you need to go to school. That building, your school, can feel like social torture for many of you. But soon you will head off to college or university, or to work or travel, and more and more you will find yourself surrounded by like-minded people. As time goes on, you will choose your own places to live and work and, again, people with similar values will surround you, or seek you out. Wonderful, lifelong friends will present themselves to you at the various stages of your life. See? It will get better.

But, for now, let's deal with what you've got today. ...

Healthy friends laugh *with* you, not *at* you.

Healthy friends don't drag you into their mistakes or miseries.

Healthy friends challenge you to look at things in a different, better light.

Healthy friends want what's best for you.

Healthy friends will try to stop you from doing stupid things.

Healthy friends will listen to what you have to say.

Healthy friends bring more joy to your life then frustration.

The Bully Circle

Let's take a look at the big picture and who's involved. When it comes to bullying, the teenagers who experience it feel helpless and trapped. But, when you look at the big picture, there are many points of intervention and healing. It is so sad that so many people suffer when it is so preventable. Children and teens can be incredibly mean to each other. The pain some people feel as a result of a bully circle can be so bad it causes them to contemplate suicide. Some actually do kill themselves. It doesn't have to be this way. The good news is there are many solutions.

The Victim

Victims and their reactions are part of the problem. If someone is trying to show they have control over you and they see you hurting, they feed on that and will continue doing it. A victim must dig down deep inside for incredible inner strength. Remain as emotionless as possible, cry at home, and let it out where it is safe. The truth is that a bully will hurt anyone who will let them. Don't take it personally. If they didn't have you to push around, they'd do it to someone else. You have become a target, a pastime for them, but it has very little to do with you and more to do with your reactions and the pain they can cause you. ***Do not suffer in silence.*** Speak up. Tell them you won't take it anymore, be assertive and be tough. If it continues, get adults involved and continue to report it every time it happens. You may have to change a few things you are doing. Many smart teens shut down their social media accounts. Then, when they rejoin, they are very selective about who they will "friend." Others change their phone number or stop texting for a while.

I read an incredible story about a mother and daughter who were so fed up with the negativity going around that they made a pact to stop texting for one year. Both reported their overall enjoyment improved greatly because they were not swept into the negative drama going on minute by minute. The daughter soon realized that the daily drama was all very temporary and meaningless. A short time later, I read another story about a teen who committed suicide because of the bullying he was receiving online. These are two extreme responses to two similar circumstances.

IMPORTANT*: When you are talking to friends or posting online, do not give bullies any fuel. Never send any nude or provocative (sexy) photos. If you are tempted to write something negative about yourself or others, don't. This can become ammunition against you – anyone who wants to, can and will, take your images or twist your words and cause you social damage.*

The pain that you feel as a victim of bullying is very deep, and I would never try to diminish your pain. It is extremely difficult to feel better right away, but, think of it this way: Think of a time when you were disagreeing with someone and then, when the answer was revealed, you were right and the other person was wrong. Remember that feeling of satisfaction, that smile that you smiled on the inside because you didn't want to gloat, but you were smiling, nonetheless? Please understand that the bullies in your life are wrong. The actions and their words are wrong. Try to smile on the inside trusting this truth. You might reply, "Yeah, but no one knows that they are wrong." Oh, yes, they do. Every single bystander knows that the bully is wrong; they are just too scared to do anything about it.

When Cindy was in Ninth Grade, she was new to her school. In one of her classes, she would witness the almost daily verbal abuse of a boy in her class from two very mean girls. She would sit silently while feeling almost sick to her stomach over the pain she was witnessing as these girls tormented the boy. She was afraid of what they would do to her if she spoke up. One day, she couldn't take it anymore, and she told them off. Immediately, Cindy became a target as the girls turned on her. She had rumors spread about her, and she felt very alone. Cindy did experience some satisfaction that the girls at least had left the boy alone. Within two years, she learned that everyone was well aware of what these girls could and would do and that no one had any respect for them. They had hurt so many people and burned so many bridges that they didn't receive any respect. In the end, the bullies suffered, burned by their own fire. To this day, Cindy is proud of herself for sticking up for that boy.

The bully is wrong, and the bystanders know this, whether they have the courage or not to stop it, they know. You are right, and they are wrong. Take solace in this. Never, ever be ashamed of who you are. Bullies will put others down to make themselves feel better. Bullies will zero in on the one thing about you that makes you unique, (it may be something that you are already sensitive about) and they'll turn it against you, if you let them. Do not let them. You are amazing! You are beautiful! You are smart! You are kind! You are right!

Do not drop to their level. So many victims become bullies, thinking that is how they get ahead – it isn't. Do not turn on others and repeat the cycle. Hold your head high. This entire book is about transforming your pain into peace.

The Bully

Yes, bullies can be mean and careless. They seem to thrive on causing pain to others. It's hard to imagine why or how people can be so cruel. In reality, all bullies are people living in pain. They have turned to power-seeking and have made it a habit to externalize their pain, putting others down to raise themselves up. They have never learned to deal with their own anger and sadness in a positive, healthy way, and they take their pain out on others. Perhaps, if we approached bullies with sympathy and an ear and shoulder, we'd get to the root of the problem. There are many anti-bullying campaigns out there. This is a great thing as all children and teens need to know what acceptable behavior is and what is not. But, I am worried about the anti-bullying approaches that alienate the bullies even more. These teens are already way over their heads with pain and sadness. Pushing them further from social acceptance will cause only more pain for them and their future victims. The best campaigns focus on reaching out to victims *and* to bullies. Get to the root of the problem. My message to the bullies: Go back and re-read the previous chapter on stress and sort through your sadness and anger. Get help if you can't control it on your own. And, understand this: apologies are an incredibly powerful start. Say sorry to those people you've hurt, and *mean* it.

The Bystanders

This is an incredibly important role. Bystanders give power to the bully. If the bully had no one watching, or no one to brag to, they often wouldn't do it. They want someone to witness their power to hurt and cause fear. It continues because the bystanders are usually too scared to speak up. Bystanders can change everything. By reporting or standing up to a bully they are saying this is not acceptable and the bully cannot get away with it. Bystanders can hold their head high. Even bullies are concerned with social acceptance. A teenager saying "stop" is more powerful than a teacher or another adult saying it. If you are reading about nasty comments on social media, you are a bystander. Do not pass it on and spread the gossip. Stop it and encourage others to stop it too. Show your parents or tell your school. Don't delete it though, until after you've reported it, so it can be used as proof.

The Bully's Friends

The friends of bullies are very interesting. They are either bullies themselves, and by sticking together, reinforce each other's actions, or they are living in fear. They figure it is safer to be on the bully's side rather than be on the receiving end of the bully's anger. They are often self-conscious about their own weaknesses, and they feel tougher in a crowd. The friends of bullies could have an incredible impact, if they could find their inner strength. They know the hurtful actions are wrong. They could steer the bully away from situations where trouble is likely to start and prevent the pain altogether. They can also use their friendship to help the bully understand that their coping strategy of externalizing their pain is not cool. These friends can help the bully find support and figure out better coping strategies and healthier ways to spend their time.

Bullying *causes* pain, is caused *by* pain, and continues *because* of pain. But, it is all entirely preventable. Every one of you can do something to make the situation better.

Toxic Friends

So many of you know that bullying is wrong, and you should stand up against it. But the meanness of friends can often go unnoticed. Many of you watch bullying happening among your friends, saying: "We're just joking around, having fun." I see it on a daily basis in high school, where "friends" are incredibly mean. Consider any action among friends and look at it this way:

If, in a circle of friends, Matt is teasing Finley and it seems pretty mean, but later on Finley teases Matt as well, because they are reciprocating the taunting you could probably assume that they are joking and having fun. But, if Matt teases Chris, and Chris does not return the prank and just laughs with everyone else, or rather pretends to laugh with everyone else because it is at his expense, then, in reality, Chris's own circle of friends are bullying him.

If you are like Matt, then wise up. Have that kind of fun only with people who can take it otherwise you are a bully. You won't know if you can truly consider those people your friends or if they are hanging out with you only because they are scared of you. That is a lonely place to be.

If you are like Finley, go ahead and have some fun with Matt but heed the same advice given for Matt.

If you are like Chris, you know that toxic friends are very frustrating, hurtful and confusing. There are two important things you can do to change how you feel and what they do to you. The first is to rearrange your circle of friends.

Think of all of the people you currently call friends, the people you hang out with. Imagine them in a circle around you. Now rearrange this circle into 3 distinct groups. They are all still your friends, but they will now have a different place in the circle.

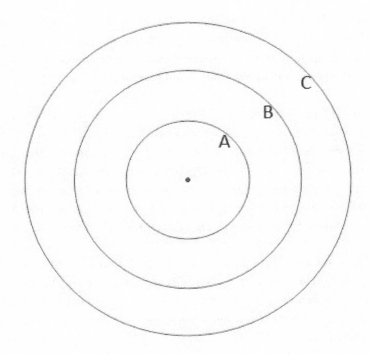

You are in the middle. Your friends surround you in 3 groupings. The closest circle to you contains the friends that bring you more joy then frustration. We'll call this circle A. The outer circle will contain the friends that bring you more frustration then joy. We'll call this circle C. The B's are in between or neutral friends, not super-close, but not causing you many frustrations either. Form these circles in your mind and carry the mental image of it wherever you go with friends. Please note these 3 points: it's OK if there are only 1 or 2 friends in circle A, cousins and siblings can count in these circles and, you may find that your friends will shift circles occasionally.

It is important that you do not let the C friends dictate how you feel about yourself. C level friends are sometimes living with their own pain and may externalize their pain onto you. Try your best to stop caring what C level friends say about you. How they make you feel on the inside is completely up to you. If you can visualize these circles of A, B, and C level friends, you can mentally protect yourself from their negative words and actions.

Why call them friends at all? Your job is to be kind to everyone as often as you can. That is your main role in this circle. Be kind and bring joy to other's lives. Be an A level friend for others. As long as you remain kind, others will recognize the C level friends for what they really are.

IMPORTANT: Just like the previous warning, there are ways to protect yourself from social harm within this circle. Do not share private information with C level friends. I'm talking about information that you wouldn't want used against you. Because C level friends might do just that.

This mental circle image will help you toughen up on the inside. But sometimes in extreme situations if the bullying doesn't stop, you'll need to take action to stand up for yourself. Think of this step as taking action to create peace. Find a time when you and Matt are <u>alone</u> (no audience), then calmly and firmly tell him that you don't like it when he does ... (fill it in). Be firm. It is better to say this when you are alone because it allows him to save face and not be singled out in a crowd, as this would put him on the defensive. Yes, I know that he singles you out in a crowd to taunt you, but go back and read the section on Power in Chapter 2. He bullies because of his own insecurities. If you take away the crowd, you can probably talk sensibly to him.

Next move – what if he doesn't stop taunting you in front of friends? At this point, in front of the friends, tell Matt off and walk away. You told him nicely once, now the time to be nice is over. Be brave. He'll most likely get the point now to stop being an ass. If he still doesn't stop, now you need to tell an adult and, in the meantime, find some other people to hang around. If you don't stand up for yourself, you will continue to be a punching bag.

<u>Note:</u> I have used guys in the above example with Matt, Finley and Chris, but this is just as easily a "Mean Girls" story among female friends, as well.

Toxic friends will also thrive on excluding others. They are using their power-seeking behavior to control what others can and cannot do. This is bullying. Are *you* a toxic friend? If you find yourself excluding others, trying to steal friends away from each other or telling others what to do, ask yourself, do you have a low tolerance for others? If they do something that annoys you, do you push them away? Work on your tolerance. Do you have insecurities? Putting others down will not make these insecurities go away. Do some soul searching of your own. You have the potential to be a good leader but only if you use that leadership role for good. Try guiding others instead or simply let them be who they are. Do not exclude others; you know it is hurtful and cruel. Do you really want to be a bully?

If you are being excluded, be brave. You have a right to ask the individual why they are excluding you. Having a face-to-face discussion may resolve the issue. If you are not happy with the result, find someone else to hang out with or find something else to do. Stay off social media so you are not watching the play-by-play of the event you weren't invited to.

Toxic friends are everywhere – it is important to know how to respond to others who are cruel to you and how to prevent the cruelty, whether you are the toxic friend or the victim.

Always Remember: when dealing with your toxic C-Level friends in your social circle, be extra careful about what you say around them and what you post on social media, because they are the kind of people who will pounce when the opportunity arises and may use your personal information against you.

[Send] ... Oops!

On the topic of social media, you have probably noticed that many adults want you to use discretion when you post online. There is an incredible irony with being a teenager and having an ability to broadcast your every thought to the world. The irony is that this is a time of your life when your thoughts and behaviors are spontaneous, fleeting and driven by emotions. All of this means your thoughts are temporary. The Internet is fast, open to everyone – and, I mean EVERYONE – completely traceable and permanent, very permanent.

I have vivid memories of the first time I had an argument with a student in class. It happened in the early years of my teaching when a student completely lost her cool and we ended up getting into a heated argument. That night, I was so bothered by what had happened that I lost a lot of sleep. I was really unsure of how things would be between us the next day in class. I was amazed the next day when the student walked in and started chatting with me like nothing had ever happened. At that moment, I remembered what hormones felt like. How easily sad turns to devastation, mad turns to verbal or physical eruptions, and how easily it all fades away, and all is forgiven or forgotten. The emotional responses can happen so quickly and be so temporary and short term – very short term.

Apply this reality of quick highs and quick lows to the immediate worldwide broadcast of the web and social media. Too many hurtful things are said; too many errors of judgment are posted, with the individuals, afterward, saying, "I didn't mean it like that." You press [Send] so quickly. Once you press [Send], it is no longer temporary; it will live on much longer than you will hold these feelings. Pressing [Send] makes it permanent. Tomorrow, you will feel better, but the anger or hurt will be out there for others to dwell on and aim back at you. Be careful.

Processing the information before you decide to make it permanent is so important. You must ask yourself, "How will this be interpreted?" "Would I show this picture to, or speak these words out loud, if all of my friends and my friends' friends and my so-called enemies and their friends, were in front of me? And to my family, and their families? Would I show this or say this over and over and over for days and weeks?" This is the reality of pressing [Send] when you are angry, or posting something inappropriate like mean words, revenge, sexual content, personal photos; and it displays it to the world. It can't go away. You cannot delete it.

There may be moments when you are feeling like, "I don't care, I don't give a crap who sees it or how long it's out there." You say that now and maybe you are right. But what if you are wrong? What if it will be a really big mistake that you will have to live with? Are you ready to face the consequences when it blows up?

Wait before you send angry or inappropriate content. There's an old saying, "Sleep on it," which means to wait until tomorrow to see if you still feel the same way. Chances are that you'll feel much more calm and wise with this little bit of thinking time.

There is also a wonderful Sufi saying that I wish I could carve into every electronic device.

It basically means we must test out words before we release them:

Our words should be released only if they pass through three gates:
Gate One: Are the words true?
Gate Two: Are the words necessary?
Gate Three: Are the words kind?
If the words can pass all three tests, you can release them.
Think about that.

A Confidant

Everyone needs a close friend they respect and in whom they can trust to tell their deepest secrets. It is crucial and healthy to have these kinds of close friends. But many of you feel that you do not have a close friend that you can respect and trust.

Girls and Their Friends

Girls are generally verbal creatures. Girls get into more trouble because they tell too many people their deepest secrets and then they get burned. Choose wisely with whom you share your innermost feelings. If you tell a friend something who then turns around and betrays your confidence, that would be very painful indeed. Be extra careful about what you post online. There are many people out there waiting to feast on your insecurities.

Guys and Their Buddies

For guys, I see a different issue. You need someone to talk to, but unfortunately many boys are not encouraged to open up and talk. They have difficulty talking with friends about their emotions because doing so is perceived as weak. So you hold it in, trying to be strong and brave and quiet.

If this is you, I want to warn you about a scenario I have seen many, many times. You get a girlfriend/partner. And slowly you open up to them. You share all of the emotions you have kept bottled up for so long. It will feel great and you will feel such a strong connection with her. Sounds great, doesn't it? But what happens if this relationship doesn't last? Guys fall very, very hard when their heart is broken. This person has become a lifeline and you feel a deep connection with this one person. It may be the only person you have ever really opened up to. The feelings of desertion and betrayal create deep wounds. To lessen the impact, here is my advice: open up to a friend. It could be male or female; just open up to someone you are not planning to date. This way they won't break up with you. Maybe even choose two friends. Hopefully one will always be a source of dependable friendship and so, if the dating relationship comes and goes, you still have a deep connection with someone close.

Who Can You Trust?

When times get really tough, as lame as it may seem, talk to one or both of your parents, or talk to a sibling or a cousin who is older or who doesn't live in the same city and doesn't know your friends. If you are choosing a friend, go back and read the chapter on Attention Seeking and Power Seeking. These individuals are more likely to misuse your information. Choose a friend who is respectful and trustworthy. You may know if you are on the right track if they also share information with you, and the two of you can have deep heart-to-heart talks. They will be much less likely to abuse your information if they have shared personal stuff with you too.

If you have an issue that you are scared about, like depression, harming yourself or another person, a crime you've committed, or a pregnancy for example, and you don't think you can talk to your parents, chose an adult you feel comfortable around. Maybe that would be an aunt or an uncle or one of your friend's parents. A coach, or a teacher, or a school counselor is another good choice. Let that person know that you are scared to talk to your own parents and why. They can help you to bridge the gap and/or lead you to the help you need.

I am directing you to choose adults with this more serious information because, honestly, you cannot handle and process this information, so how can your friends handle it? They are more likely to keep a secret for you and hold your pain and be too scared to do something about it. They likely are not going to be able to provide the best advice at this critical time. If you are dealing with one of those serious issues, you need more than a friend to talk to; you need someone who can help you. Don't be afraid to talk to an adult you trust. Remember that you are supposed to be happy and you can be so again. Ask for help, and help will be given. It is OK to ask for help. That is what we are supposed to do, but sometimes, when we feel bad, we forget that. Helpful contact information is located at the back of this book.

The Constant Complainer

If you are going to listen to someone complain, go ahead and listen, but be careful. It is easy to get wrapped up in their emotions and blindly agree with them. Ask yourself if you are making their situation better. You might think that you are supporting them by agreeing with them, and temporarily you are, but it encourages them to come back and complain about the next thing and the next thing.

If this happens, you have become an enabler. You are enabling their "poor me" habit. They are not actually doing anything to improve their situation. They have become addicted to complaining and to anyone who will listen to them.

When you agree with them, you are throwing fuel on their fire. You are validating their habitual negativity. If you really want to help this person who is constantly complaining, then challenge them to make their life better. Offer solutions, encourage them to move past this event, talk them *out of* angry reactions like seeking revenge and remind them to look on the bright side, "Yeah, but have you ever thought about this ... ?"

Friends can play an important role in challenging us to move away from our victim story, from our "poor-me" thinking. Friends can challenge us to become better people. Of course, the main question is, do *you* really like sitting there listening to them complain all the time? If you don't, then taking these positive actions will end in one of two directions:

1. They take your advice and take steps to improve their life and their outlook on it.

OR

2. They will realize they cannot count on you to enable their habit, and add fuel to their fire, so they won't come to you with their complaints, which is better for you anyway. You will still be friends, but you won't have to play the role of the pillow anymore.

Feeling Like You Don't Fit In

If you don't feel like you fit in anywhere, please understand you are not alone. I mentioned earlier that high school can be like social torture for many teens. It won't always be this way, hold on life gets better. While you are trying to navigate these teenage years there are a few strategies you can try out:

1. Join something at school. Every school offers clubs for students to join on a wide variety of great topics. Pick one that sounds like it could be interesting to you and find out where they

meet and when, and talk to the teacher who organizes the club. For most clubs, it doesn't matter if you join part way through the year.

2. Talk to a teacher about feeling like you don't fit in. Ask them for advice. They may be able to connect you with a really nice group of teens who can welcome you in.

3. Bring a book to school and find a quiet place to read at lunch every once in a while.

4. Volunteer. There are groups in your school, and in your community, that would love to have your help. Ask a teacher, a guidance counselor or at the main office.

5. Be brave. If you notice someone else sitting alone, join them, introduce yourself, and see if you have anything in common. It could mark the start of an amazing new friendship.

If you are shy these suggestions might seem too difficult, but you have inner strength inside of you. You can rise to the challenge.

Family Ties (Or Chains)

N.B. *It is important to note that the following section on parents assumes that you have had a relatively healthy family life. That your parents have met your needs of food, clothing, shelter, safety, role models, and that they have cared for and loved you to the best of their ability up to this point in your life. If you come from a home where your basic needs have not been met, then the role of improving your own self-esteem is at an even more critical point for you. I have had many teens confess to me what their home life is really like, having been neglected, seeing their parents drunk or high too often, having parents who steal their things to sell for money, having most household chores put on them including caring for siblings. Some of you have been forced to be the more responsible person in a home where your caregivers are not able to properly care for you. Abuse comes in many forms. If you are coming from a household that is very unhealthy, then please reach out to a caring adult, to a teacher, a coach, a school counselor, your doctor, or all of the above.*

Explain what you are going through, be truthful. You have endured so much. Living this way is almost over for you, you will be able to move out soon. Your goal should be to seek help and heal yourself from the inside, so you do not repeat the mistakes of others. I encourage you to take what you can from this book and any other reliable sources, seek help from reliable adults and begin your journey to heal yourself and take control of your future.

Your Parents

Potentially the biggest influences in your life are your parents. They should be. After all, friends will come and go but family is forever. I know your relationship with your parents is challenging at times when you are a teenager. I will bet that they care more about you then you can ever imagine. Yes, you will have issues, but the tricky part to understand is that there is no perfect parent. Parents are all new at the role they are in and, as you grow up, their role constantly changes. Sometimes they can handle the issues facing them and sometimes they can't. Being a good parent is the most challenging role you will ever experience.

There are seven main factors I see that impact a parent's ability to be a solid, consistent and positive parent.

1. The degree of positive parenting they learned from their parents.
2. How prepared they were for becoming parents – were you a planned baby or a surprise?
3. Personal stress going on in their lives, i.e. divorce, job loss, death in the family, health issues, financial troubles.
4. Support around them to bounce parenting questions off of such as a spouse, family, close friends, or professional support from family counsellors or doctors and the like.
5. Their state of mental health.
6. The degree of challenges their children throw at them.
7. Their self-esteem – yeah, the stuff we've been talking about.

So, before you judge them and get angry at the world for how you were raised, take a few minutes to think about the challenges your parents were faced with. In order for you to move past their mistakes and move on, there might have to be a bit of forgiveness.

If you really want to decrease the stress and arguing with or between your parents, then be helpful at home. Running a household is a huge amount of work and now that you are a teen you are as physically capable as any adult to help out with most of the things that need to be done around the house. Amaze your parents by doing something helpful *without* having to be asked. See what happens when you show them what you did. Offer to take on specific chores. If you have good parents, they have been increasing your responsibilities at home. It doesn't matter if you like it or not, they are preparing you for life. Remember that you want your freedom. You want them to treat you like an adult. Well this is a big part of it. If you haven't done your chores and you want to go out to a friend's house, do you think you should be allowed to go? If you are weaselling out of chores, who does the work fall on? How does that make you feel as you manipulate your parents? Growing up is about learning to be selfless instead of selfish. Until you are a parent yourself, you will have no idea of the thousands of ways your parents put you first. This is a small way to say thank you. Step up. Help out at home.

What You Want, What Your Parents Want.

You want freedom. You are practically an adult and you deserve a chance to make decisions for yourself. Valid.

They want to protect you, keep you safe from harm and pain. Valid.

Why it is so hard for parents.

I did not understand this until I had my own children. I will share with you what I have learned. From the moment you were conceived, your parents have been caring for you, watching over you, *protecting* you. As a child they choose your clothes, your food, your friends, your TV shows, and your bedtime. They constantly sacrifice their own wants and needs so you can have the best life they can provide. They put themselves in control of most aspects of your life to keep you safe and healthy and happy. But you grow up and want to make all of these decisions, and more, for yourself. Some are easy to let go of, but some are not. And so, teenagers and parents since the beginning of time, and until the end of time, will argue over control. You are entitled to freedom on some accounts, and later on in this chapter, I'll discuss how to get your way. But some aspects of your life you might be tempted to keep secret from your parents. These are decisions that you think your parents should not be involved in.

Here is a list of items you should <u>never hide</u> from your parents.
1. Your grades at school
2. Your options for post-secondary schools, jobs, etc.
3. If you are involved in a crime
4. Who your friends are
5. Who you are dating
6. If you are in an unhealthy relationship, examples would be secret online connections with strangers, or verbal, emotional, physical, or sexual abuse
7. If you are receiving threats or being bullied, online or otherwise
8. If you are mistreated at work
9. If you feel unsafe in a situation
10. If you have health problems
11. If you or your partner is pregnant

Just tell them. Even if you think your parents have enough to deal with and you don't want to burden them. Even if you know you will get in trouble once they know. In these situations, and many more, they have every right to be involved. If I spend 15 years trying to provide the most for my children and then in the critical years they jeopardize their future, I want to know. Yes, it may be heated at first, but eventually the topics can be discussed calmly and resolved before any careless decisions are made.

Maybe in the end the parents are the ones who need to adjust their expectations, but this can only be done if they are aware of what is going on. If you want to be treated respectfully then you must treat your parents with the respect they deserve. Open the door.

Note to teens: To your parents you've become a stranger. Preadolescence is a time when you can actually relate to your parents. You see the world view and you want to make it a better place. You act with fewer inhibitions. Then the teenage years hit and your desire to fit in, to belong, takes over. Societal values and pressures, especially those coming to us through the media, mean everything to you. In fact, social values become more important than family values. The way you look and behave is of utmost importance. It is all about image and the way you are perceived by others. Things your parents did to make you laugh a few years ago, you beg them not to do in public because it is so embarrassing. Mom and Dad cannot relate to your new values and so you think they cannot understand you. You yell at them, "You just don't understand!"

The good news is that when you hit your late teens and early 20's, if the bridges in the relationship haven't all been burned, the dust begins to settle, and you hopefully begin to see through the superficial values of society. The fog is lifted, and you can once again form a wonderful relationship with Mom and Dad and see them as good human beings again, not mortal enemies.

I don't want to trivialize your daily issues, but it is important to understand that you are on a journey and you are only experiencing one small part of life. Next time you find yourself in an argument with Mom and/or Dad, try to see it from their viewpoint. Know that they have lived through the teen years with significant challenges of their own and they made it through.

Parenting Styles

Regardless of the style of parents you have, please understand that they do love you and want the best for you. As you read about these 3 parenting modes, remember it is possible for your parents to adapt and change their parenting style depending on what is going on in their lives and with you, their child. As an introduction to the type of household your parents create, I often use the example of the police showing up at a party that has gotten out of hand, announcing that they are arresting you and calling your parents from the police station. Some kids will be like, "Oh shit," but remain relatively calm. Others will say, "Go ahead, they're not gonna care." And others that will be having heart palpitations, repeating over and over, "I'm dead. Oh God, I'm dead. I'm dead. They're gonna kill me."

The responses to this scenario are quite telling about family life at home. Let's take a look at three basic parenting styles. Think of them as extremes:

- Far left
- Far right
- Middle

Let's rewind to earlier this same evening, when the teens are asking their parents if they can go to the party.

Style #1 – Strict: "No, you can't go to the party."

In this house, parents are oppressive and over-controlling. *(now I think all teens believe their parents are strict, so before you go assuming this is your household, read the first paragraph or more from Parenting style #3 – Democratic).*

If you really are in an authoritarian, inflexible, strict household, where rules are enforced but not explained, you may be tempted towards rebellion, or worse, *quiet* rebellion. Quiet rebellion is when some teens start doing extreme things behind their parents' back.

Sneaking out of the house when they were told not to go out. And once they are out, "Hell, I'm already in trouble, so I may as well burn the candle at both ends." And then the night out includes drugs, alcohol or other risky behavior. Eventually this teen, let's say it's a boy in this example, gets caught and the parents pull the reigns even tighter. Remember they are already non-trusting so this only makes it worse. More parental restrictions follow, which breeds more rebellions. This spiral goes on and on, getting worse and worse until there is no trust and no respect in the relationship. The situation has deteriorated so far that the teen moves out. Moving out, of course, does not solve anything. Now he is out in the world with complete freedom but has not been taught how to safely handle it.

Usually the "vice", for example drugs, takes over because it is the only comfort he knows. In the worst-case scenario, after bouncing from friend's house to friend's house, he winds up living on the street. Of course, this is the worst-case scenario. Most teens will not rebel to this extent, but will still try desperately to exert independence.

I had a student whose mother was very strict. She was a single mom. The teen wanted to get her belly button pierced but the mother was adamant. "Absolutely not." Over and over the daughter asked and the answer never changed. "But Why?" she would ask. "Because I said so," was the reply. Eventually the teen did it anyway and kept it hidden. Over time, she also rebelled by having her eyebrow pierced and her nose, which for some reason the mother was ok with. But when I last saw the girl the mom still did not know about the belly button piercing. The constant fear of being found out, along with the guilt of having tricked her Mom, was wearing the girl down and stressing her out.

You can spot teens from a strict house fairly easily. They can appear very tough and fearless, but dig a little and you see they are extremely fearful of what goes on at home. Back to the example at the beginning, when the cops show up at the party, these teens will be the ones repeating over and over, "I'm dead. They're gonna kill me. I'm dead." They were not supposed to be there at all.

Many times, strict parents give rise to stubborn kids who have not learned to be flexible. I remember a student who was having a lot of trouble at home. Her dad was very strict, and he was adamant that his daughter go into the medical field. For years she had wanted only one career, to be a hair stylist. She was really good at it. Her marks could not have supported the career choice that her father wanted for her and her chosen career path seemed to make her happy. The debate over this issue, on top of other disagreements, fuelled a separation between them that led to her moving out and living with a friend's family. She completely disconnected from her own family for months. This was a case of two people being amazingly stubborn about a small issue that got way out of control.

Another student, named Nick, was extremely rude in my class and made numerous attempts to bully me as a teacher. I eventually called the father and informed him of his son's behaviour. The very next day it was like a different student was in the class. His behaviour was completely changed. It made me wonder what actually went on at home. In class, Nick once spoke about life at home and he informed us that his dad never physically hurt them, but he had a really bad temper and yelled a lot and was very strict. In talking to another teacher who had taught Nick in the past, she told me that he responded well to strict teachers, but my democratic classroom style he probably had no respect for. I understood him to respect only people he feared, which in turn, worried me about the kind of adult or parent he would become as he would eventually want others to respect him. Unfortunately, his family moved out of our school zone and I never saw him again.

If you are in a strict home, I highly recommend you read the upcoming section *Why are parents Rules so important* AND *How to Win...Eventually.*

There is one specific issue regarding strict parenting that I find particularly difficult and that is cultural differences. When families move to North America and raise their children here, common difficulties surface in the teenage years. Parents are used to the societal expectations from their home country and yet their children are growing up in our "loose" North American society. I can understand both sides here and can blame neither poor parenting, nor rebellious child for the confrontations. I believe that independence in the teenage years is important, but I completely agree that our North American society offers too much, too fast, and we have turned into a society without strong morals and values. I think some families manage to find a happy medium. Success seems to come with joining community events with others of the same cultural background. It takes a village to raise a child, as the old saying goes. Well, if you can create your own village, all the better. Everyone needs to feel like they belong to something. So, the next time Mom and Dad ask you to attend a family or cultural gathering, don't give them a hard time. They are trying their best to create a network of safety and cultural familiarity around you, upon which you can depend.

Style #2 – Laissez-Faire: "Can I go to the party?" "I don't care if you go, just get the f*#ing car home before I have to leave for work in the morning."

—— —— —— —— —— —— —— —— —— —— ——

—— —— —— —— —— —— —— —— —— —— ——

This is also a difficult household to grow up in. In fact, I would say this might be the most damaging to a child or teen. The perceived benefits of this arrangement are deceiving. Many friends of this teen might be jealous of the freedom that their friend has and so they become "famous" for their lack of rules and curfews. If you take a closer look, you see that the parents are often neglecting the child's basic needs for attention and guidance. The lack of rules, which seem so appealing to other teens, actually make the child feel small and unsafe. Emotionally they feel unworthy, not worth protecting, not worth loving. These children and teens will opt for any attention they can get and it doesn't matter if it is negative attention. They often get into a great deal of trouble, and eventually dive into multiple vices, which I will discuss in the next chapter. You might think, "If you [meaning your parents] are pissed at me or yelling at me, in some twisted way it lets me know that you notice me and that I exist. And possibly that you care about what I do. And maybe that means you care about me."

When these parents are asked the question, "Can I go to the party?" and the parents respond, "I don't care if you go, just get the car home before I have to leave for work in the morning," they are letting the teenager know that the car is more important than they are. When the cops arrive, this teen will say, "Go ahead, arrest me, my parents are not gonna care." They have no fear of the consequence, as it will force their parents to give them attention, even if it's negative.

Sometimes, good parents slip and slide into Laisse-Faire parenting. Sometimes the parents are too busy or caught up in their own drama and vices to notice the child/teen who needs their guidance so desperately. Unfortunately, this is becoming more common in our society as the demands on the adults in our society become more intense. Concerns over money, job security, personal relationships, concerns for their aging parents, and being physically and emotionally exhausted from their workday can cause parental disengagement. They may feel they do not have the time or energy to give an open ear, or assistance or guidance for their child and so the child begins to slip through the cracks. It amazes me how many families I have observed where the parents over compensate with material things. The latest clothing brands, latest electronic gadgets, whatever it takes to make up for time they cannot spend with their child.

It also may be the case that the parent or parents did not have good parental models themselves and never learned to communicate with their children in a constructive and healthy way. Parents need to learn too. None of us know what we are doing when we start having kids. There is no required course on parenting. We have to learn as we go. We learn from our own parents, from our family and friends and from reading books and articles on how to do things better. Some parents are more open to learning than others.

Sometimes a perceived lack of interest and a lack of rules can have a very negative affect. The parents might be trying their best but are caught up in their own situations and are unable to provide the emotional support and guidance when their children need it. In the case of one friend's upbringing, during the years of his parents' divorce he felt non-existent. He was incredibly intelligent, and his marks were very high, during the early years of high school he had hopes of going into mechanical engineering. As his self-image plummeted with the lack of attention from his parents, he let out his cry for help. He let his marks drop in his final high school year. His parents did not notice, the marks dropped lower and lower. In fact, he went from an average in the 90%'s the year before to a 60%'s average just when he wanted to apply to university. His parents still didn't recognize this as a cry for help. In the end, he crushed his own dreams for the future and has regretted it ever since.

It is important to recognize that the ways that we try to get back at our parents inevitably hurt us in the end. There are much healthier ways to resolve the pain.

Authority Figures

Many teens have a difficult time with authority figures, especially those who have grown up in a laisse-faire or overly strict household. It is entirely possible that you do not respect authority because, quite simply, the authority figures from your childhood, usually your parents, were not setting very good examples and therefore they did not deserve your respect. (We'll come back to this.) Many teens translate that into a lack of respect for all authority figures. Being rude to those in a position to help you is a damaging way to go through life.

The beginning of this process might not be obvious. It may start with a parent simply wanting to be their child's friend. With this kind of parenting error, they often try to protect you from suffering the consequences of your actions. Case in point: in the schools, we see it far too often where a student, breaks or bends the rules at school. Your parents receive a phone call about the issue. Over the phone, or if they really want to make an impression they'll do it in person, your parents actually defend or make excuses for you and your actions. In their mind they are helping you, protecting you. They assume that the school staff could not possibly understand your life like they do, with all its stresses and pressures. So, they protect you from whatever consequences your actions should have caused you.

Unfortunately, their attempt at being your friend will actually damage your relationship with them. The earlier you experience it, the worse it is. The reason for this is that in school, the teachers, administrators and support staff, are the authority figures in your school life. When your parents oppose people in these positions and defend you, they are teaching you that authority figures, and their rules, do not matter. They are teaching you that you can get out of punishment with excuses, arguing, lying, or blaming others. They are teaching you that you can avoid consequences. It is not their intention and they don't mean to do this, but through their actions, that is what they are doing. Eventually you are dealing with bigger issues and bigger authority figures. It could be your high school principal or VP, your boss at work, a police officer. You get the idea. You will still have it in your head that you don't have to listen to these people, you don't have to follow the rules and that you can avoid consequences.

How does this damage your relationship with your parents? Well, eventually, the authority figure you will oppose will be them! They have unwittingly taught you to disrespect authority and set you up to disrespect them. This hits most often in the teenage years and suddenly you are in major conflicts with your parents and they don't know what went wrong. They were only trying to protect you.

Strict or over controlling parents may also raise their children with this unintended message. Perhaps they are very assertive about their own rules, but they will leap on anyone else who wants to give you a consequence, because they believe your punishment is their job.

Kara was a student who hated her mom. I first met her in Grade Nine. I was on detention duty every second day and I could not believe how often this girl was in there. Many teachers were very put off by Kara. She opposed their every rule. She was defiant in every way she could think of. The teachers laid down consequences on her and what followed was a battle over pride and power with neither side backing down. Every teacher agreed that she was very smart, but she had failed so many courses because she constantly skipped or refused to hand in assignments or do what was expected. Eventually, I started to talk to her about what was going on. She told me about a rough life at home, single mom, drugs, alcohol, and no guidance. After many talks we got on the topic of authority figures and how she felt about her teachers. She said that usually she likes them at first, but eventually their responses to her rule breaking actions forces her into battles. She would tell me the long list of teachers and VP's she hated along with her mother. I asked her if things were always like this with her mom. She told me, "No,

*things were great when I was younger. I could do anything I wanted
and all the kids at school thought that my freedom was so cool." I
asked if her mother ever made excuses for her in elementary school,
so she would avoid the consequences of her actions. She laughed,
rolled her eyes and answered, "All the time." When I explained to
her what I had observed in these situations and how it eventually
turns on the parents, she was amazed at how true it was for her life.*

Consequences Are a Part of Life

We learn from our mistakes because of the price that we pay.
Parents should not try to prevent consequences for their child's
actions. By protecting you from consequences your parents are
ENABLING you to continue your actions.

If you sleep in and you are late for school, then you should serve
the detention. It is a lesson in life that negative actions have
negative consequences. It is true for school, for relationships, for
part time jobs, for careers, for communities, for the law, and for
families. If you go through life disrespecting the rules and the
people who enforce them, you are in for a rough ride.

Why do we even have rules? Many teens have a belief that
everyone should be able to do what they want and that everyone is
equal. That is not true.

Everyone deserves respect but not everyone is equal.

In a democratic society, there are hierarchies of authority. In
order for civilization, and by this, I mean where everyone is
civilized, to be successful, rules have to be applied to keep people
safe and on task. A society is an interconnected maze where we
depend on each other. If one area is not pulling their weight, then
the whole of the society suffers. Areas of society include businesses
and workplaces, banks, city workers, schools, and individual family
homes, for example. All of these areas have to maintain rules to
keep their members safe and doing what they should be doing.
School rules are a big part of this. Many kids think they don't have
to follow the rules.

Read on a little further to find out why parents' rules are so important.

The Rule of Voice

Speak to all authority figures in a respectful tone, even if their tone is assertive. Imagine you are babysitting in your neighbourhood. You have two kids in your care and you are responsible for their safety. One kid starts to act up and is doing something dangerous. So, you, as the authority figure, tell them to stop. They do not, so you raise your voice and become more assertive. You are not bullying them. This is what you have to do to get their attention and to let them know you are serious. It is their responsibility to listen to you and your rules. Now imagine that that kid gets their back up when you got mad and they start raising their voice at you – they are becoming aggressive. This is completely out of line and extremely disrespectful to you, the authority figure who was only trying to maintain a safe environment for them. Do they have the right to speak to you that way? No. Do you both deserve respect? Yes. Are you equal? No.

When you are a student at school, a son or daughter in your home, a younger individual in society, you are not the authority figure. It is your responsibility to follow the rules and speak respectfully to everyone, especially the authority figures. It is actually in your best interest to do this because in addition to enforcing the rules, authority figures all have the power and discretion to assist you when you need a favour or a break. Any authority figure will be eager to help out a polite, friendly teen. On the other hand, any authority figure will be much less likely to help out a rude, selfish, aggressive teen. So how you behave to them affects *You* negatively or positively much more then it affects them.

Some authority figures do not deserve the role they have. They abuse their power and are aggressive and rude to others. Let's say it's a boss or a teacher who screams and yells and puts you or others down. You still must behave respectfully to them. *You must respect the position even if you do not respect the person in the position.* In extreme cases, you can go to other higher authority figures and report on what is going on. If you are not dealing with an extreme case, then try your best to minimize your contact and confrontations with them, and keep your cool. Do not lower yourself to their level. Either way it is not your job to stand up to them – don't try to be a hero. If they really are abusing their power position, eventually they will get what they deserve from people higher up the chain.

What if a rule is really stupid? Instead of simply breaking the rule, ask why the rule is there in the first place. Most rules need to be questioned every once in a while. Maybe it's an old rule that needs to be adapted and you can be a part of that process. Maybe the authority figure can explain something about the rule that you were not aware of and that helps you to understand why it is important to follow it.

For example: most schools have a no hats rule. Many students think it's a stupid rule and often try to get away with wearing one. I tell them the story of working in a rough school that didn't enforce this rule. A student owed a lot of money to a drug dealer, one day these guys walked right into the school and grabbed the kid near his locker and took him outside and beat him up. They were all wearing hats and so they could not be identified accurately on the school security cameras. This hits home with the students and they say, "OK, I didn't think of it that way." Then they are much more likely to obey the rule because they understand why it's there.

I always find it hilarious when students act out and misbehave, and then when they get in trouble, they are so mad at the authority figures, they actually believe they personally are the victims! The excuses, blame, and lies start flying. It's a little embarrassing to watch. It's quite a spectacle.

Parents, and sometimes even teachers, often rush to explain this behaviour. The lamest excuse I have ever heard are the words, "He doesn't do well with authority figures."

Huh?

What the hell does that mean?

Basically, that means he wants to do whatever he wants to do, doesn't want to pay consequences and hates anyone who tries to give him one. Let's face it. That is what it means. Now back to my initial reaction – "What the Hell?"

What kind of rock is he going to hide under for the rest of his life so that he doesn't have to deal with authority figures? They are EVERYWHERE! Learn to deal with them, learn your role and their role and learn to be respectful. We live in a civilized society. You may think that everyone should be equal, but that leads to one thing – anarchy, which is a disordered society that is anything but civilized.

Style #3 – Democratic: adaptive and flexible, yet firm on big issues.

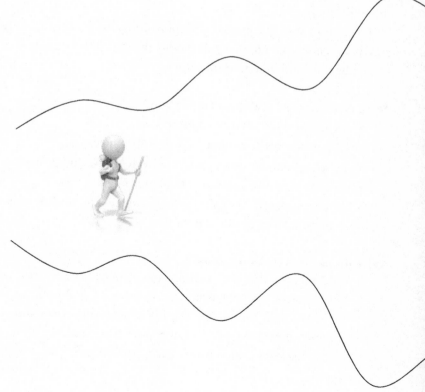

These are the best authority figures that parents can be. In this household, parents allow freedom on small matters, but when lines are crossed with regards to safety, or family morals and values, the democratic parent is quick to put their foot down. Parents will consider each situation independently and weigh the consequences carefully. The teenagers in this house will complain about the inconsistency, for example, "Michael got to do it when he was my age," and often say, "It's not fair." But in reality, this is a stable place to grow up in. Fights will happen, but if the kids start to get into trouble, on a deep level, the level that helps to form your understanding of your place in the world, the rules that are set in place bring comfort to you. If you live in this household, you might notice that friends of yours who come from laisse-faire households like to come and hang out at your house. They feel safe and protected there.

Over time it is the parent's responsibility to loosen the reigns slowly and allow you to make decisions for yourself, to guide you to a safe, healthy and independent future.

Why Are Parents' Rules So Important?
- They provide safety and protection.
- Give us a pathway that leads towards success.
- Create boundaries that allow us to feel safe and protected.
- Teach flexibility and how to compromise
- Help us learn to make personal decisions and accept the consequences of our actions.

Why do parents insist on rules?
- Because there are certain big consequences that your parents do not ever want you to have to deal with, so they will put their foot down, even if it means upsetting you.
- Your parents have spent the past 14+ years of your life keeping you safe from harm, protecting you, making

decisions for you so you could, and can in the future, move easily and happily through life.

- They are not saying "no" to you because they want to hurt you. They are saying no because they want to protect you from being hurt. But, let's face it, you want to have it your way – you want to win.

How to Win... Eventually

- Acknowledge their fears; lay out all of the possible things that could go wrong, so they know that you are aware of their concerns.

- Establish a plan of responsible behaviour to handle the situations.

- If you really think you are mature enough to look after your own safety, then DEMONSTRATE that to your parents. Suggest some solutions/examples of guidelines you will set for yourself. Be truthful.

- If you are requesting joining a social event, suggest how you will get home, and what time would be a reasonable curfew. Talk openly about how taking alcohol and/or drugs may affect your decision making for the plan you have established. Discuss a plan for that too.

- Leave them alone to discuss what you have said. Let them talk it over, or if there is only one parent at the time, let them think it over.

- Be calm and ready to accept whatever they decide. Like a lawyer, you have stated your case, now it's up the Judge.

- Let them approach you with their offer. It will probably not be exactly what you asked for but a compromise is good.

- Take it. Do not push further at this time.

- Live up to their expectation. Show them you ARE trustworthy and responsible.

- Slowly with each request, and responsible behaviour on your part, they will loosen their grip *and* you will have learned to stay safe.
- Remember: if you mess up, you have to deal with the consequence of less freedom next time. End of story.

How NOT to Win (but Think that You Are)

- Disobey your parents by doing something after they say no. This just proves to them that you are not trustworthy or responsible.
- When they find out you went against their wishes, you argue, scream and fight, and complain that it's not fair instead of admitting maybe you made a mistake.
- Tell your parents you are not going to listen to them.
- When they put a tighter hold on you – because now they cannot trust you – you repeat the cycle and damage the relationship further.
- Resent your parents and now live in a home that's become a battlefield.

When you really need your parents to trust and help you in the future, be prepared for disappointment. That's when you will feel the kick of the above actions. Your parents still love you but you've created mistrust and lost their respect.

In chapter five we will discuss the importance of trust and respect with boyfriends and girlfriends. The same is true for every other relationship. Consider the relationships with your friends, siblings, teachers, boss at work, and your parents and know that at the core of any good relationship is trust and respect – on both sides.

Growing up in a community north of Toronto, there were many nights in my teenage years when I came home a little later than I should have. My parents were pretty reasonable about curfew times, but they always asked that I call them if I was going to be late. I wasn't great at this and actually felt like my parents were treating me a bit like a baby and not trusting me. I mean, I always made it home eventually didn't I? One Saturday night, when I was 16, I was babysitting my little sister while my parents went out for dinner in the city. They said they'd be home by midnight and not to wait up. Keep in mind this is a time before cell phones.

I looked after my sister and put her to bed. She was 7 at the time. I watched a movie and it ended close to midnight, so I decided to stay up and wait for my parents. I started reading in the living room, but with every minute that passed I became more anxious. My mind started to wander to dark places. My imagination created horrible scenes of why they were late. After about an hour and a half I was losing my mind! I truly believed my parents were dead! I was going to have to raise my little sister and my older sister was going to have to quit university to support us! I was fully expecting to hear the knock on the door and face a policeman telling me the grim news. Then I hear the keys in the door and I raced to face them as they came in. Before they could get a single word in, I was tearing a strip up and down them. "Why are you so late? Why didn't you call? I thought you were dead!" My dad took one look at me and said calmly, "OK, now you know what it feels like." They didn't stay out late on purpose just to get back at me, they expected me to be asleep, but when they saw my reaction it was all too familiar to them. From that night on, I always called them when I was going to be late.

This experience was the beginning of a new kind of thinking for me. Of course, they had explained to me before why they worried, and it made sense, but it didn't really hit home until I experienced it first-hand. I was truly becoming aware of the concept of consequences of actions. I needed to earn the trust of my parents and I needed to be respectful of their rules.

Divorce

When conflicts at home become more than your parents can handle, divorce becomes a viable option. There is no way to imagine how hard this decision is for them. I do believe that far too many families quit too soon. All relationships have struggles – there are no perfect couples out there, and no perfect families. All members of a family have to work at their relationships to support each other, appreciate each other and to challenge each other to be better people. If you have watched your parents try very hard to make things work, but the problems continue, you may be forced to endure one of the most challenging things a family can go through. Divorce is extremely difficult on everyone involved. Your parents are splitting up because they are deeply unhappy with each other, and oftentimes themselves too. You can do your best to appreciate what they do for you each day, and to love them both. You are still going to be loved and cared for. You will get through this.

Be careful that you do not get in the middle of their arguments and issues. If they ask you to get involved and pit one against the other, that is not fair. If one parent is often complaining or saying bad things about the other parent to you. Tell mom/dad to vent to their friends, not to you, and that you still love the other parent too. The divorced families who are most happy are those who allow the children to love both parents separately.

Many times, teens will manipulate parents and play one against the other, telling one parent one thing and something different to the other parent. This is extremely disrespectful and selfish. You are adding fuel to a fire. You can't possibly feel good about those actions therefore you can't possibly feel good. Throwing more pain on top of pain yields nothing but greater pain. Your parents love you and they are going through something very difficult. Set higher standards for yourself and choose actions that make family life easier for everyone.

School

School is an obvious source of stress for so many teens. School has so many rules and expectations. Sometimes it is really hard to keep up. When you are having a hard time with one aspect of life, sometimes it helps to look at the big picture to try to understand why you have to get through this challenge.

Here is the big picture of school: School is where we learn about society. We learn how it functions and the incredibly complex network of people in diverse roles required for it to function well. Society is dependent upon its citizens' contributions, and healthy societies thrive when people work together. It is strange how many people view life in the opposite way, thinking that we are all in competition with each other. No, we *depend* on each other.

I am not surprised that teens have a competitive view of the world. We don't really create a system in schools where you rely on the talents of your peers, where you are encouraged to appreciate the diversity of interests and skills without jealousy. I wish we did a better job of that. In the context of society, if one person is incredibly talented, we all benefit from the improvements they help bring to society. We should be celebrating when someone is good at something we are not good at. We each contribute, and we benefit from the contributions of everyone else.

As an example of this collaboration, let's look at the making of a great action movie. After a movie ends, most people get up and leave the theatre while the final credits are rolling, but if you stay, you see a very long list of incredibly talented people. Each of these people bring different talents to the film.

Your drama enthusiasts are of course the actors, the high tech people bring fantastic animations, graphics and special FX's, the mathematically-talented work out the budget and financing, the engineers, technicians, trades people and manufacturers build the sets and props, the athletic gurus are the stunt doubles, the creative writing stars write the script, the multi-linguists translate the movie for subtitles, the business minded work the marketing and promotions, the science buffs and cultural historians make sure details are authentic, artists work the make up, costumes, hair, and scenery, the animal lovers bring the trained animals, musicians provide the soundtracks, culinary experts provide wonderful food to fuel everyone during the long days at work, and on top of all of these experts, there are many assistants, runners and drivers.

Each, and every diverse skill set is important in the making of this movie. Did you recognize your high school subjects? Can you pick out subjects you like and don't like? Can you think of people who do well in subjects that you are not so great at? Look at the movie example again. Do you see that these skilled workers are not in competition with each other? This is just one little example, but society is just like this. We all depend on each others' unique skills. We depend on diversity of interests, experiences, skills, and strengths.

In addition to contributions through our paid work in our careers, there are many other ways we can contribute to society. It can be through a part time job, volunteer work, financial donations, charity work, paying tax dollars, raising awareness of important issues, helping others to learn skills, being an informed voter, helping to keep communities clean and safe, through our ability to be responsible, law-abiding citizens, and most importantly, by showing love and kindness to others.

It is in school that you learn about your interests, your skills and your talents. At the same time, you are also learning about the world and humanity, about global challenges and successes. Through all of this, the hope is that you can see your value, that you will learn how you can contribute to make the world a better place.

School is about your capacity to learn. Unfortunately, the content can sometimes seem irrelevant. The most important thing is that you are training your brain to learn. As you get higher up in the grades, it is expected that you can learn more challenging information. The traditional classroom setting may not be for everyone, but as long as you can be open to learning, that is the most important thing. A closed mind will hold you back. We are always learning throughout our entire lives. The more open we are to new information the more we can learn and grow. When we are in school, we are teaching our young brain to collect, store and sort new information, but we are also training our developing brain how to learn so that we can continue to do it effectively throughout life.

With regards to the content, *what* you are learning is secondary to the fact that you are learning something. That's the training. The multitude of subjects and curriculum topics are there to offer you a possible area that you are interested in. You don't need to be interested in everything. It's OK, just keep learning.

Consider the analogy of learning to walk. Once you've mastered walking you move on to running, jumping, playing sports, and possibly playing sports at a high level. If you were to say, "This is stupid, I don't need to learn how to walk," or, if you give up and say, "I'm no good at walking," then you would be cutting yourself off from all of the wonderful future experiences that stem from walking. The same goes for your brain. Stay open, and get help with the tough stuff. You may have a lot of negative ideas about school but think of it this way, school is a place where young brains are growing.

On the first day of school, in every one of my classes, I go through my 10 rules for school and life. I am continually pleased by the responses I get from students who are new to me. If the students are not new to me, they continue to appreciate the reassurances.

Rules for School and Life

1. BEHAVE IN WAYS THAT ALLOW YOU TO RESPECT YOURSELF

   - It seems that fitting in with the crowd is more important than doing what you are comfortable with, and it is easy to lose respect for yourself.
   - Once you lose your self-respect, it's is a slippery slope.
   - You cannot expect others to respect you if you don't respect yourself.

2. DON'T CHEAT, DON'T LIE

   - You have to live with yourself in the end.

- People who cheat believe they are not capable of learning. That is sad.
- People who lie are proving to others that they cannot be trusted. That is sad.
- People learn at different rates, it's OK, keep trying

3. BE AWARE OF YOUR ACTIONS AND THEIR IMPACT ON OTHERS
- All actions have impacts on others.
- Good actions have positive impacts.
- Poor actions have negative impacts.
- Use good judgment.

4. TAKE RESPONSIBILITY FOR YOUR ACTIONS – DO NOT LAY BLAME
- All actions have consequences.
- Never blame someone else for your actions or the consequences of those actions.
- Never try to weasel out of your consequences.

5. DON'T FOLLOW THE CROWD – DO WHAT IS BEST FOR YOU
- When you try too hard to fit in with people who don't share your goals in life, you will never reach those goals.
- Whether it is help with a test or help with a personal problem, ask for help when you need it.

6. GET INVOLVED
- There is so much more to school than classes.
- Join a team or a club.
- Try something new.
- Step outside of your comfort zone and discover your amazing potential.

7. WHEN YOU MAKE A COMMITMENT – BE COMMITTED
- Don't sign up for something and then quit partway through.

- If you cannot follow through on a commitment, be mature and go talk to the person you are accountable to. Do not be a coward.

8. REMEMBER: PROBLEMS AREN'T REALLY PROBLEMS; THEY'RE "IDEA EMERGENCIES*" (*from the (network) TV show *Imagination Movers*)
   - Never give up. Use your brain, use your textbook, use research, ask your parents, ask peers, ask the teacher.
   - Challenges are life's way of strengthening you from the inside.

9. TRY YOUR BEST. WORK HARD
   - You get out what you put in.
   - Poor effort yields poor results.
   - Never Ever Quit!
   - Whether it is doing your best in sports, in school, in music or the arts, in relationships, in life, *if something is hard, then try harder.*

10. BELIEVE IN YOURSELF
    - *"Whether you think you can or you think you can't, Either way, you are right!"* — Henry Ford

It doesn't just take intelligence to get through high school, it takes support. Support can come in many forms. At home, your parents are the obvious and easiest source. But not all of you have that support structure going on. If that is your situation, it's good to know that many others can become support for your success. Teachers, guidance counselors, resource teachers, VPs and principals are all people who can act as supports. The unfortunate part is that some of you are so angry that you view these individuals as your enemies instead of potential branches of support. When you are angry with these people, you think that you are hurting them, but in reality, it is you, and only you, who suffers in the long run.

Often, students see authority figures as enemies whose rules are meant to be broken. This comes from a deep-seated lack of respect for authority.

Jenny, a Grade 9 student, snuck out of class on the way to an assembly. After the assembly, she didn't return to class on time, but instead told a friend to tell Ms. Wilson that she was feeling ill in the bathroom. Ms. Wilson appeared sympathetic to Jenny on her return, but kept an eye on her. For the next few weeks, she stuck close to Jenny at other assemblies, making sure she followed all instructions and was there to remind her if she didn't. Later on, when Jenny asked for an extension on an assignment, Ms. Wilson said, "No." Jenny got really annoyed at Ms. Wilson and often said, "Ms. Wilson picks on me. She hates me. It doesn't matter though because I hate her, too."

Again, as with all other relationships we will discuss, it comes down to two things: respect and trust. Whether it is with your parents, your teachers, your employers, your friends, coworkers or romantic partners, healthy relationships must be based on RESPECT and TRUST. Respect is something you LEARN, trust is something you EARN.

Let's back up and examine both sides.

When Jenny skipped out after the assembly, Ms. Wilson knew and immediately became suspicious of Jenny. Upon hearing that Jenny is ill, the teacher's first thought is, "She's faking – I don't trust her." The teacher has every right to think this way because she has witnessed a breach of trust already. Her instinct is to watch Jenny more closely.

When it comes time for Jenny to ask for a favour or break from the teacher, the answer is no. Why? Because the teacher feels she doesn't deserve it. Valid.

Jenny has laid the foundation of the relationship by breaking trust. Unfortunately, when Jenny needs a break from her teacher she won't get it because the teacher thinks Jenny will take advantage of the situation.

Jenny is like so many adolescents testing out the waters in different kinds of relationships. How much can I get away with? How can I cheat the system? How can I get my way?

The problem with this way of thinking is that when you cheat people they eventually find out. They automatically lose trust in you and feel suspicious about you.

They will either hold on tighter (parents, teacher) or they will drop you (friends, partners), either way you come out of it feeling like they are being unfair and don't like you.

You end up feeling negative towards them and the relationship spirals downward.

When you really do need a favour, they will be very reluctant to give in to you and rightly so. You have not proven to them that you are trustworthy. Every action has a consequence. Are you ready to take responsibility for your actions?

If school is an area that you struggle in, you have to first take a good long look in the mirror and decide if you believe that you can succeed in school. If I have a student who is not doing well and not paying attention in class, I always ask, "Who is in charge of your learning?" They always answer, "You are," (meaning me, the teacher) and I say, "No – I am not in charge of your learning, you are!" Your teachers are there to provide information; it is up to the student to learn the information. The biggest barrier to the learning process is if the kid simply doesn't *believe* that they can learn. If a student feels bad about their academic performance, that can define the type of student they are. They don't believe they can do any better. If I can encourage you to understand your role in the learning process and how it is in your control, and that you are capable of learning, then you can find incredible success in school. Once you decide that it is possible, then you can seek the help that is necessary for you to succeed.

Support can come in so many forms. Your first line of support could be parents, teachers, guidance counsellors, resource teachers, tutors, or VPs and principals. In tough times, you can also find support from foster parents, addiction counselors, teen help hotlines, police services, and student welfare agencies. If you can be open to these resources, you can create success for yourself even if there isn't support at home.

Asking for help seems hard at first, but once you have opened up a connection with one or more of these influential people, asking for (and receiving) help gets easier and easier and more and more success comes your way.

It's all about making your life better.

You are more successful if you ask for help when you need it. This is not a sign of weakness; it is a sign of wisdom.

Future Career Paths

This section is for any of you out there who don't yet have a career path and, as a result, are starting to feel pressure for a decision from home and school. Career decisions can be stressful because so often you see people who hate their jobs, and you do not want to end up like them.

Job dissatisfaction is so common, and many people wander aimlessly from job to job.

Many adults in the work force wake up every day hating their jobs, dreading going to work, wishing they could stay in bed. Maybe you can recognize this in your own parents.

People who are unhappy at work may not have always been unhappy. Their job may, at one time, have excited them. Maybe it came around at the right time and was a good salary. And maybe that gave them freedom they didn't have before, or brought them status, or perhaps it was the only option they had at the time. But if they are not passionate about what they are doing, over time the excitement turns to emptiness as they begin to question their worth in the world. Only then do they look around and say, "Is this all there is?"

Sure, you might start out seeking things like salary and perks like cars or electronic devices, and that's fine, but be sure to consider things that will fit with the lifestyle you want, like hours, work conditions, and holidays. Talk to the adults in your life about what they like and don't like about their jobs. Every job will have its ups and downs, but if you really like what you are doing on a daily basis, it is much easier to get through the parts of the job that are less appealing.

I often talk to my grade 11 and 12 students about career paths. If they are feeling lost, I tell them about three paths to being passionate in your career. You can try to find something you love to do, something that you want to change, or something that helps others, and then make that a career. Inspiration, motivation, and appreciation are three paths that can lead to a satisfying career.

1. **Inspiration**. Think back on something, anything you have experienced or learned, maybe in a class, that made you say, "Wow." It could be a favourite course, or a show that you watched, or an assignment you did, or a sport you played. One way to know you are on the right track is that when you are doing that action or learning that information, it doesn't feel like work. That is a "spark." Sparks lead to passions, so follow that interest and let it lead you. Then you end up loving what you do because it brings you joy while you are doing it.

2. **Motivation**. The second way to find a passion is to consider something that you know about the world that you disagree with. Maybe it even angers you. You can turn that awareness, that inner fire, into a form of contribution where you are improving society. The world changes constantly, it never stays still. It is the changemakers that create the steps forward. Changemakers are very passionate about what they

do because they know they are making a difference and that is incredibly joyful and satisfying.

3. **Appreciation**. The third way is to view every job as valuable. When you are in that job you can see that it is important. Consider the person who serves your coffee with a smile. That is an important job and we all notice when they enjoy what they do and when they don't. They affect us while we are interacting with them. Consider the job of a garbage collector. This might not be your first choice in careers, but it is an incredibly important job. Imagine life without them! So, if you are ever in a job that seems less than desirable, look hard to see the value of the job and then do it with pride.

Tips to finding and living a happy, rewarding career path:
1. stop being boring – try new things, learn about new things
2. keep track of your skills and interests and strengths
3. volunteer, this allows you to try a career path
4. follow your passion – there are hundreds of jobs in this area that you don't know about yet
5. Work to the best of your ability. Be proud. Work as if others are depending on you – they are!
6. Once you are in your chosen career, use your creativity, awareness and conscience to make improvements to your workplace, your industry, your community.

Number 6 might sound hokey, but it isn't. Use your creativity and the knowledge of your industry to make the world a better place. Think expertise + awareness = innovation. Now that is a recipe for a fulfilling career.

When considering your career, ask yourself, "How could I use this career to make the world a better place?" It is all too easy to get caught up in how much money you can make. But at some point in your life, you will ask yourself what you added to the world. Your day to day existence should be rewarding for you on a deeper level. Choose wisely. Remember, once you are in that field you don't have to follow what others have always done. Carve your own path. Innovation is the key to the future. The world will be healed by people who focus their efforts on positive change.

Making the World a better place is easier then you'd think. You don't have to be a philanthropist or a human rights crusader to make the world a better place. Each and every one of us has an opportunity within our own career area. Making the world a better place could be done by improving a product or service, requesting recycling or compost bins at work, improving individuals health or health care as a whole, helping a person reach their full potential, improving laws or environmental initiatives, improving manufacturing efficiency or materials, helping to preserve nature and animal rights, or human rights, improving access to accurate information, filling communities with beautiful art and music, improving quality of life for co-workers, parents and children, and of course providing happy, helpful customer service with a smile. Making the world a better place is possible for all of us.

This book is about building self-esteem and understanding your self-worth. Most people currently do not work on improving the world through their careers and unfortunately it shows. It is obvious when you meet them personally, but it is also obvious when you look at the world. They don't know how, or can't be bothered, to improve their own lives so how can they gather the energy to improve the world. In Chapter 1 we discussed the secondary benefits of realizing your own self-worth. Waking up to your own worth wakes you up to the worth of everyone else around you and to that of every other living thing. This gives people amazing energy to become innovative in their career field because they want to make a difference. Just imagine what the world would be like if more and more people made this a priority. Imagine how it feels to wake up every day feeling good, feeling proud, and knowing you are making a difference.

I know because I live it and let me tell you, it feels amazing!

Not everyone is destined to have an incredibly high-ranking job, but whatever job you are in, do the best that you can do. Be proud of your efforts, be proud of your contribution and personal reward will come in the form of job satisfaction.

During a conversation on this topic years ago, a wonderful colleague of mine reminded me of this quote by Dr. Martin Luther King Jr:

"If a man is called to be a street sweeper, he should sweep streets even as Michelangelo painted, or Beethoven composed music, or Shakespeare wrote poetry. He should sweep streets so well that all the hosts of heaven and earth will pause to say, here lived a great street sweeper who did his job well."

Big-Picture Points

- *Parents are the most common source of conflict in a teen's life. It is important to compare what you want with what they want. You want freedom – you are practically an adult and you deserve a chance to make decisions for yourself. Valid. They want to continue to protect you, keep you safe from harm and pain. Valid.*

- *It is possible to get what you want, but it involves making wise decisions and accepting responsibility for your actions and accepting the consequences of your actions.*

- *Consequences are a part of life. We learn from our mistakes. Do not get upset if your parents do not stick up for you. Parents should not try to prevent consequences for their child's negative actions. By protecting you from consequences, your parents are ENABLING you to continue your actions. It is a lesson in life. Negative Actions have Negative Consequences.*

- *It is incredibly important to have respect for authority. You don't have to like the person or their decisions, but you do have to be respectful of the position of authority that they hold. This includes parents, police, a boss at work, coaches, teachers, principals, and so on.*

- *Rules are there to keep us all safe and keep us on task so we can achieve success. Rules help us to feel protected. If you were raised with very few rules, you feel uncared for and unguided.*

- *Bullying between friends is incredibly common. You don't have to put up with it.*

- *Your current friends are not necessarily lifelong friends. Right now, in high school, you are all crammed together in one building because you have two things in common: your age and where you live. Your interests and ideas, beliefs and lifestyles could be incredibly different, and you are forced to be around each other daily. That is like social torture for many of you.*

- *Wonderful lifelong friends will present themselves to you at various stages in your life. It will get better after high school.*

- *School will challenge you in many ways. It is your job to rise to the challenge. Remember: It doesn't take brains to get through high school, it takes support. Support can come in many forms. Seek help when you need it.*

CHAPTER 5
Sex, Love and Relationships

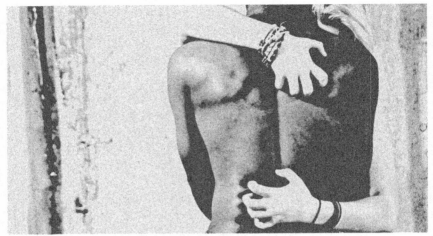

Photograph by Olivia Giroux

This Chapter is dedicated to sifting through the crap, and getting to the core of what really matters.

Do you want to hurt others who are close to you?

Do you want to hurt yourself to please someone else?

Do you want to get married?

Do you want to get divorced?

Do you want to have a family?

Do you want to use people for your own pleasure?

Do you want to let others use you?

Do you want to pretend to be something you're not?

Do you want to be secure and happy in your relationships?

You may have many different views on the questions above, but at the very least, I hope you answered "No" to the first two questions and "Yes" to the last one.

Whatever your answers, I bet that a significant amount of the stress and frustration in your life revolves around relationships. Relationships you have, or relationships you don't have. Relationships that you love one day and hate the next, relationships that exhaust you or that make you feel insecure, relationships that are fake, relationships that are harmful, that stress you out, or relationships that you run to as an escape. These are all what I call *Relationshits*!

What Is Love?

Media does a great job of convincing us what love is. The scenes we see in videos, movies, TV, Magazines, or online are constantly deceiving us. We have been convinced by a great deal of media that love is about being beautiful, sexy, sexual, and all of that equals love and happiness. Nope, sorry, all that equals is lust and it is really easy to confuse the two. These media sources convince you of what love "looks" like because it cannot tell you how it "feels." So, it is easy to see how so many people cannot tell the difference between love and lust. The unfortunate part is that relationships based on lust, even if the two people think it's love, always end in disaster.

And there is a lot more lust out there than love. So, the question really is, "How do you tell love and lust apart?" You know it's love when you feel secure and healthy and happy. With love, you do not hide who you are, and you truly trust this person with your heart.

If you listen to the lyrics of songs that deal with relationships, they seem to have four common themes:

1. Songs about hooking up. "I have no idea who you are, but damn you're sexy and I want you now."

2. Songs about cheating and mistrust, i.e. being cheated on or getting caught.

3. Songs about temptation. "Your boyfriend/girlfriend don't treat you right, they don't love you like I do, come to me."

4. Songs about using someone. "On your knees, B**CH!"

When these are the main messages, is it any wonder that our society has a warped view of relationships? When you really think about music and how it influences our lives, it is easy to see that we get caught up in what we think is the "real world." Well here's your first tip. That is not the real world. In addition to hearing what they sing about, you can read about these celebrities and all of their failed relationships over and over again in magazines. Hopefully at some point you say, "OK, that doesn't work."

What is the one thing that all people want to experience regardless of our backgrounds? Deep down we all want to love and be loved.

A Broken Heart

Let's face it. The worst feeling in the world is a broken heart. Anyone who has ever had a parent leave, had a loved one die, lost a pet, or had their heart broken by a boyfriend or girlfriend knows the full, gut wrenching pain these events can cause. It's a pain that seems like it will last forever. In classes when we are discussing sexual health and healthy relationships, I ask every student in every class the same question. I ask them what scares them the most about dating. Regardless of whether it's a boys' class or a girls' class, overwhelmingly they give me the same answer. I get some responses about sex or liking someone who their friends or family don't approve of, but the number one response I hear is, "I'm afraid of getting rejected," or, "I'm afraid of getting dumped." That is an amazing response to that question. And one that all of us face.

The reality is that relationships begin and end at some point and someone is probably going to wind up hurt. But for some people it happens a lot more often than for others. Some people, and you probably know some, seem to forever be falling for one person only to get their heart steamrolled, then fall for someone else and go through it again, and again, and again. You might even be the one experiencing this rollercoaster of agony, and find yourself thinking, "What is the matter with me? Am I doomed to have a broken heart or to keep breaking the hearts of those I care about?" The answer is NO! You can get off that track or prevent yourself from falling into that brutal cycle in the first place.

Another common fear many teens have is not ever finding the right person and being alone forever.

Whether they are afraid of commitment for the fear of eventually having their heart broken or fear of being alone, some teens try to avoid the dating scene only to "hook up," thinking that if they aren't officially dating then the pain of ending it will be less severe. But, as you will find out in this chapter, this pattern of hook ups will send you into a real cycle of self-loathing.

Two Magic Ingredients for a Happy, Solid Relationship

Many adults believe that teenagers are too young and immature to experience true love. I do not agree. I do believe that teens can fall in love – in fact I know from experience.

What is true of Teenagers is that you can easily confuse "infatuation" for love or "lust" for love. But is it possible to know the difference? Well I didn't know the difference when I was your age, but now I do. And since I'm going to explain it to you, the answer is, YES!

To begin with, we need to be careful how we define love. Let's first look at infatuation. This is an emotional state that would include thinking about your partner constantly and wanting to be around them all the time. OK, that's kind of what love is like in the beginning, but infatuation generally comes with insecurity. You may want to be with them all the time because when you are apart, your imagination takes over and you get nervous about what they might be doing behind your back. Or, you spend so much time together that you start to lose your own identity. This is not love and it certainly is not a healthy, happy relationship.

If we take a look at lust, we see two people who are incredibly attracted to each other, but their main interests are physical. It is obvious that you will have physical attraction, but for true love you have to have two key ingredients, and they are genuine TRUST and RESPECT for each other!

I define Trust as confidence that your partner is loyal to you and will not be swayed by temptation. You have confidence in them that they will make decisions that are beneficial to your relationship. When you are apart, you are still 100% confident in the relationship and you can carry on with your day to day life without insecurities.

I define Respect as a genuine admiration for the values and actions of this person. You not only approve of the way they think and act, but you both actively encourage each other to evolve and grow into better people.

You probably have a list of features you'd like to have in a partner. This is great and important as it shows you what you want and don't want in a partner which helps you to narrow down your search. Please understand that even if you have everything on your list, attractive, smart, funny, for example, if you don't have BOTH Trust *and* Respect for each other, this relationship will not last – I promise you that.

So, you need to ask yourself, "Do I trust this person completely? Do I respect the way they live their life?" But also, "Does this person trust me? Do they respect me and the way I live my life?" In other words, "Do I feel trusted, do I feel respected?"

Respect for Yourself

One of the biggest mistakes I see teens make is to believe that a partner will complete them. You walk around the hall of your high school or mope in your rooms because you don't have a boyfriend or girlfriend, or your jump from one partner to the next because being alone terrifies you.

I will emphasize a few key points throughout this book, but truly none is more important than this: Love comes from within. This goes back to the earlier concepts of self-esteem.

If you are single, then this is a crucial time for you to get to know yourself. Try getting involved in things that interest you and invest some time in yourself. Take time to read, exercise, eat well, forgive yourself for errors in your past and, as corny as this sounds, fall in love with yourself. Get happy on your own, before you get into a relationship.

So many people jump into bad relationships because they are trying to fill a void. If you can fill your void on your own, you will be less hurried and more careful with your heart and who you share it with. Slow down. Love comes from within first. Period.

When you are doing things that you enjoy, you might meet someone with the same interests. I mean, if you are out there doing what you love, and they are doing what they love, and it just happens to be the same thing – well that's an excellent base for a happy relationship. So, join that drama or art club or sports team, or singing class, ski club or math club or whatever is your thing and explore who you are and what is important and enjoyable to you.

When I was growing up, I had 2 very long-term relationships. After the second one ended, I remember being in my late 20's and going through a down time and I was complaining because I was single. My older sister said something to me that has stuck ever since. She said, "You can't expect a happy, confident guy to be attracted to you when you are in this sad, depressed state. Get out there and have fun with life. When you are happy, you are so much more attractive to other happy people." I took her advice. I spent close to a year soul searching for the real me, which, because of my many years in relationships, I had never done before. I learned so much about myself and I learned to be truly content with "single me." It just so happened that this happy, content me, met the wonderful guy who later became my husband.

If you are in a relationship now, you can still get to know and love yourself. It involves spending time alone, away from your partner. It could be a specific night of the week, or a night when your partner goes out with their friends, which is also very healthy by the way. When I say time alone, I don't mean with your friends or family, I really mean time by yourself. What do you truly enjoy doing that you haven't done in a while? This is your chance to do what you love because you love to do it.

It is very easy to get lost in what others want. Who you are will surface at some point, but if you've been hiding it or ignoring it, when it does show up, you and your partner will both be scratching your heads saying, "What happened to you? You've changed."

The more you do the things you love to do, the more confident you'll be with yourself and the less fearful you will be of being alone. This last point is crucial. Many people stay in the wrong relationships because to them any relationship is better than no relationship. This is a dangerous way to think. It causes us to cling to love that isn't there, to stay in painful relationships and to jump from one disastrous partner to another, and after yet another break-up, cry out, "Why does this always happen to me?"

After a break up, declare yourself "off limits." And that includes the recent Ex. Don't go running back to each other until you've both done some independent soul searching. That break up happened for a reason. See it as an opportunity for self-improvement. Whether you get back together or not, you will be approaching the dating scene better prepared and confident with who you are and what you want.

Cheating - When the Heart Ignores the Mind

Without the input of the mind, the heart is like an untrained dog. Looks cute and harmless enough until it starts shitting and peeing all over the place, barking uncontrollably in the middle of the night, jumping up on guests and, "Oh my gawd, is he really...?" Yes – humping their leg.

The heart is wild and doesn't have the means to show restraint. That is why it is so easily hurt. It is your job to train the heart and be careful with it. It is true that you can't control what your heart feels and who you like, but you can control what you say, your body language, what actions you take and what thoughts and feelings you keep to yourself. Case in point and rule number Two: Never go after someone who is currently in a relationship!!!

NB: As you read this case study about Tim, Kaitlyn and Amy, maybe reversing the roles of guys and girls might be more applicable to your experiences. Feel free to interpret it the other way around.

Case study:

Tim and Kaitlyn are dating, and Amy finds herself extremely attracted to Tim. She thinks he's hot and they have even flirted together which makes her think that he likes her too, possibly more than he likes Kaitlyn. An opportunity arises when Amy and Tim can get together behind Kaitlyn's back. What should Amy do?

Well if we let the mind take hold of the situation then the obvious answer is Stop. Remove herself from contact with Tim and move on. If we let the heart take over and start manipulating her mind.... well, *here is how it plays out: What does Amy really want – to be loved. Attention makes her feel good. Attention from someone else's guy makes her feel strangely powerful, like she's in control of the whole situation. False. In the worst-case scenario, Tim and Kaitlyn don't break up, Amy is left alone, rejected and now carrying a reputation. But let's look at Amy's "best case scenario" after the cheating. Let's say Tim and Kaitlyn break up and Amy and Tim start dating. OK that sounds good – Amy has "won." Well, what exactly has she "won?" Amy is now in Kaitlyn's position, think about it. Remember you need <u>trust</u> and <u>respect</u> in the relationship to have true love. Could Amy and Tim ever achieve that? The only known factor is that Amy will be justifiably insecure about Tim. She knows firsthand that he is capable of cheating on his girlfriend so what's to stop him from repeating it when temptation arises? Nothing! Whether Tim ever cheats on her or not, Amy can never truly trust him and if you recall, trust is one of the two most important ingredients of a happy, healthy, long term relationship. Nope, Amy and Tim are doomed. And the misery was preventable. All she had to do was let her mind guide her heart. So, if we go back in time to before the cheating incident, what should Amy do? Acknowledge to herself that she likes another girl's guy, accept the pain and wait silently, patiently for one of two things to happen. 1) She moves on and lets go of her feelings for Tim, or 2) if Tim and Kaitlyn were not meant to be together then guess what, they'll eventually break up and then Amy can enter the scene with a clear conscience and trust in her partner.*

It amazes me the number of people who cheat in relationships, and it also amazes me the number of teens who think it is completely acceptable. I guess in an age when the divorce rate is higher than 50% and songs constantly sing out emotions from all sides of the love triangle, it somehow has become a normal part of dating. I must honestly say that regardless of the age of the participants, I have never once seen cheating work out in anyone's favour. Cheating is completely avoidable and doing so allows you to protect your heart and the hearts of others. Have faith. The right person will come along at the right time for both of you – be patient.

This scenario also opens the door to a common interaction among girls. When hearts are at stake in a love triangle, girls blame the "other girl" and not their boyfriend. Many times, I have heard about threats towards a girl for looking at someone's boyfriend. Cat fights are insane if you really think about what is going on. Let's develop the characters from the example above and focus on Kaitlyn. In this case study, as the original relationship between Kaitlyn and Tim dissolves, it is easy for Kaitlyn to place all the blame on Amy. Kaitlyn might get all of her friends involved, the texts and electronic messages start flying, and Amy receives threats at school, in the middle of the night, or in person from a group of Kaitlyn's friends. Amy is in the wrong, but so is Tim! The Kaitlyn's of the world are more apt to want to please their boyfriends and not blame him for fear of losing him. Kaitlyn aims all of her anger and pain at one target – the other girl. Unable to consciously come to grips with the pain of Tim not wanting her any more.

If the flirting is one way, say from Amy to Tim, and Tim doesn't return the flirting, then Kaitlyn has nothing to worry about and would continue to feel secure in her relationship knowing that Amy will move on. But if Tim reciprocates then Kaitlyn blames Amy for making her feel insecure about her relationship. Amy might be the catalyst, but if the relationship was true love with trust and respect, then Tim would not be flirting, and Kaitlyn would not be feeling insecure. If your boyfriend looks around or flirts, then your issue is with your boyfriend. Don't misdirect your anger toward another girl while putting your boyfriend on a pedestal. He is equally to blame and should not be treated like you are protecting him from the evil temptress. So, what do you do? First acknowledge that the real issue is *within* – on two levels.

First, the issue is within you. Are you truly content with yourself at this time? Do you love yourself? Are you clinging to this partner because they make you feel complete somehow? Second, look closely at your relationship. Do you both feel deep trust and respect towards each other? If the answers to any of these questions cause doubt, then you should take this situation and turn it around for the better. Instead of aiming your energy at the outsider, you should turn that energy into something beneficial and take steps to work on improving your relationship with yourself. Ask yourself, "Do I want to be in a relationship that makes me feel insecure?" Address your own healing. Maybe it's time to get out of that relationship and focus on you – single you. Even if you scare Amy away with threats, if the healing within doesn't happen, then the same situation will be around the corner with another girl. Inner healing is necessary for you. Threats, anger, and blame toward another will not fix your pain. Deal with the source of your insecurity. Really, deal with it.

Let's look at this from Tim's angle. If he is truly in love with Kaitlyn, with trust and respect for her then he would not feel the desire to look around. Also, the thought of hurting her would stop any stupid actions. But what if he actually is interested in Amy? Getting to know Amy while still in the relationship with Kaitlyn is nothing but cowardly and selfish. Fear of being alone without either girl might prompt him to cheat. Maybe he's gotten away with it in the past, maybe his parents or siblings have cheated. In this case he probably doesn't trust himself and might eventually think girls who date him are doing so at their own risk – it might become acceptable for him to be a "heartbreaker." But maybe it's his first time cheating. In that case it's time to learn right from wrong. If he is really interested in Amy, then that should be the first sign that things are not right between himself and Kaitlyn. You can't be perfectly content and search outside at the same time. Before any action with Amy, Tim has to be respectful to himself and Kaitlyn and end their relationship. I have been stressing the importance of trust and respect in a relationship, but really that has to apply to you too. In order for any partner to trust and respect you, you have to trust and respect yourself. Tim has to either stop flirting with Amy and work things out with Kaitlyn, or he has to end his current relationship. Yup, hard work either way, but that's what love is.

In order to Trust and Respect your partner and expect that they feel the same towards you, you have to first TRUST and RESPECT yourself.

Breaking Up

A student let me in on what she was going through in her relationship. She was really upset about what she was feeling. She'd been in this relationship for almost two years, but for the past few months she had been feeling like she was no longer in love with her boyfriend. There seemed to be no reason why she was feeling this way. She sometimes was completely happy with him, but other times she wanted to end it. She didn't know what to do. I gave her some advice that seemed to help her to make up her mind. We talked about how relationships can become a little dull after a while. My concern was that this would happen to her in other relationships too and that she really needed to look inside before she let go of a good thing simply because she was bored.

So here was my advice: "Don't dump him yet. Instead take the next month to work really hard at making the relationship great. Do wonderful things for him, plan nice dates, spice it up a bit. Really dive in and work at making things fun again. Hopefully it won't feel like work. If at the end of the month you still feel the same, then I would say that you've given it your best shot and then you could end the relationship with little doubt."

She was quite happy with the idea and when I chatted with her a few months later, she was still with him and much more content in the relationship.

What if you realize that breaking up is the right move. How do you go about doing this? One word – respectfully. Unless your partner did something horrible to you, it is your duty to be respectful with their heart at this painful time.

Timing - it must be about considering *Their* situations, NOT *Your* convenience.

Break ups should happen <u>face to face</u> when you are <u>alone</u> together, when you are <u>sober</u>, at a reasonable <u>time</u>, and the partner is in a <u>safe</u> location. It would be better after school, <u>not</u> just before bed or a work shift, <u>not</u> during school. Let them save face. They should not have to return to a group or go immediately to a class. They should be able to experience their pain quietly on their own or with close friends or family.

Rule: It should <u>never</u> happen <u>electronically</u>, i.e. texting. Electronic break-ups are cowardly, inconsiderate and disrespectful. That is all about your convenience, not their situation. When you press send, you have no idea what situation they will be in when they receive it.

There are no specific words I can tell you to say, but I can tell you to be truthful. Honesty will pay off in the end as they can continue to know you are a trustworthy person. Lastly, leave them alone. Do not call them to see if they are OK, do not flirt with them at parties, and do not "hook up" with them. This only drags them along and prolongs their pain. Casual conversations at school after a few weeks or months are enough. Let them move on. It is also important to not concern yourself with who they date afterwards. Avoid feeling jealousy or anger. If you want to move on, they can too. End of story.

How does self-esteem fit in? Regardless of the role you play in this mess, self-esteem drives your decisions. If you believe that being alone is worse than being in a dysfunctional relationship, then that is a dead giveaway to how you feel about yourself. The "truth of who you are," which we will examine in the final chapters, is that you deserve respect and love – not only from others, but also from yourself. If you can't love and respect yourself, then how can you expect others to? If you do not love and respect yourself, then you will end up making bad decisions; decisions that will result in others choosing not to respect you or trust you. Believe in your own worth, believe in the worth of others, and act on those beliefs. Live happily and confidently.

Playing Roles

Media sets up male image, female image, like game pieces and teens happily, or not so happily, play along. Do you have to buy into this? Apparently, most of you think you do.

Female role – sexy, petite, graceful, confident yet vulnerable, emotional, in need of a man.

Male role – buff, strong, tough, sex addict, determined, confident and independent, rescuer of women.

But what if you don't fit that mold? Well, the bad news is, it is tougher for you to feel confident in who you are if you compare yourself to these stereotypes. The good news is you are not alone. Most guys and girls are extremely insecure about fitting into this mold. It either makes them feel uncomfortable or they simply do not have the looks or interests to fit them. If you don't fit the media mold, then you have two options. One, you can feel miserable and sad and complain, or, two, you can say, "Screw the mold," and be yourself and aim for a chance at inner happiness. This goes back to the idea of living life for you, doing what you love, and getting to know what is important to you.

Teens are not the only ones affected by these stereotypes. Are there any adults you can think of that are almost obsessed with their appearance and behaviour in front of others? Almost like they are always performing and never relaxing and letting their true self show? For example, if it is a woman, is she someone who would never leave the house unless she was in full make up and dressed in the latest fashions? If it is a man, is he always "on," always looking his best, always coming across as confident and strong in social situations? Does he always need a beautiful woman around?

182

What does that say about how they view themselves? Are they unhappy with what's inside? We can assume they are, otherwise why would they try so hard to cover it up? Go back and read about DAP in Chapter 3. The fact that they are adults tells us that they have been feeling this way for a very long time, and that their beliefs are deeply rooted. They will probably not be able to change their actions easily, as it is so difficult for adults to change their ways. They have fallen into the trap of the "false esteem" that we discussed in the first chapter. It's a sad place to be. But *You* have a great opportunity to break free from these molds before they become deeply rooted beliefs. You can save yourself now.

For the next section, I will speak to girls and guys separately.

To the Girls

Being Cute-iful. (*My daughter made up this word when she was three.*)

I am amazed at the lengths to which girls will go to try to impress boys. You regard your appearance so highly. But take note, all of the things that you do to look pretty, they are to please the "girl half" of the population. You may have grown up with the princess concepts, but do you remember most boys never played with that kind of stuff? The reason is because this stuff doesn't impress them. It doesn't interest them. You will never hear a boy say, "Oh she's not wearing enough make up," or, "Her hair is messy," or, "Gross, she's all sweaty from playing sports." Why? Because boys don't care about half the things you think they care about. It is strange because it's like girls are reinforcing these beliefs in each other. You are competing with each other, to get the attention of the boys, when in reality the boys don't understand or care about this stuff. You don't have to look princess perfect. If you want to impress a boy then you'd better try to understand what interests them, and stop trying to be something that you're not – because that definitely doesn't interest them.

To the Boys

It is difficult at best for you to fit the mold that society deems to be sexy for guys. It is all about muscle and body size, but time is not on your side for most of you. Your bodies will become much more muscular and larger in your late teens, and through your 20's. I constantly see guys trying to build muscle in the school gyms. Exercise is great, keep going! But do it for *You*, not for the girls. Any girl who likes you only for your body is not one worth working out for.

Attracted to Trouble?

So many girls choose to go after the "bad boys" and don't even blink at the nice guys. Why is that? For some it is the social status that they gain by association with this guy, for others it is to get back at parents by dating someone they know mom and dad would not approve of. There are many ways to look at this, but after many discussions with my students, I have to lean in one specific direction. Girls like to help others. Girls innately play the mothering role and think that we can help this poor lost soul. Girls are often invited past the tough exterior and shown the softer side of these guys and then fall for them with the belief that we can fix their problems. Hell, *they* might even believe you can fix them. But this thinking is forever flawed, and the relationship is destined for a crash landing.

It comes down to this. **You cannot fix another person**. You can guide them, you can point them in the right direction, but the "fixing" has to come from within. Only that troubled person can heal their own wounds. Let them read this book, particularly the chapter on Vices. If you think you can save them, you might wind up with a person who clings to you for salvation, or maybe they let you down over and over because that's what they are used to doing. Either way this emotionally draining relationship is destined for failure or an eternity of fights and heartaches. If you truly care about this individual, point them in the right direction and tell them you'll wait for them to sort their struggles out. This is one path they need to travel on their own.

OK, it's time to put this "attracted to trouble" thing into perspective for the boys. Let's face it there are a lot of hot girls out there. They are in your face in all forms of media, at the clubs, at school. Looks are so incredibly important to girls. Check out the media messages aimed at girls, watch commercials on TV, and notice how many times a relationship is shown where both the guy and the girl are hot. This sends a huge message to you guys, as well as the girls. BUT also notice how many relationships on TV are between an OK looking guy and a hot girl. It is rarely, if ever, seen the other way around. So, the message that gets out is it is of utmost importance for girls to be attractive before any other trait. Right now, you, as a guy, might be smiling because, hey, you're in the winning seat up to this point in the conversation. You are thinking, "I can be great looking or even OK looking and I can score a hottie!"

Remember that dating is practice for marriage, for most people. I am not saying you have to consider marrying every girl you date. Far from it. But you should be *learning* from every relationship so that you can be sure of what you want in a relationship, and more importantly, what you DON'T want in a relationship. So, as you are considering a girl as someone you might want to date, think of it this way. Eventually you have to choose someone who you will be making all of your life decisions with. Your decisions on finances, career, raising children, and rough times in life such as losing a job, or facing illness and death. You need to be each other's best friends. Listen man, she needs to be more then hot! There are so many girls out there that focus on their looks, at the expense of every other important trait. There are far too many hot "twits" out there and many guys, and society, encourage them, date them, learn nothing from the relationships, get addicted to looks and lust, and then they are on a straight road to marrying one of these hot, insecure, twits. Good luck. You're going to need it. Do you respect her? Do you trust her? Does she trust you? Sure, she's pretty, but these relationships are not smooth rides and they don't end in a very pretty way.

The good news is there are tons of amazing girls out there. They are happy, fun, confident, doing what they love, playing sports, joining clubs, being healthy, not dating guys that are idiots, and they are not wearing slutty clothes to attract guys. They do not need to be saved by you because they have already learned to figure things out. They are awesome, and these are the ones that you will have a great relationship with.

Guys are victims of the media's curse just as much as girls are. Many boys grow up with the notion that girls are objects for their physical pleasure. It is everywhere, and it can become part of your identity. If you don't have strong role models at home demonstrating healthy relationships, then girls can only become objects.

John sits a party and laughs with his buddies, he has just sent out four separate text messages each to a different girl. In each text he tells the girl he misses her and wants to come and pick her up tonight – can she sneak out?

He confidently tells his buddies that he's going to get laid tonight. "With who?" they ask. He replies, "Whichever one texts me back first."

Are these guys truly happy? How can they be? True love is something that everyone seeks deep down, but if the two most important components to true love are trust and respect, how could anyone really love them deep down. They are so afraid of never finding someone and being alone that they ensure they are never "physically alone," even if it is only in bed. They may look like they have it all together, but make no mistake this is not a happy place.

One side note that all guys should be aware of: Consent for Sex. If a girl says yes but she is drunk or high when she says yes,

or she says yes and then passes out, you do not have her consent. You can be charged with rape.

Sexuality and Self-Punishment

Don't judge overly sexual people – you don't know their past. Don't judge seemingly frigid people – you don't know their past. Some people use their sexuality as a form of self-punishment.

Jenny has had a troubled past, and her self-esteem is at an all-time low. In her past, she experienced childhood sexual assault. She identifies herself as a victim but worse still, when the world teaches her that to have sexual attention makes you a tease and to have sex makes you a slut, she identifies herself as a tease and slut. Jenny may drown herself in the role of a slut. "This is who I am, this is where I belong." It is her self-punishment and her comfort all at the same time. Along the way Jenny will be used by many people to get what they want and get out of there. Every boy who has sex with her is essentially adding another nail to her coffin, for their own pleasure.

Jenny may also meet someone nice who wants to save her from her pain and poor decisions. Like the situation described above, Jenny might cling to this person and drain them emotionally or she may feel she does not deserve him and might purposefully do something wrong to cause the person to leave her – that is what she is used to. This is another example of self-punishment and comfort all at the same time. Jenny needs to heal herself from the inside, but all the boys in Jenny's life need to recognize that she is in pain and not add fuel to her fire.

There are also victims of sexual abuse who will go to the other end of the sexual behaviour spectrum.

Ida was a victim of sexual assault when she was as a child. Now, as a teen, she wants to have a relationship like everyone else, but she is extremely uncomfortable with physical contact and sexual advances. Too scared to talk about her past, she gains a reputation of being frigid and then no guys want to date her.

I repeat:
Don't judge overly sexual people – you don't know their past.
Don't judge seemingly frigid people – you don't know their past.

Gay Relationships

It's time to mention the inner turmoil of young people who are questioning their sexual orientation and/or gender identification. Forgive me for using male - female relationships in the earlier case studies. It could have just as easily been cheating between Ben, Jeff and Tyrone or Cindy, Keesha and Alicia. Any of the previous examples can easily apply to gay relationships. Regardless of your beliefs on the topic of gay relationships, they happen, and they are just as confusing and heartbreaking as a straight relationship. But they are WAY more complicated because of the pressures that come from *outside* of the relationship.

Let's clear up two important terms: Gender Identity and Sexual Orientation. These are the two main ways people struggle with sexuality. The first is Gender Identity, this refers to who (what grouping) a person self-identifies with. For example, traditionally if you are born with a penis then you emotionally connect yourself with being male. They just seem to go together. Well that isn't always the case. Gender Identity refers to a disconnect between who you feel you are and what sex your body tells the world you are. This has nothing to do with who you are attracted to. This has everything to with how you feel on the inside about yourself and your gender. It is possible for someone to feel they are male, female, both or neither.

Sexual Orientation is a different issue altogether, it refers to who (what grouping) someone is attracted to. Traditionally we think of a female being attracted to a male, but who (what grouping) people are attracted to is not set by choice. It is possible for someone to be attracted to males, females, both or neither.

In my many years of teaching, I have met many teens who struggle with gender identity and/or sexual orientation. In talking with them it becomes obvious that this is not a choice for them but a complicated inner struggle.

Once you delve into the many combinations of gender identity and sexual orientation there are many specific terms that surface. I don't want to insult anyone, and I apologize if my over-simplification does. Please forgive me as I, for the sake of ease of reading, will for the next few paragraphs refer to anyone struggling with their sexuality as the term gay.

Note: If you are homophobic as a teenager, and reading this part makes you feel uncomfortable, then I want to challenge you to question your opinions and beliefs. The strong feelings you have, are they your *own* thoughts? Did you decide that gay is wrong completely on your own? OR did these ideas and opinions come from the opinions of others? Perhaps your parents' ideas, or your religion? I am asking you to question this because I would venture to say that in your life, gays have not attempted to harm you or convert you. And yet you think it's fine that you make their lives miserable? What does it matter to you? At this point you can rationalize all you want, but in the end the answer is, it doesn't matter to you. So, leave them alone. Life is hard if you are questioning your sexual orientation, and nobody needs an individual in their life making it worse. Do you think cruel actions will scare them into being straight? I am a firm believer that people do not choose to be gay and they certainly can't choose to be Not gay. From a biological standpoint, there are many examples in nature of homosexual tendencies. We are a part of nature too, our functions controlled by the inner workings of our genetics. Be open to the possibility that others may not be able to choose to be straight and get on with your own life. Otherwise you are a bully, which means, as we've discussed already, that you need to examine where your own pain comes from as you act on the impulse to push others down in order to raise yourself up.

If it is you who is questioning your sexual orientation or gender identity, stay strong. The road ahead is a tough one, but it gets easier. Most gay adults would agree that the teenage years are the toughest. After that you can find social groups in colleges and universities, at work or in your community. Be as honest as you can with yourself and your family but be patient with the rest of the people in your life. While it is common for people to do some experimenting with partners of the same sex, individuals who are truly homosexual generally know they have interests that are not traditional. Listen to gay adults and their experiences. Some say they had known from childhood or as an early teen that they were different, while others say it took a very long time and many relationships to figure it out. Some resisted their feelings, thinking they could change how they felt. In the end, if you do come to terms with accepting who you are, it makes it easier on you. The most difficult years will most likely be the teenage years, because in high school, everyone around you is trying to fit in. They are very judgemental of themselves and also of everyone else too. It truly is *their* problem first and foremost; don't make it *your* problem. Please understand that everything I have written about relationships so far, the importance of feeling comfortable with who you are, having trust and respect for your partner, cherishing alone time, following your interests, it all applies to you too. As does any advice that will follow. A relationship is a relationship. Regardless of the type, they build up and fall down the same way. Stay Strong.

Sex

WARNING! "AwkWeird" Moment coming! You may feel a little uncomfortable reading this stuff. That's normal. Of course, you can skip this part if you want to.

Obviously, there is a very specific purpose for sex: procreation. Yes, sex creates a baby, but there is another, not well known but fascinating, role of intimacy. Nature is amazing. Intimacy not only creates a family, it helps to maintain the bond between parents. This bond is similar to the bond that is formed between mother and child, after a child is born.

When a mother has a baby, and begins feeding and caring for her baby, she becomes bonded with that child. It is nature's design. The bonding experience is rooted in the chemistry of the mother's brain. Through the good times and the bad times, she will care for that child. Fathers go through it too. The more time they spend caring for the child, the stronger the bond. But our brain chemistry is also guiding the entire family unit.

As long as parents remain intimate in their relationship, they are strengthening their emotional bond. When parents are intimate together, their brain chemistry reinforces their bonding as a couple, and therefore reinforces the strength of the family unit. They will care for each other and their children through good times and bad. Loving intimacy between parents helps a family unit to remain together and strong for life. In his 2015 *Making Sense of Adolescence* video course, Dr. Gordon Neufeld refers to sex and intimacy as "super-glue" for the relationship. This works as long as the intimacy is respectful and loving. But there is catch…

Brain chemistry is fascinating but here is how it can backfire. If a person has had too many short-term sexual partners, sharing intimacy with many different people, the brain makes an attempt to protect itself. Break ups are emotionally wounding events, especially if sex was a part of the relationship. So, if it happens repeatedly, the brain will try to prevent that pain. It responds defensively and decreases the bonding capacity, so that when you break up, it will be less painful. Unfortunately, it becomes harder for you to emotionally bond to a partner when you really want to. Then, instead of sex being an experience that reinforces long term connection, it becomes a purely physical connection, not an emotional one. Essentially, it becomes harder to fall in love. So, if a person is seeking intimacy and a long-term connection, but they have already slept around, their capacity to create a long-term emotional bond is impaired.

This decrease in "super-glue" can also occur in those who have experienced trauma and/or abuse associated with sex and sexual activity. The brain's defensive response is designed to prevent further emotional pain by creating numbness and non-attachment.

Have you ever heard about a person who sleeps around a lot, but can't seem to fully commit to anyone? Often falling in lust, but not falling in love? This is the neuroscience behind that phenomenon. They seem unable to faithfully maintain long-term relationships. They move from one partner to another, unable to deeply connect, because their "super-glue" is currently not working.

Note: Be careful if you are interested in a person who seems to "get around" a lot. Chances are, you will not be able to hold on to them. You may bond to them, but they can't emotionally bond to you. Before long, they'll end the relationship or cheat on you.

If it is *you* who have found yourself getting involved in one relationship after another, sleeping with each partner, but finding none of these relationships are "sticking", your brain chemistry needs time to reset. So, take a break. If you want long-term commitment in the future, consider yourself off-limits for a while.

As a modern society, we've lost the understanding of the role of intimacy to secure long-term relationships and we are paying a big price for it. As a young person, take it slow. Be aware and respectful to yourself and to others. Rushing into a sexual relationship will backfire on you. Take your time, get to know your partner as a person. Do you want them as a life-long partner? Do you want them as a "right now" partner? If you select too many "right now" partners, you are decreasing your chance of being able to bond with a life long partner when you want to. Conserve your "super-glue".

Know Your Sexual Limitations

So many couples miss out on a healthy and enjoyable progression of intimacy. Healthy relationships progress through the physical stuff <u>slowly</u> over a *very* long period of time. It is vital that young couples don't go further than they are comfortable with. Setting limits is critical. Intimacy is supposed to be a pleasurable experience. If you are uncomfortable, it is your brain and body's way of saying this isn't right for you right now. Step back and slow down. Set your sexual limits. The right partner will wait for when you are ready.

Below is a list I call Progression of Intimacy. Consider it a general guideline of suggestions for how a healthy intimate relationship could progress slowly over time.

- Flirting
- Getting to know each other (talking/texts/online chats/phone calls)
- Establishing interest in each other, and <u>trust</u> and <u>respect</u> for each other
- Dating (friends and family are aware)
- Holding hands
- Kissing
- Becoming intimate (dim lights during movie, cuddling)
- Sharing intimate words
- Touching each other through clothes
- Touching under clothes
- Seeing each other naked
- Manual stimulation (hands)
- Oral stimulation (mouth)
- Intercourse

In a healthy relationship, eventually sex might be part of it, but it isn't rushed. As you look back at that list, the Progression of Intimacy, consider these important guidelines:

1. **Time frames** of weeks, months or years exist between each stage.

2. Constant **communication** is essential so that both partners indicate their comfort level.

3. If one partner is **not comfortable** with any intimate activity, the other partner does not pressure them to go further. Intimacy is supposed to be a loving and respectful experience. If the actions don't make you feel that way, slow down!

4. It is critical that **both partners are comfortable, trustful and respectful of each other.** The relationship continues and regularly encompasses the previous stages.

5. Partners regularly reassess **trust and respect** for each other.

6. If a couple moves into a sexual relationship, they continue to communicate their comfort level. **Healthy partners** do not make you do something you don't want to do.

NOTE: Alcohol and marijuana (or any substance use for that matter) will blur the lines of your sexual limits. It is very important to make sure if you are choosing to use substances, that you have a friend who will make sure you get home safely without engaging in risky sexual behaviour you would otherwise regret. Keep in mind, your "friend" cannot be your romantic partner (*that's a conflict of interest*).

What You See, What You Don't

Some young couples rush to oral sex and sexual intercourse and they miss out on all of the amazing stuff that builds the foundation of their relationship. Media doesn't help in this regard. In many TV shows, movies, and music videos, couples rush and go from flirting to intercourse <u>in one night!</u> We see it so often it's really easy for you to think that is normal. Is this the path to a strong relationship? You meet, you flirt, you go all the way. Now what? If all you want (and all they want) is sex, then this is not a problem (although it becomes a problem later on when you really do want to stay with one person – remember that "superglue" stuff?).

It is important to note that just because a couple has sex does not mean they go on to the degrading and disrespectful actions shown in some types of pornography. Trust and respect are important in all areas of healthy long-term (and short-term) relationships, including the physical/sexual aspects of the relationship. I don't think the people who create porn or who are displayed in it, have much of nature's superglue instincts happening anymore. Sadly, when sex cannot be relied on for creating connection, it is pursued as a means of an adrenalin rush. As with any adrenalin addiction, the actions need to push the boundaries to get the desired experience. I fear for young people being exposed to the extremes demonstrated by adults chasing adrenalin rushes. If Porn is where you are getting your sexual information from, be careful. It can decrease your chances of being satisfied with a long-term healthy, respectful relationship.

Some people, subconsciously, engage in certain aspects of extreme sex as an adrenaline rush. They can't bond emotionally, but they are aroused and get a rush. Unfortunately, a relationship that is based on sex in this way can be emotionally painful to partners, and eventually becomes boring. Staying with the same partner leads to the adrenalin rush decreasing and when the bonding does not take hold, sometimes a person begins to question why they are staying. They may start to wonder what a different relationship would be like. Would another relationship be more exciting? Maybe, they think. So, they dump this one and try a new partner. But, if they still just chase sex, the same thing happens again and again. Remember the bonding "superglue"? The more you get around, the less you can truly connect for the long term. Chasing extreme sex is not a recipe for a healthy, secure relationship, and it's definitely not a recipe for true happiness.

Benefits of Slowing Down the Physical Stuff

You may feel pressured from the outside world, but it isn't a race. It's wise to slow down the physical stuff. If you take your time (weeks, months, years) and communicate openly about how comfortable you are feeling, you can both get to know each other. You can remain in control and reduce the chance of regretting your actions later on. And, you get to enjoy the wonderful time spent on the falling in love stages: the text messages and talks, the flirting, the hand holding, the dating. Not secret dating, but the kind of dating where all of your friends know you are dating, and you can all hang out together.

Once you've had sex, regardless of whether you are a guy or a girl, there is no turning back the clock. And once word gets out, and the word will get out, if the relationship doesn't work out, your future partner's expectations of you are entirely different. It is much easier for a virgin to say no to sex with their next partner. It is much harder for a non-virgin to say no to the next partner. Once you open yourself up to sex, if you are not careful, you are likely to be opening yourself up to sex with every person you date. And possibly with people you are *not* dating. The goal of healthy self-esteem means that you respect yourself. Can you see the dilemma?

What if you are reading this and you have already had sex? What if you have already begun to experience the negative side of sex with everyone who asks? Turn yourself into a Born Again Virgin. Declare yourself off limits. Fly solo for a while and reassess what you really want in a relationship and Be Strong. Once you do find someone you are interested in, start back at the beginning and navigate carefully from one intimacy step to the next. If your partner can be patient with you, this will help you to know if they are in it for the right reasons. If you want to date someone who respects you, then you have to respect yourself first. There is no other way around it.

Tamara was known for getting around. After a class, when I was talking about the progression of intimacy, she told me that she missed out on the flirty stuff at the top and that was what she really wanted. She told me that the last two guys she was "seeing" would text her at night, sometimes in the middle of the night, and say they missed her and wanted to come and pick her up – right away. They were completely fine with having sex with her, but they wouldn't take her out on a date, or hang out with her friends, or hold hands with her in public or ask how her day was. She wanted advice.

I asked her what she wanted in a relationship. At first, she said she wanted to be loved, but then she said she wasn't aware until this class about trust and respect. She said, "Now I know I want to be respected."

So, I asked her, "Are you behaving in a way that allows you to respect yourself?"

She looked down and said, "No."

"Well, do you think that anyone else can respect you right now?" I asked.

She looked up with tears in her eyes and shook her head. "No."

"So, what do you need to do next time they call?"

We discussed telling them that their arrangement was over, telling them not to text anymore, also not answering their texts, blocking their number and turning off her phone at night. We discussed how she might feel lonely, but strong, and that she should connect with her old friends more often.

Respect yourself and you will attract people who will respect you, you set the pace and others will follow.

Oh Baby!

The most serious reality of teen sex is teenage pregnancy. **This single topic may be the most crucial of all.** With most things in this book I will ask you to rethink situations so you yourself can avoid pain and suffering. Now I will ask you to rethink your actions so that a completely innocent person - a child - can avoid pain and suffering. Before you read any further, I am fully aware that some of you will disagree with what I am saying on the topic and you will say, "But I know someone who got pregnant when they were a teen and they kept the baby and had the support of the parents (now grandparents) and everything worked out fine." There are exceptional cases where this can work out, but you must understand that these are **exceptions**. The vast majority of teenage pregnancies are incredibly difficult and the child in the end grows up to be a teenager who has seen too much fighting, violence, neglect, poor healthcare, and questionable discipline, if any at all. They grow up so unsure of how they fit in to the world that they can't help but be swept up in crisis after crisis. I work constantly with students who have grown up in that situation. Many don't even think it's a problem. Many times, in school the most troubled kids in the class are children of teenage parents. As we discuss teenage pregnancies, they may call out, "My mom was a teenager when she had me and I worked out just fine." And then the rest of the class looks at me with a look of, "OK – I get it."

If you are having sex or thinking about having sex then you and your partner need to be dealing with the question of, "What will we do if we get pregnant?" Do not avoid this question – don't say we will deal with that when it happens.

I hear teens talk about when they become parents how they will be such a "cool mom" or a "cool dad." They fantasize about being the parent that they want to have right now. Letting their kids do things that they think are cool. How they would discipline. If you fantasize about this, you need to know the truth about parenting. The cool parent you dream of being is the parent of a teenager. You have to be a parent for 13 years before you get to parent a teenager. You cannot be a "cool" parent of young children and make wise decisions for their success. Young children need firm guidelines for them to follow. If you are too relaxed, they receive too much freedom and not enough attention and guidance. It leaves them wondering who really cares about them. Go back and re-read the section on parenting styles specifically Laisse-Faire parenting. Good parents are selfless, they put their children's needs ahead of their own, they let go of their own ego, and they let go of needing to be viewed as "cool."

If you are considering keeping the baby, I want to bring you back to the main theme of this book: Self-Esteem. The main concept is that either "low" or "false" esteem affects every decision in life. If you bring an unwanted child into the world what do you think their life will be like? Some of you might say, "But I actually do 'want' the baby." Maybe because you have this dream of someone (your child) actually loving you when you feel that no one else has. Don't fall into la-la land!

Love is not enough!

What does a baby need? You have probably already heard how expensive babies are. As well as a parent with a stable income, a baby needs love, unconditional love. It also needs safety, protection from harm, daily routine, health care, healthy food, attention, stimulation, and age appropriate play. All of these things may seem easy enough, but the tough part it is that they need this *constantly*, which is incredibly exhausting. There is no break for you. Let me repeat that point. There is no break for you. While your friends are out shopping, socializing and partying, you will not be. You will not be able to do these things and continue to be a responsible parent. Resentment will grow toward this child who took your freedom away. But remember this child is completely innocent. YOU brought it into this world. YOU chose to keep it. YOU gave up your freedom. This tiny creature will wake you up so many times in the night that you feel like you are being tortured with sleep deprivation. It will poop when you are in a rush to get out the door, it will scream in a store if you are 10 minutes late feeding it. It will throw food on the floor after you've just spent half an hour making it. You will lose it. And yet, you still have to keep it safe and protect it from harm and love it unconditionally and it is hard!

And if you don't do all these things, they will learn from you that they are not worth protecting, not worth keeping safe, not worth loving.

Loving a child does not mean buying them the things they want or letting them watch the shows they want to see or letting them stay up late with you as you do the things you want to do. It means being with them, playing with them, doing age-appropriate thing with them, setting rules and boundaries and following through with consequences. The only thing a child wants is your time, attention and love, but you need to provide much more than that to keep them safe and feeling protected. Have children only when you are ready to be *SELFLESS*. Until then either use birth control or don't have sex!

In 2011, I heard statistics about 750,000 babies born to teenage moms in the US in 2010 alone, and that the vast majority of those moms would choose to keep their babies. That saddens me to the point of tears. That so many babies could be at risk for growing into emotionally lost children every year is heartbreaking. Is there any connection between the growing issues in the world and the number of children growing up without enough love? Poor self-esteem breeding poor self-esteem. Tragic.

Some people think that keeping the baby is akin to dealing with the consequence of your behaviour. I completely disagree. That argument works for getting an STD. Yes, there are consequences to stupid decisions, but if the bad decision is not putting on a condom, I don't see how ruining the life of an innocent child matches up! In my opinion, the pain of pregnancy, labour, and the heartache of giving a child up for adoption is consequence enough. *Your* error, *your* pain. NOT *your* error, pain transferred to an innocent child.

I knew a young girl who got pregnant when she was 15. She convinced everyone around her that she would return to school after the baby was born. She even convinced herself. Things were not going very well at home with this newborn and she moved out of her dad's house and in with her birth mother, who had also been a teenage mom. By the time she was 16, after much conflict, she moved out and got her own apartment. When she was 18, a friend went to see her and found that she now had three children and was living in a tiny apartment and was on welfare. The children apparently were in rough condition, acting up and starving for their mother's love and attention. The building was also in rough condition. There was no hot water and she was trying to bath her screaming children in cold water. Her visiting friend, only 17 at the time, was crushed to see this young mom and her children in the state they were in.

If there is not supportive family helping young parents to raise their child, adoption is the best answer but the hardest to deal with at the time. It is the most selfless, mature decision you can make. As an adult, I have come to know friends who are on adoption waiting lists. They are wonderful people, secure as a couple, secure financially, and are healthy, happy individuals. They sincerely want to have children but are unable to have children of their own. They do the most compassionate thing, they chose to love and raise a child through adoption. They spend thousands of dollars and they wait and wait, years and years. All the while babies are born to teenagers everyday who think they are fine to parent babies. It is so sad.

If you truly love this baby, and you don't have the family support around you, then do what is best for the baby. Adoption is hard but it is truly the right thing to do. In this day and age, you can even make arrangements to be a part of your baby's life. Be selfless.

If you (or your partner) do get pregnant, I must stress the importance of looking after your (or her) health.

You are in charge of the health and well-being of this child and that responsibility begins with conception. Everything you eat or drink, every medication or recreational drug or alcohol you put into your body you share with this innocent developing child. As their brain, heart, bones, hormones, organs are forming, you are in complete control of whether this child develops in an unhealthy state or a healthy one. There are so many young children and teens whose lives are extremely challenging because of the way that their mothers treated themselves while pregnant. Smoking, drinking, drugs, addictions, staying in abusive relationships, stress and anxiety, poor nutrition, all affect a developing baby. Everything unhealthy thing you do to your body during pregnancy will surface at some point in your child's life. Be selfless. For nine months, you have to be an angel. When you bring this child into the world, even if you give it up for adoption, you need to give it the best start possible. Then be proud of the gift of health you gave this child.

Abortion is a horrible thing for anyone to go through. The thought of it makes most people cringe and many people cannot even talk about it as a consideration. In reality, many teens turn to abortion. It allows them to carry on without anyone knowing they were pregnant. I have met young teens who have had two or more abortions! I am not here to debate for or against abortion. The reality is abortions happen whether they are legal or not. It's just safer for the mother if it's a legal procedure. I personally wish we didn't have to consider it at all. I wish we as a society would take all of the energy we spend in the pro-life/pro-choice debate and instead put it towards prevention of unwanted pregnancies. Get to the heart of the issue.

I have a wish list about teen pregnancy choices:
1. I wish that teenagers and ill prepared individuals would simply not have sex.
2. But, if sex is going to happen, I wish that anyone who didn't want a baby would use birth control every time.
3. If they did accidentally get pregnant, I wish they have loving, solid, supportive and healthy families. I wish they have the courage to talk openly with their families to

collectively make a group decision about raising this child with love and support. (you and your partner must be open to their advice and help being offered along the way, because they've done this before and you haven't)

4. If they do not have the support of a loving caring healthy family, or if the loving family decides they are unprepared to support a baby at this time, I wish they had the courage to give the baby to a healthy happy, prepared adoptive family.

5. If none of these measures are taken and a young couple refuses to go through adoption, if they are trying to decide between raising the baby themselves and aborting, I wish they would consider the next point.

6. If you do not have the support of family around you and you will be facing raising this child alone, here is my advice to you. If you have already been living in sadness and anger and you believe that having this baby will take away your sadness and anger, that this child will make your life better, you are not ready to be a parent. A baby will challenge you in ways you cannot yet imagine and so it will add to your sadness and anger. What emotional state do you think a child will grow up with when they are raised by sad, angry parents? Keeping the baby in this situation is selfish. The best parents are Selfless – at the other end of the spectrum.

7. If #6 above applies to you, before you choose Abortion. Please carefully consider Adoption.

Good Orgasm Does Not Equal Good Parent!

How Do I Know When I'm Ready?

I am constantly asked in every sexual health class, "How do you know when you are ready?" I love this question. The easy answer comes from parents, religion/faith, family morals and values and that answer is, "When you are married!" It truly is an easy answer. The students I have met who are choosing to wait until marriage are much more relaxed. Truly, they don't have to worry about the decisions about sex because their minds are already made up. If your choice is to wait until marriage, then you can set aside a lot of worry and regret! By choosing to wait to have intercourse, you can still enjoy the other physical pleasures on the upper end of the progression of intimacy list discussed earlier, but you can avoid the one area that comes with the biggest consequences.

For many teens, the path of waiting until marriage is not the one they will follow. I am not passing judgement on anyone, it's your choice. My only hope is that you take time to consider what you are getting into. When we talk about the question, "How do you know when you're ready for sex?" Many students who ask the question tell me they've previously been told by others, "You'll just know."

Brutal!!!

That's basically taking one of the biggest decisions you will make in the teenage years and leaving it up to your hormones.

When the blasé answer "you'll just know" is what young people hear, is it any wonder that we have a world full of regrets, STD's, rape, criminal charges for sexual assaults, unwanted pregnancies, abortions as a form of birth control, teen pregnancies, child abuse and more. Few decisions in your teenage years have the potential to alter your life more than mistakes related to sex.

In reality, your hormones at some point are going to be screaming out at you, but intercourse is not the only way to satisfy those hormonal urges, to achieve an orgasm. Look back at the "Healthy Progression of Intimacy" list and consider those options, including masturbation. The urges will come and go, but the consequences of how you satisfy those urges can be much bigger. Hormones are nature's way of ensuring reproduction, ensuring that a species survives. Hormones do not care about your goals and dreams for your future.

The bottom line is this. You are in control of your actions and *you are responsible* for the outcomes that follow.

So, let's deal with the question head on, so to speak. How do you know when you are ready for sex? It's a big question, so let's hit some background details first.

When we live in a society where sex is constantly in our faces, it is difficult to understand the importance of being cautious about your bedfellows. Movies, TV, music videos, song lyrics, and magazines, all scream out, "Just Do It!"

It is important to understand that the people who send those messages do not know you, they do not care about you and they certainly do not care about the consequences you live out if you do have sex. To help out the young people who are considering having sex, and for those teens that already had sex but were questioning if it was the right thing to do, I created a little questionnaire to help them decide if they are ready. It's called Don't Be a Fence Sitter.

A fence sitter is someone who has not yet thought about the options or made a decision. Sitting on the fence is a dangerous place to be. Let me explain. If you go to a party and you get drunk or high and horny (gawd, did I just use that word?) and the offer of sex is presented to you, if you are a fence sitter you'll likely fall towards the "Yes" side and have sex. When the negative consequences come, and they will, you will feel regretful and resentful and ill-prepared. You didn't really know what you were getting into and the event "just happened."

Get off the fence! A non-fence sitter will be either on the "Yes" side or the "No" side. They will decide this *before* the party. If they are on the "Yes" side, they have carefully weighed all of the consequences and decided that they can accept everything that comes along with sexual activity tonight. Later that night when the offer is there, they can move forward without regrets, knowing they were prepared. And prepared does not simply mean bringing a condom! Conversely, a person on the "No" side, has thought it through, weighed the consequences and has decided they are not ready to have sex tonight. So when the offer is there they can firmly say no and hold to it. They also will have no regrets. Fence sitters live in a world of regret and self-pity. The following chart is by no means a rule of thumb, but it is helpful when you are wondering what it means to be ready to have sex. It is meant for those of you who are thinking you will not wait until you are married. It's also meant for those of you who have already had sex, but are wondering if you should be continuing to have sex with every partner. Take the questionnaire with this day, today, in mind. What is true for you right now? Take the questionnaire and then read about the scoring underneath.

Don't Be A Fence Sitter

???

F
E
N
C
E

YES		NO
I am Ready		I am NOT Ready

<u>Degrees of Readiness for Sexual Intercourse</u>

YES   NO

_____ _____ I am in a committed relationship

_____ _____ I truly care about my partner's well being

_____ _____ We are not making this decision while under the influence of drugs or alcohol

_____ _____ We can openly discuss sex, contraception, and the risks involved

_____ _____ I have discussed post-intercourse relationship expectations with my partner

_____ _____ I would not (and I feel confident that my partner would not) discuss our intimacy with friends

_____ _____ We have discussed pregnancy options and feel confident in our ability to handle the situation

_____ _____ I feel totally comfortable with my naked body

_____ _____I feel confident enough to discuss, choose, purchase and use contraception

_____ _____I know my partner's sexual history, I am confident they haven't had a bunch of partners in the past and jeopardized their "superglue" ability to connect long term

_____ _____I feel confident requesting STD tests, and/or getting one myself

_____ _____I am prepared for my relationship to change

_____ _____I understand we might be going against the values of my parents, church, siblings, close friends

_____ _____I am prepared for social repercussions, such as a damaged reputation

_____ _____I am aware that I can re-evaluate these questions at ANY point in my life

So how did you score? If you answered **"No" to ANY of the questions** above, then the answer to the question, "Am I ready for sex?" is: <u>No, not yet. If you go ahead and engage in sex, you could seriously regret it.</u>

I ask my class to take this questionnaire on a Friday, then ask them, "OK, who is ready to have sex this weekend?" Technically, I am asking if anyone had all Yes's. The look of shock on their faces at first, turns to smiles of relief as they can finally be confident with their answer – 99% of the time it is "No." Know your limits.

The good news is this – even if you are not ready to have sex, you can go back to that list of progression of intimacy and know that you are not ready to do the *last* thing on that list. All of the other stages are great ways to have intimacy in a healthy relationship.

For those of you who have already done it, just because you have had sex doesn't mean you have to continue to have sex with every partner. As I mentioned before, you can re-evaluate anytime you want and make the best decisions for you. If you are saying yes to sex, then consider the above questionnaire and be confident in your decision. Be safe and be wise.

I will end this chapter with a few more practical tips to consider...

Dating and Relationship Advice
Being Single....

- Understand it's OK to be single, in fact it's better than OK, it's great to be single – enjoy that time to yourself, no matter what age you are.
- Do what you love.
- Maintain self-respect at all times. Treat yourself the way you want to be treated by others.
- Be respectful of those around you. Treat others the way you want to be treated.
- Understand that love isn't something that you can only get from someone else.
- Fill yourself up with love, both self-love and self-respect. Then, what is overflowing you give to others. This way you won't go searching for love in desperation.
- No one else is responsible for your happiness except you.

Looking for the Right Person....

- Nice guys and nice girls DO exist. Here are a few ways to weed out the "not-so-nice ones."
- Look closely at their parents and how they interact. This is a clue as to how you'll be treated.
- Girls: Listen carefully to his views about women – does he respect them?
- Listen to your parents, don't fight them if they don't like him/her, they have excellent intuition and remember they are looking out for your best interests.
- Listen to your close friends – same reason as above.

- Remember, love makes us blind. Your family and close friends can see dangers that you are oblivious to.
- If he/she tries to pull you away from your friends and family – RUN!!!!!!!!!!!!
- Talk about cheating – don't assume it won't happen. Make sure they know you'll drop them right away if they stray.
- Find out about their past relationships and what happened. Your relationship may be part of a predictable pattern.
- Do NOT go after anyone who is already involved!!! Move On. END OF STORY!!
- More than Looks. Go for people with personality, goals, and aspirations.
- Go for people who have interests in common with you.
- Anyone who is interested in you growing as a person, your goals and dreams, they are the ones who will truly grow to love you.
- Ask yourself, "Do I respect them?" You can't truly be happy and "in love" if you don't respect your partner.
- What aspect of "you" are you promoting on the dating scene? Think of your clothing and conversation as your resume. Relationships that are based on physical affection always end in heartache. LUST does not equal LOVE.
- Be wary if they treat you differently when you two are alone vs. in a crowd. If they are rude to you in public – RUN!

In A Relationship....
- Remember that EVERY relationship requires hard work to keep it running smoothly.
- Whether it's a relationship with your parents, siblings, friends, boyfriends/girlfriends, spouse or children, life's daily events pile up like dust and dull it down. But love is always there. You need to polish it to let the love shine through.

- Communication is the key to success.
- Trust and Respect are the most important attributes for happy relationships.
- Don't forget to spend time alone, by yourself, doing the things you like to do.
- Don't forget to spend time with your friends and family, without your girlfriend/boyfriend.
- Everyone needs a support NETWORK, not a single thread.
- Remember you cannot "fix" someone, you can help them to <u>fix themselves</u> but only if they are willing.
- Regardless of your age, you are both growing and evolving. Both of you should be encouraging each other to become better people in the world.

Breaking Up

- Hearts are vulnerable. Love hurts at some point or another, if you follow these pieces of advice you'll simply hurt less often. Break ups are part of dating.
- Break up with maturity. That means privately, and <u>face to face</u>. Not on the phone or text or email or any other form of technology. Be respectful of the person's feelings. Be mature.
- Dumped?? You are amazing – if they choose not to keep you in their life that is their LOSS!! Now there is room in your life for someone better.
- If you are tempted to cheat on your partner, it's time to break up. You are no longer in love.
- Do not get into a "rebound relationship." You need time alone to get happy and comfortable with yourself. See Being Single.

Project: Self

- To quote Fergie, "Myself and I, we've got some straightening out to do."

- What doesn't kill you makes you stronger. Learn from your experiences and do not repeat mistakes.
- AND, if you've made errors, then learn from them and *forgive yourself*. It's time to move on.
- Do not *define* yourself by your past actions or things that have happened to you.
- That was who you *WERE*, **not** who you *ARE*!!!
- You are worthy of a wonderful respectful partner. Believe it. Act like it. Love yourself and the right person will show up and love you too.
- **You cannot love another person or truly allow them to love you if you do not love yourself. So, start here.**

Big Picture Points

- *No one else can make you happy. Only you can do that.*
- *It is really easy to mix up Lust with Love. It is entirely possible for teenagers to be in love. When you are in love you both feel secure and healthy about the relationship*
- *Relationships can have many ingredients for success, but there are only two critical ingredients. If either of these two ingredients is not there, the relationship will most likely not last. For true love, you have to have genuine TRUST in, and RESPECT for, each other!*
- *Trust is confidence that your partner is loyal and will not be swayed by temptation. You have confidence that they will make decisions that are beneficial to your relationship. You do not feel insecure.*
- *Respect is a genuine admiration for the values and actions of this person. You not only approve of the way they think and act, but you both actively encourage each other to evolve and grow into better people.*
- *In order to have trust and respect with someone else, you must trust and respect yourself.*
- *Never go after someone who is in a relationship. A healthy relationship based on respect and trust cannot begin with cheating.*
- *If you decide that breaking up is the right move for you, how do you do it? One word – Respectfully. Unless your partner did something horrible to you, it is your duty to be respectful with their heart at this painful time. Timing must be about considering Their situations, NOT Your convenience.*
- *If you are single, then this is a crucial time for you to get to know yourself. Get involved in things that interest you, take time to read, exercise, eat well, forgive yourself for errors in your past and, as corny as this sounds, fall in love with yourself. Get happy on your own. Before you get into a relationship. Your happy, healthy state, will attract others in a happy healthy state, and that is a great beginning for a happy, healthy relationship.*
- *All of these things apply to straight and gay relationships.*
- *Teenage Pregnancy. This single topic may very well be the most crucial of all in this book. With most things in this book, you are challenged to rethink situations, so you can avoid pain and suffering. Here you need to rethink your actions so that a completely innocent person, a baby, can avoid pain and suffering.*

CHAPTER 6
Food and Your Body

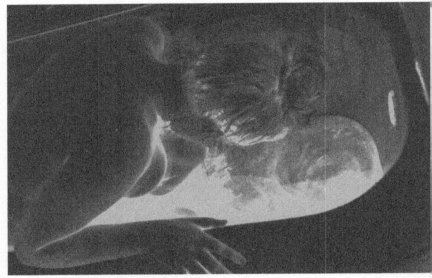

Photograph by Olivia Giroux

"I want to be a person who looks into the mirror and is happy because she is healthy."
   - Gr 11 student

We have a strange relationship with our bodies. The body is a tool to experience life with. It does billions of amazing things for you every day and yet many of you openly say you hate your bodies. This is crazy. Consider the senses that guide you, the muscles, bones and joints that allow you to move, the skin that protects you from everything you come in contact with. You spend so much time obsessing about what you don't like about your body you completely ignore the amazing machine working so hard for you all the time.

Consider a pimple: You zoom in and agonize over one pore in your skin, meanwhile completely ignoring the millions of other pores that are working perfectly. Consider an injury. You sprain your ankle and hobble around on crutches cursing your body and the pain it brings you, while you completely ignore the rest of your perfectly functioning joints; joints that move easily and painlessly. There is so much to be grateful for, and yet it is just taken for granted.

Instead of appreciating your body you find endless ways to punish yourself and hurt it. Maybe you engage in dangerous acts that result in injury, or hurtful self-talk because you wish you had a different body, or you inject ink into your skin (multiple tattoos) and pierce your body in multiple places creating holes in the most important protective barrier you have – your skin. Or maybe you harm your body by taking drugs, or abusing alcohol, the list goes on and on. But do you know what the most common form of self-punishment is? What you eat.

The Food You Eat

Teenagers are notorious for having poor eating habits. New found freedom includes making your own meals and snacks. A part-time job and not a lot of time mean you eat quick easy food on the run. And, with a driver's licence, fast food restaurants are only minutes away. Combine this with the desire for "taste first" food considerations, and this means you are often stuffing yourself full of sugar, fat, and salt. With over 65% of Americans and 55% of Canadians classifying as overweight or obese, statistically this will not work in your favour.

On the other extreme, are fad diets and eating disorders, which are rampant among teens. Dieting is something deeply engrained in our society. You see it everywhere. So many of you alter your food intake simply because you think it is the "normal" thing to do. Society and the media sources tell you it's the thing to do.

Subliminal messages are much more powerful than you can imagine. They are so powerful that if suddenly there were images of people doing cocaine in magazine ads, videos, TV commercials, newspaper ads, we would eventually become numb to it. We would start thinking, "Well it can't be that bad." Absurd as this may seem, we would begin to ask ourselves why we aren't doing it too. It's like this with the messages we continually receive regarding body image. We actually believe we can all – make that, should all – look like the people in magazines and movies. Never mind the fact that many of them harm their bodies in the process of looking that way. When some celebrities talk about their bodies, they quickly reveal an obsession with food and body size. In constant striving for perfection on the outside, they are left never truly happy with their bodies or themselves. But we think, "No matter, let's put them on the pedestal anyway because they *look* happy."

Why We Eat What We Eat
- Hunger/fullness
- Taste
- Convenience
- Emotional response to stress
- To alter or maintain body shape
- Athletic performance
- Health
- Because that's what my mom or dad made for me

You are quickly coming to a point in your life when the last point will decrease and stop altogether.

Think about your last meal or snack. Why did you eat it?

If your answer is "taste," you are a typical teenage eater. But consider this fact. Taste is a sense determined by taste buds on your tongue. Think of the size of your tongue. You are letting a part of your body, smaller than the palm of your hand, make all the nutritional decisions for your ENTIRE BODY!

Perhaps a bit of self-control needs to enter in? The tastiest flavours come from sugar and fat and salt, a threesome I call SFS. The tastiest foods are full of them. When you achieve healthy self-esteem, you will realize that one of the key factors is respecting your body. Having some self-control from SFS is critical.

Even if you genetically have a fast metabolism, and you don't gain weight easily, you are still stuffing yourself full of SFS which offer the lowest nutritional value. Nutritional value? Huh? Oh yeah, the fuel that makes your amazing body function. I'll come back to this.

Metabolism and Food

Anyone who wants to change their body wants to alter their metabolism, whether it is to gain weight, lose weight, or simply to get fit. What is metabolism, you ask? It is the rate at which your body uses energy. Think of it as the manager of all energy resources. It has to dole out energy as the various body systems demand fuel. If someone has a fast metabolism, then the body's cells are going to use energy very quickly. Think of people who can eat a lot but remain thin. They also have a difficult time gaining weight. If someone has a slow metabolism, then the body uses energy slowly so the extra energy consumed is stored. And the way our bodies store extra energy is as fat. Those with a slow metabolism tend to be heavier and/or gain weight quickly. So really anyone who wants to gain or lose weight actually wants to change their metabolism. Food containing vitamins and minerals is vital to the functioning of your body and your metabolism controls this critical fuel. When and what you eat greatly affects how your metabolism functions. It is reliant on regular deposits of healthy food.

Your metabolism is critical to your survival. In nature, every animal experiences times when food is scarce. The metabolism of an animal's body slows down when food is scarce, or activity is low, like during hibernation, and stores what it can in fat cells. It then rations out the available energy to the most vital systems to keep the body alive. Your body works the same. Your metabolism doesn't know that you have a grocery store that is well stocked and open year-round.

Metabolism is in charge of rationing the body's available energy. When energy reserves are low, it switches into the conservation mode and slows down the energy export/usage. Only the most important "vital to survival" systems get the priority, receiving the majority of the available energy. These vital systems are: the nervous system, the cardiovascular system and the respiratory system.

The metabolism attempts to take care of these systems because, if it doesn't, the entire body goes into failure. Let's just say at that point the metabolism is out of a job. That's a lot of pressure! If the food arrives while the metabolism is in slow conservation mode, it does not speed up right away. Instead it says, "FINALLY!! Ok! But just in case this happens again we need to stash the energy away, so we can continue to ration until things return to normal around here. Put the fuel into storage!" it yells. Where exactly is "storage"? Fat cells.

So, a slow metabolism will readily fill fat cells. It's like putting cash in the bank and rationing it carefully after you've had the experience of being broke. Fat cells are a key part of the metabolic process. They are amazing cells that can increase or decrease in size depending on how much energy is being eaten and used by the body.

If you skip meals, if you diet, if you stop eating, if you miss breakfast, if you eat really poor quality food with very low nutrition (full of SFS and not much else), the vital energy reserves are arriving sporadically or unpredictably. The metabolism will switch to its storage mode and slow down, carefully rationing the energy as if to say, "We don't know when the next shipment is arriving, so we better be careful." When food energy does arrive, it is horded in the fat cells again. Your Metabolism loves regular, predictable deposits of food; healthy food full of a variety of vitamins and minerals. The number one goal of the metabolism is to keep you alive and it does this by making sure the vital systems have what they need. All other systems have to wait.

The **essential systems,** also known as the vital systems, are:

- The nervous system (your brain and all of its vital communications to maintain organ functions)
- The cardiovascular system (your heart, blood, blood vessels)
- The respiratory system (your lungs)

The **non-essential systems** are areas such as:

- Hormonal and reproductive system (regulating hormones)
- Muscular and skeletal systems (exercise and general energy level)
- Repair and growth (immune function and healing, building strong new cells)
- Cognitive functions (thinking and decision making)
- The Digestive system (this one is tricky, I will explain it within the topic of skipping breakfast)

Once you understand it, you can see your metabolism at work as you listen to your body and become aware of how it feels when you feed it and when you don't. If your eating is not regular or healthy, you will notice the effects in the non-essential systems. When not enough energy, protein, vitamins and minerals are available, the metabolism takes from the non-essential systems and gives to the essential systems. If you are not eating right, you may notice moodiness and irritability, lack of energy, decreased strength and endurance, increased injuries and longer healing time, longer and frequent illnesses, decreased concentration, and frustration when dealing with decisions. All of these are the result of your body saying, "There is not enough good to go around."

All of this can dramatically impact your mood and therefore how you feel about day to day life and about yourself. Conversely if you don't feel good about yourself, you may not be motivated to eat well, having regular and healthy meals. Any way you look at it, food is directly tied to self-esteem.

Skipping Breakfast

Skipping any meal is problematic but breakfast is the most commonly skipped meal and it is the worst meal to miss.

One reason skipping breakfast is a really bad idea for you, is that it affects your ability to learn. Remember, cognitive functions (thinking and decision making) are a non-essential system. So if you regularly skip breakfast, your cognitive centers of your brain will not be turned on in the morning. This could contribute to the feeling that you are "not a morning person," and possibly negatively affect your grades. You could find yourself taking a hit to your self-esteem both from a lack of nutrients, which can directly affect your mood, and from a feeling that you are struggling in school because you are having trouble focusing and completing class work because you haven't given your body enough food in the morning to turn on these areas of your brain.

People skip breakfast for a variety of reasons:

- they wake up too late and don't have the time to eat
- they want to start with a coffee and will rely on the late morning break to provide the first solid food
- they want to consume less food and this is the easiest meal to miss
- some people feel physically ill if they eat in the morning

Let's deal with the last one first. When you sleep at night, your metabolism decreases, and the body relies on breakfast and exercise to get it rolling again. If you regularly skip breakfast and get a ride to school (no exercise), then your metabolism stays slow and continues to focus on your essential systems and limit the non-essential ones. For immediate survival, your digestive system is a non-essential system and it takes a great deal of energy to make it go, so when energy is low, this system is sacrificed. If you have a habit of skipping breakfast, then your body has a habit of limiting energy to the digestive system. If you do try to surprise your body with food when you wake up, there will not be enough energy going to these organs to function properly and so they will let you know they can't handle the food yet. Then you will "feel sick." This reinforces the feeling you shouldn't eat breakfast, so then you carry on through your day, except that your metabolism is still low. How can you tell if you have created a slow metabolism for yourself? Answer this question: Are you hungry at lunch? Most people who skip breakfast could also easily skip lunch too – they really are not hungry. Slow metabolism.

People who eat breakfast every day are really hungry by lunch. Their metabolism is functioning at a much higher level. Trusting that good, healthy food is on its way, their body doesn't ration, and instead it uses up the energy and asks for more. In the body of the breakfast skipper and dieter, the body is saying, "I don't have enough to go around, and I don't know when the next meal is coming so I'd better store what I can in my fat cells and ration it out slowly."

So, to make a long story short, if you want to feel great each day, feel like you have lots of energy, heal quickly and stay healthy, the quickest way is to eat a good breakfast.

If you are one of those people who feels sick when you try to eat in the morning? Set of goal of eating a healthy breakfast every day, and start *slowly*, start with a piece of fruit every morning this week, then add a breakfast bar for the next week, then try making a healthy smoothie, or a whole grain toast, try to include a source of protein with your breakfast, (remember to avoid SFS). You will feel sick for the first week, but slowly your metabolism will begin to trust you and it will gradually increase to meet the food that it comes to expect. You will know it is working when you are really hungry at lunch. Then keep it up every day.

Other Factors Affecting Metabolism

There are other factors that affect metabolism, such as height, body composition and age. Let's talk about height. People who are tall actually have more surface area (think skin) and that means they have more places for heat to escape from their body. Tall people, therefore, have faster metabolisms because their bodies have to work harder to stay warm. That is why it is more common for tall people to be thin. The thing is, while you may be able to change your metabolism, you can't change your height.

Age is another factor that you cannot control so it is important to be aware of the affect it has on your metabolism. Metabolism slows as you age. As teens, you are growing and many of you are extremely active, but this will likely change as you get older. The appetite you have now is not the same as the appetite you will have later on. If you try to continue eating the way you do now when you are in your twenties you will be in for some serious weight gain. Right now, your body needs extra energy, healthy energy from foods full of nutrients, then later on you will need the same stuff just less of it. So, you can't control your height and you can't control your age, but you can control your food intake and you can control the composition of your body.

Body Composition has a big impact on metabolism. The more you exercise, the more muscle or lean body mass you gain. Muscle cells are "hungrier" then fat cells. They run at a higher metabolic rate, so the more you exercise, the faster your metabolism will be. There are a few things to keep in mind here. One, if you are trying to gain muscle, as some girls and many guys are trying to do, you will have to exercise more and eat more and choose really high quality foods. To gain weight you need to consume more then you use, but exercise is key so that the extra energy will not be converted to fat. If you want to lose weight, exercise is key as well in order to increase the lean muscle mass and increase your metabolism, BUT you should not go from the gym to McDonalds. Many teens think, "Oh, I worked out today, so I can afford to eat this fast food." Wrong. If you are trying to get fit, stuffing yourself full of crap will negate the positive effect of the workout.

Weight Gain and Weight Loss

I am continually disturbed at the weight I see many teens gain in the 4 years of high school. I get really pissed off at the fact that fast food businesses will capitalize on the locations of high schools to set up their new restaurants. Money and health are thrown out the window. Weight gain happens very easily in the teenage years. Let me explain. Fat cell production occurs quickly during puberty, so as you are filling up on SFS, this is a time when your fat cells are ready and willing to multiply.

As a fat cell is filled up it will stretch and stretch, but eventually it cannot get bigger, so it divides and forms two new cells. The worst aspect of this is, once a new fat cell is created/duplicated, it will never go away. Fat cells can get bigger and smaller, but they will never go away. So, when you fill up more than your body needs for that day, taking in more energy than the fat cells can store, the body creates more fat cells. Now you have a huge number of fat cells. On a small scale, think of 10 fat cells being stuffed and then overstuffed, then they divide to create 20 fat cells. Even if you diet, and seem to be losing weight, the fats cells decrease in size but not in number – remember they will never go away. When you go back to your "regular" eating the fat cells are happy to fill again but now there are 20 cells to fill instead of 10, so more fat is gained back.

So many people yo-yo their weight by going on diet after diet. They make strange deals with themselves thinking, "Before I go on this diet I'll eat all the things I soon won't be able to." So, they overeat to compensate for the soon-to-be restrictions. All this overeating causes the fat cells to divide, but the individual won't notice this right away. They happily hop on the diet train and the weight begins to fall off – but only temporarily because they won't stay on the diet for long. When they return to their "normal" eating habits, those hungry fat cells fill up again except this time there are more of them. And remember, because the metabolism will be slow coming off the diet, the body will send the new fuel reserves straight to the fat cells. The weight not only returns, but now there is more fat on the body than if they had never gone on the diet in the first place. Dieting does not work. Fad Diets have been around for decades and decades and our society just keeps getting fatter and fatter. At some point, we need to wake up and realize that temporary diets don't work.

In class, I get this question all the time:

Q – *"So how does someone lose weight in a safe, effective and permanent way without increasing the number of fat cells?"*

A – First off, it is extremely common for an already healthy person to view themselves as fat, so it is entirely possible that you should not try to change your weight. You may want to change your body composition, which you can do through regular exercise.

If you truly need to lose weight for your health, then the key is small changes, and long timelines for goals. It took many years for things to get out of balance in your body. A quick fix is not possible if you want it to last. Behaviour modification is the key, but before you change the way you behave, with respect to food and exercise, you must change the way you think. Go back to the concept of loving yourself first. At the end of the food section of this chapter, I will give specific examples of good nutritional habits. See if you can fit them in to your lifestyle. The important thing to remember is this: every change you make has to become a *lifelong* change so you must do this forever.

If you say I want to give up ice cream – ask, "Could I do this forever?" No.

If you say I want to switch to skim or 1% milk – ask, "Could I do this forever?" Yes.

I want to go to the gym 6 times a week – ask, "Could I do this forever?" No.

I want to walk or run around the neighbourhood 2 times a week and work out 2 times per week – ask, "Could I do this forever?" Yes.

Do you get the idea? Small permanent changes yield small permanent results. The longer you keep at it the more it changes for the better. Your goal is to create lifelong healthy HABITS.

Eating Disorders

There are four main types of eating disorders:

- Anorexia – extremely low energy consumption
- Bulimia – extreme efforts to rid the body of calories consumed
- Compulsive Overeating – extreme levels of food consumption
- Muscle Dysmorphia – extreme efforts to gain muscle

All eating disorders are equally sad. Food is one of life's greatest pleasures; trying new recipes, experiencing wonderful taste sensations, the social enjoyment of sharing meal time together, experiencing multicultural flavours and traditions. Food is one of the wonderful ways to experience life, but not for someone suffering from an eating disorder. This is a day to day struggle with food. It is an addiction, but worse than most addictions because you cannot escape from food. We all have to eat, and so every day they have to face their tormentor. These individuals are so obsessed with body shape that they will repeatedly harm themselves. They have an inner turmoil of worrying so much about how the body looks while having a total disregard for how the body functions.

Eating disorders are food obsessions and I have never ever met anyone who was obsessed with anything and was truly happy with life. Steer clear of this pathway. Diets are a huge risk factor for all eating disorders. Please do not diet. Use the tips in this chapter to develop a healthy relationship with your body and strive for lifelong healthy eating habits. For those of you who are already on the slippery slope of an eating disorder, seek professional counselling. You are suffering from a true mental health disorder. At the same time, decide that you are worth saving and that life can be wonderful. You can achieve a healthy relationship with food and with your body. You don't have to hurt yourself anymore. This is your personal challenge – you can do it.

Learn about the body and how amazing it is and then use that to motivate yourself to treat this incredible miracle with the respect that it deserves. Instead of looking at your shape, understand that you are more than skin and surface beauty. Seek the true, deep happiness within you. Once you have found acceptance of who you are, you can move towards inner peace and joy. Here you learn to respect your body, and all of its incredible functions, and treat it with love, respect, good healthy food and exercise.

Healthy Mind, Healthy Body

What you eat and how you feel about food may have more to do with your self-esteem than with hunger, cravings and food likes and dislikes. I'd venture to say that nine out of ten teens are unhappy with their bodies. Just think of that. In the classes that I've taught it didn't seem to matter what the students looked like or what their body shape was, they all felt insecure about their bodies. So if it doesn't matter what you look like, then it must matter how you think and feel. As teens, you are visually bombarded with so called beautiful bodies – which of course you are supposed to emulate. Many insecure individuals go online and are hurting themselves, putting themselves down, or making comments about their own and other's bodies. As a teen when you are witnessing others' critical comments and insecurities it may fuel your own insecurities.

Healthy teens and adults are able to move beyond the media's image of perfection and grow into a true acceptance of their bodies. How do they do it and why is it so hard for some teens to feel comfortable in their own skin (and muscle and fat)? I too felt horribly insecure about my own body as a teen, even though as I look back on pictures now, I see a beautiful, healthy girl. I am bigger and softer then I was as a teen yet I feel amazingly confident and comfortable with my body now, so what changed? And, more importantly, is it possible to feel great as a teen? To this second question I answer, absolutely. I know teens that live this way. Beauty is on the inside.

Love Your Body

To the average person, food intake, what and how much you eat, would seem to be the main contributor of body shape and size. And so if you desire to change your shape or size, you'd consider altering your food intake. This seems straight forward, but in reality, most of the changes that people make completely back fire on them, many times having an effect opposite to what they desired, not to mention creating a negative cycle of self-pity and unhappiness.

It all starts with self-esteem. My goal is to get you to love your current body – I really mean it – Love your Body! If you can do this, everything will change for you, *including your body.*

Consider this: if a teenager (guy or girl) is unhappy inside, they may blame their body. They will look at the celebrities or even the beautiful "perfect" teenagers at school and think, "They look so happy. If I could just gain some muscle, gain weight OR lose fat or lose weight [whatever the goal may be], I'd be happy too." So, they start by hating their current body, begin an exercise regime, pushing themselves beyond the enjoyment of the activity. They will deny themselves their favourite foods, and despise what they see in the mirror to motivate themselves forward on their path to the ideal body. They will alter their intake of food, dieting, restricting certain foods, taking supplements instead of real food, become addicted to the gym, over exercising. They ignore the messages their body is sending them in the form of hunger, fullness, injuries, fatigue. In essence, they are punishing their body.

Hmmm, let's think about that... punish your body to make it beautiful, and then you'll be happy.

When you lay it out this way you begin to see the underlying physiological absurdity. Most people begin this miserable cycle only to find it too difficult and they give up. "Great now in addition to being _____(scrawny/fat, you fill in the blank) now I'm weak too. Excuse me while I drown my sorrows in a bag of Doritos." But what if you did it? Obviously, some people succeed in transforming their bodies using this method. Could you ever be truly happy if the ideal body *was* achieved this way? No, it's impossible. Instead you end up living in constant fear of losing what you have worked for.

Eckhart Tolle uses a term called surface happy. Surface happy is happiness that comes from looking great today but next week feeling weak and scrawny or fat and bloated. It is an endless rollercoaster of ups and downs and the fleeting ups are perceived as happiness. It always has a polar opposite that surfaces at some point, and even when you are "up" you are constantly trying to avoid the lows by using food restrictions and exercise to keep the outer body you've created. That's not happiness, it is fear. Your obsession with your "new" body will cause the self-punishments to continue. Happiness? Sorry not down this road.

By the way, to give you some more perspective, if you rewind to when you were looking at those people with perfect bodies, thinking they look so happy, chances are you were seeing their "surface happy." It's sad to think that you wanted to emulate them, as they mask their pain.

Start Happy to End Happy

Instead, try the concept of loving your current body, then feeding your body wonderful, healthy things and exercising because that is what your body needs to function and feel great. Guess what happens when you take this action? You start to look and feel great! Be happy *first*, feel beautiful on the inside and *then* look great on the outside. Happiness comes from within not from without.

Sure, that sounds nice, but how realistic is it for you to change your thinking from one extreme to the other? How can you go from hating your body to loving your body quickly enough to start treating it well and reaping the rewards? How can you start? Follow me on this journey and see where it takes you.

First consider this. Think of five things about your body that you are incredibly grateful for. For some of you this may be difficult, but try anyway. Consider your sight, close your eyes and imagine your life without sight, or hearing, or without feet or hands or a fully functioning brain. You see, your body is so much more than what fits in a swimsuit.

Grab a pen and paper.

Seriously! Do it! If you haven't yet, stop reading and go get a pen and paper.

Now write out that list. I'll wait while you write it. Start with, "I am so grateful for my......"

***

OK, the next step is to really *be* grateful for them. For a few minutes close your eyes and think about all of the amazing experiences these things give you every day. Get happy, smile, feel the gratitude – really feel the love for these areas of your body. Think of how amazing your body is.

Now what if I told you there was a magic combination of foods and exercises that could make each of these areas function even better. Would you choose to eat these miracle foods and do the exercises, or would you punish your body instead by depriving these areas of what they need to function? The obvious answer is you'd choose to eat them, right? If you take it down to the basic levels of gratitude then you will realize that it is your duty, your responsibility to be good to your body. Would you treat a child in a way that deprives them of healthy food and good exercise? Of course not. You have been given this incredible form so you can experience life. Be grateful for it and love it and be good to it!

I hope to get you to the point where you love every part of your body so much that you choose to feed it wonderful and healthy food.

So, what about those tasty treats that are full of SFS? If you are being good to your body, do you have to give those up completely? Of course not! Food is one of life's greatest pleasures. Food is meant to be enjoyed. All types of tastes and textures should be enjoyed. The goal is to be happy not unhappy. Do not deny yourself the wonderful tastes of your favourite foods. Just enjoy them in *moderation*. If someone were to tell me that I couldn't have ice cream anymore, guess what? I would want to eat more. No food should be forbidden if you enjoy it. Just think about Health first – that must be the priority.

Here are some tips:

1. Eat healthy things first. Before you pull out your favourite SFS snack, ask, "Have I had enough fruit or vegetables today?" By eating something healthy first, then going for your favourite snack, you are giving your body important vitamins and minerals to function well. By always eating the healthiest things first, when it comes time for the treats and desserts, you can control the amount that you eat because you won't be as hungry.

2. Slow down. Savour the food, enjoy it on your tongue. The 12th chip tastes the same as the 200th chip. If you slow down and really taste your favourite foods, you will enjoy the moment, feel more peaceful, and you will eat less. It takes about 20 minutes for your body to process the fullness sensation. If you slow down, you can listen to your body and stop when you are full.

3. Eat Breakfast. Let's be even more specific, eat a healthy breakfast. Fruit, whole grains, nuts, seeds, add a protein source like eggs. This will set you up for feeling great all day.

4. Don't eat out of packages. Prepare a bowl or a plate, put the rest away, sit down, breathe, eat slowly, enjoy the moment, then get up and do something else.

5. Don't eat in front of **a TV/screen**. Once in a while is OK, for example during a movie. Unfortunately, far too many people eat meals in front of a screen. Mindless hand to mouth munching is a habit that takes control and awareness away from the eater - "did we eat that entire bag?!" - And did you really take time to enjoy it?

6. Learn to cook and try new recipes. When you are a part of the cooking process you can control what goes into your food and you can use wonderful healthy fresh ingredients. You can avoid additives and preservatives, and unhealthy 'filler' ingredients. You are also more likely to slow down and appreciate the food if you are aware of the effort that goes into preparing it.

7. Learn about food. Read about healthy foods. Do not read about Diets! Read about great foods, how they help your body and how to cook and prepare them.

8. Warning – another AwkWeird moment! **Be grateful.** In my house, when we sit down to a family meal, we often take time to appreciate our meal but it's not in a traditional form of grace. In addition to thanking the cook (usually dad) we give our gratitude to the farmers, and to the cow (or the chicken or the fish) to the bees that pollinate the plants, to the seeds that miraculously form the vegetables and the fruit. When my kids were young they would often add, "We thank mother nature and father time." When you try to be consciously aware of the journey the food has taken to get to your plate – the number of steps, conditions, and people involved in the making of your food – you are less likely to shovel it in and take it for granted.

Your Body, Your Miracle

From a biological standpoint, you are a living breathing miracle. To simplify things, your body contains two things: cells and water. But those cells, they are amazing. Right now, at this very instant, you have trillions of functions happening to keep you alive. You have approximately 100 trillion cells in your body! Every minute close to 3 billion cells die; they've come to the end of their long and important lives and need to be replaced. Where do the new cells come from? Your food. You are truly what you eat!

Food is made of basically six things:

- Carbohydrates
- Proteins
- Fats
- Vitamins
- Minerals
- Water

The first three provide us with energy – calories – while the last three do not. All six are absolutely essential. Many of you out there reading the word calories think this is a bad word, but you need to understand that a calorie is simply a measurement of energy and our body uses thousands of calories every day to function. So, calories are good – energy is good. Think Energy = energetic!

So, what do all of these items do to help you?

Think back to all of those three billion cells per minute needing to be replaced. There are many different kinds of cells: bone cells, liver cells, skin cells, muscle cells, fat cells, blood cells, you get the idea, and they all are created from the food you eat.

Here is an analogy for you. Imagine workers building a house. The project needs some essential things, materials like bricks, workers, lunch and snacks for the workers, and materials need to be taken to and from the work site. Well this is just like building a cell (actually billions of them) and all of the things required for the project come from your food.

- The <u>protein</u> you eat gets broken down and forms the **bricks**. Think of how important the bricks are in building a house! Protein must be consumed every day! It's so critical.

- <u>Vitamins & minerals</u> become the **workers,** but these workers are specific to building only one type of house - the bone house, the liver house, and the skin house – so we need many different kinds of workers (think of all of the different types of vitamins and minerals.)

- <u>Carbs and Fats</u> can sometimes act as the building materials too, but mostly they are the food for the workers. They provide the **fuel/meals** for the construction project and the general maintenance of the new building (cell) and how it functions.

- <u>Water</u>, hmm, what doesn't it do? It provides transportation of materials to the worksite, cools the construction zone, regulating temperature throughout the body, and plays countless roles/functions within these houses/cells. Water is so important that without sufficient amounts, all other processes fail.

So, when you put it all together, you truly "Are What You Eat." I can look at my arm, consider my skin cells and say, "There's the chicken fajita I had last week."

If you continue to let your taste buds make all the nutritional choices for you, feeding yourself full of sugar, fat and salt OR if you continue to deprive yourself of enough food or enough healthy foods, you *still* Are What You Eat. If you put crap in your car or don't give it fuel at all, what can that car do for you? How far will you get before it breaks down? Or put it another way: crap in, crap out.

If you have any ounce of love for your body, you soon realize, "Hey, I want to treat it well and feed it well." And guess what happens next – your body thanks you! You actually feel good. You feel better – more energetic and more capable. Hey, you may even feel happier! Throw in healthy amounts of exercise and a combination of gratitude, love, healthy food and exercise and, wow, you have a recipe for a healthy fit body! When you compare it to the absurdity of the previous *"hate your body, punish your body to find happiness,"* it's worth a try, don't you think?

So, here's your recipe...

Step One: Love yourself/respect your body and all that it does for you

Step Two: Eat well and exercise because you know it's good for your body

Step Three: Reap the benefits – feel good and look good

Step Four: Repeat steps 1-4

Exercise

Reasons to Exercise

1. Sports – because you love your sport, and you want to get better – *great keep it up!*

2. Health – to improve your health because your doctor told you to, or to maintain your health – *great keep it up!*

3. To feel good, to de-stress – *amazing!*

4. As Transportation – walk, bike, rollerblade, or skateboard, simply to get around – *fantastic!*

5. Looks – to look good –....... *worst reason ever!*

Let's focus on the last one since it is the most common. Exercising for your looks.

I would say most people who exercise do it for the wrong reason (for looks.) They feel that they have to exercise. Many people even hate exercising while they are doing it. They are just trying to "get through" their workout and this is why they never stick to exercise for very long.

Yes, you are motivated, but will you stick with it?.......

What if the results don't happen as quickly as you want them to? What if it is harder than you think? What if it hurts? What if you really don't like it? What if you are not able to maintain the results you want?

I'll tell you where you're headed, you will quit! Just like millions of people before you did when they chose this as their number one reason. Exercising for this reason is tough. You go on and off the wagon so often and your body never really gets used to it. This is a recipe for injuries and disappointment. The problem is that this reason is totally externally motivated. You need to find internal motivation. Find it inside!

I will say one positive thing, there is a chance that you might notice how *good you feel* when you exercise. If this thought enters you head – let it grow. This awakening is the doorway to a healthy lifestyle – exercising for the sake of feeling good, not looking good. With this mindset, you will commit to making exercise a habit. Once it becomes a habit, if you fall off the wagon you will feel it. You will go back to being tired and cranky, emotional, and stressed. You will crave the feeling of being fresh, energetic and happy. This minor slip-up will be quickly recognized for what it is and you will be back at it, sweating with a grin.

I made up a little saying for my students to keep the right perspective:

Exercise for how it makes you feel on the inside, not for how it makes you look on the outside.

Stop Being Lazy

Let's face it there is a huge population of you out there that simply do not get enough, if any, exercise, or you exercise inconsistently. I want you to think of why exercise is important.

Consider your pet – say a family dog. You love it – you feed it healthy food, you feed it regularly and you take it for walks. Why do you do these things? Well, because you love your dog and you know that good food and exercise are essential for the dog's health. If you didn't do these things, you'd have a very depressed and sick dog. You are no different.

Your body is not supposed to be weak, it is not supposed to be lazy, and it is not supposed to be stiff. You are an animal – no really, you are! Humans = Homo sapiens from the kingdom Animalia – key characteristic of this kingdom... locomotion. You are designed to move. So, get up and move around. Seriously stand up right now, move your body. Feel your muscles, touch them as you move, move your joints feel them on the inside. Your body is designed to move. Your body is not designed to sit on your couch or sit in the car or sit at your desk, it wants to move.

You are probably aware that muscle cells can get stronger or weaker, bigger or smaller. Every muscle cell inside every muscle in your body is connected to nerves that are controlled by your central nervous system. As soon as you tell your muscle to move the message is communicated through your nervous system. If you stop asking that muscle to move, however, the nervous system decreases the connection between the nerve cells and the muscle cells and you can no longer rapidly control all of the muscle cells inside your muscle. This happens naturally as we age. Take Grandpa for a walk. If he's not active regularly, he'll be slower than you, weaker than you, because the nerves have disconnected. But at your age all of yours should be connected. Throughout time, people in their teens and 20's have been the strongest members of our species. Thanks to increased "screen time," that's not the case anymore. Unless you are seriously active, your nerves have started to disconnect. They simply are not needed while you play computer games or eat chips on the couch or get drives to school, so they've become redundant.

The good news is this is all reversible. If you do decide to get up and move your body, it will step up! Yes, it is hard at first because nerve connections are not used to stimulating these muscle fibres, and the fibres are weak. Keep it up, however, and they'll reconnect and strengthen. While you've been lazy, your heart and lungs have not had to work hard to provide oxygen and nutrients to all of your muscle cells, but if you begin to exercise *and you keep at it*, they will get stronger and more efficient. Once all of these systems start working better, because you challenge them to do so, the muscle cells will get stronger and stronger and movement will get easier and easier. Remember you were designed for movement. Move it! I do need to warn you of a few things. Exercise will seem really hard at first. That is why so many people quit saying, "I'm not cut out for this." Stick with it! Exercise gets easier every time you do it. Your amazing body will adapt. When you are sore, that is OK. Muscle pain is normal when you ask muscles to do something new. Every time you exercise you are breaking down the weakest muscle cells and they will be replaced by new stronger cells. Fit people know that pain is a good pain and they are not afraid of it. Unfit people are scared that they have harmed themselves and done something wrong. If it hurts in the middle of the muscle, that's good, it will go away. If it hurts inside the joints, that is not so good. If that is the case, try starting with lower impact exercises like walking and cycling.

Tips for starting out:

- Exercise regularly, aim for 4 times a week to start off.
- Start off easy – for example, walking for 30 minutes.
- You should feel challenged – move at a pace that makes you breath heavy – then you will know you are really working.
- Sweat is good – it's your body trying to cool off. Your muscles are generating a lot of heat. Take a shower when you are done, or at the very least change your shirt and slap on some deodorant.
- Be prepared for muscle pain one or three days after you've worked out. Instead of cursing your body for the pain, thank it for building new stronger muscles. Stretch, take a bath, walk – all of these will help the muscle soreness. If, when you are starting a new exercise regime, you don't feel any soreness afterwards you are probably not working hard enough. Challenge yourself a little more.
- Eat healthy – you do not need to eat to replace the calories. Just because you worked out doesn't mean it's OK to go to

go out to your favourite fast food restaurant now. Give your body good healthy foods, like fruits and vegetables, whole grains and legumes and/or lean meats, and lots and lots of water. Of course, treats are OK once in a while, but you don't have the treat *because* you've exercised. Be aware of your portions.

- Make Exercise a habit – Exercise is not a short-term goal. Do not exercise to get in shape for the summer or for that vacation or for prom. Exercise for life. Exercise for health, to feel good every day. Yes, looking good, looking healthy will come, but that should never be the ultimate goal.

- Most importantly, be aware of how you *feel*. Sure, it's hard while you are doing it, but know you will feel awesome when you are done. Once you get exercising regularly, you will be amazed at how it transforms every area of your life – the way you think, your confidence, the way you sleep, the way you feel about things you used to be scared to do, the energy you have every day.

I'll say it again,

Exercise for how it makes you feel on the inside, not for how it makes you look on the outside.

This book is all about how to be your own hero. On this journey towards healthy self-esteem, regular exercise is a critical life-long habit to pick up.

Sleep

As a teenager, there is a pretty good chance that you are sleep deprived. Years ago, I would have said that TV was the biggest culprit, but now it is more likely to be your cell phone or another electronic device.

Getting enough sleep is of equal importance to getting enough exercise and food. Sleep is absolutely vital to the overall health of our body as well as our mental and emotional states. You might think you are dead to the world snoring away but in reality, while the conscious part of your brain shuts down, every other part of you is working very hard. In order for your body to grow, repair, and heal, incredible amounts of energy are required. The body cannot do these tasks while you are awake and making other demands on your body. It has to wait until the conscious portion of the brain shuts down. Until the demanding master is sleeping and it can truly get to work. Sleep deprivation is cruel torture for your body and its pain surfaces in many ways, such as irritability, mood swings, concentration difficulties, poor healing, frequent illnesses and infections, poor growth and depression.

If you are suffering from self-esteem issues or depression I would highly recommend that you take a close look at your sleep patterns. Are you getting between nine and ten hours of sleep every night? This is the amount that the American Sleep Disorders Association recommends for teenagers. Check this website for more information:

http://parentingteens.about.com/cs/teensandsleep/a/teenssleepwell.htm

Tips for Good night's sleep.......

- Get fresh air and exercise during the day
- Go to sleep at the same time each night, create a routine
- Turn off electronic devices by 10pm and charge them somewhere else in the house so you are not tempted – get an alarm clock so you don't rely on your phone
- Read at night – if you are really having trouble sleeping, read a school textbook (so boring – it works every time)
- Try foam earplugs if there is noise in your house or in your neighbourhood
- Part time jobs should have work shifts that end no later than 10pm on a school night
- If you are stressed, write about it, deal with it on paper so you can release it from your mind
- Make a list in your mind about things you are grateful for, think of them all one by one and fall asleep happy

- Focus on the here and now. If you are bothered by something that happened (past) or worried about something that is going to happen (future) focus on the present – which is real. Focus on your cozy bed, your sheets, your pillow, your safe home, and so on.

Healthy Body, Healthy Mind

Most people will tell you that self-esteem is a mental issue. Well if your physical body is suffering because of poor nutrition, lack of exercise, or lack of sleep, you will not be able to feel good mentally.

Set a goal right here, right now…

I will take these steps ………. To improve the health of my body and my mind.

Big Picture Points

- *We have a strange relationship with our bodies. Your body is your tool to experience life with. It does billions of things for you every day. And yet many of you openly say you hate your body. That is crazy.*

- *It all starts with self-esteem. The goal should be to love your current body. Yes, to really Love your Body! If you can do this, everything will change for you, including your body.*

- *Many people believe if they change the look of their body then they will be happy. They alter their intake of food, diet, restrict certain foods, take supplements instead of real food, don't exercise, or over exercise and become addicted to the gym. They ignore the messages their body is sending them in the form of hunger, fullness, injuries, fatigue. In essence, they are punishing their body.*

  Hmmm, think about that...hate your body, so you punish your body to make it beautiful, and then you expect to be happy. That's Crazy!

- *Instead, Start Happy to End Happy. Try loving your current body, then feeding your body wonderful, healthy things and exercising because that is what your body needs to function and feel great. Guess what happens? You start to look and feel great! Be happy first, feel beautiful on the inside and then look great on the outside. Happiness comes from within not from without.*

- *If Change is what you want, your goal should be to create life-long healthy habits.*

- *Exercise for sports, for fun, for transportation, for the great way it makes you feel. Exercise for how you feel on the inside, not for how it makes you look on the outside*

- *If you really want the fastest way to feel better, then get enough SLEEP. That means turning off your electronic devices at night!*

CHAPTER 7
Drugs and Alcohol

Photograph by Olivia Giroux

Life is meant to be fun. For some people, part of that fun includes alcohol and/or certain soft drugs such as Marijuana. Alcohol and drug use can, however, destroy lives. Drug and alcohol abuse changes the lives of the users in very sad ways and is deeply connected to conflicts in families and relationships, divorce, neglect, child abuse, school failures, drop outs, job loss, financial strain, and poor health.

The distinction is all in the control. Who has it? Are you in control of your drug/alcohol use or is your drug/alcohol use in control of you?

Let's go back to the very first question I asked you at the beginning of this book, "Do you want life to get better?" If your answer was yes, then ask yourself "is the alcohol/drug use adding to your wonderful future or is it leading you away from your wonderful future?"

It is true that we all learn from our mistakes, but mistakes with drugs and alcohol, like unprotected sex, come at a much higher price than all other forms of mistakes. Unprotected sex, by the way, often happens because of drug and alcohol use.

This chapter is about catching yourself before it's too late and changing your actions before irreversible damage is done.

Awareness and Prevention

Letting loose on the weekends in the senior years of high school, or in college or university is something that students have done for generations. If you are in the senior years of high school and only partying on the odd Friday or Saturday night or drinking at special celebrations, and you are able to meet the responsibilities of everything else in your life, then that is considered by many in our society, to be acceptable. The biggest concern is for those of you for whom drinking and/or drug use has crept its way into less socially acceptable times.

I am not saying partying is harmless. There are risks of fights, accidents, overdoses, and other horrible outcomes. There are always dangers from using alcohol and drugs, after all they change how your brain functions; they change how you think. This means that you cannot trust your judgement in any given situation. This doesn't matter to many teens. You may feel like, "If drugs and alcohol were safe, using them wouldn't be much of a rebellion would it." Ok, but the rules of your home, school and community are not there to keep you from having fun, they are there to help keep you safe. Remember that accidents are just that – accidents. You don't plan on them happening. However, there are actions that can and will increase your risk. There are also ways you can reduce your risks, but accidents can still happen. At the end of this chapter I will mention some basic considerations for partying a little bit safer, but drugs and alcohol will forever be "use at your own risk."

I will not use this chapter to outline all of the ways that drugs and alcohol harm your body. You can learn about that in school. I am sure you are aware that drugs and alcohol are very bad for your body. In my experience, teaching scare tactics only works on teens that probably were not going to have drug and alcohol problems in the first place. Teens with healthy self-esteem say, "Oh, it does that to my body, to my brain? I'm not going to use drugs." But this tactic doesn't work on teens who feel low.

Telling teens who don't like themselves, or who think life sucks, about the ways that drugs and alcohol can harm them is an invitation to use it and abuse it. I quickly changed the way I taught this topic. I dedicate the first few days to self-esteem and making connections between self-esteem and the decisions you make in your life. Why do you choose to go beyond the socially acceptable level of consumption? Why do you choose to harm your brain, the most critical organ in your body? Why do you harm yourself on purpose? Why do you feel so low? I ask my students the same powerful question I asked you at the beginning of this book: *Do you want life to get better?* Of course, they answer, "Yes." From there I talk about how drug and alcohol abuse will never let that happen. This is the focus of this chapter – to show you how abusing drugs and alcohol will always keep you down.

The Slippery Slope

Drugs and alcohol are used often in place of healthy coping strategies. Look at images of young people partying, smiling, having fun, laughing. Even think of the word "partying." It's all about letting go of the issues in your life, letting loose, relaxing, and having a good time. It is engrained in our society as a way to get away from our stress and have fun. When it's presented to you in this way, who wouldn't want to join in? It's easy to see how you could slip too far into an unhealthy relationship with drugs and alcohol. The problem is that it's easy to attach to this as a coping strategy when life's issues and stresses become too big to deal with. It is a slippery slope. Once you turn to alcohol and drugs more often, then you need it in higher and higher amounts and often end up experimenting with different forms of release.

Generally people use recreational drugs for 4 reasons: because their friends are doing it/social connection, to take away a sensation (including pain), to create a sensation, and/or because they are addicted.

Many young people are feeling overwhelmed or stressed. That is normal. But some turn to substances like alcohol or marijuana (cannabis) to take away those negative feelings. Let's go back to that physiology stuff.

Do you remember the physiological changes we discussed in the stress chapter? That information on the sympathetic (SNS) and parasympathetic (PNS) nervous systems will connect deeply to what we are dealing with in this chapter. You may want to go back and re-read that section. Level One Threat/Emotional Pain can trigger an innate desire to follow others as a safety seeking measure. If the people you are hanging out with are experimenting with drugs, you are likely to do that too (keep in mind that the decision to do this is subconscious). This is also the stress stage where our brain wants to kick start the digestive system, so we can activate the rest and digest parasympathetic nervous system. So, smoking and vaping are subconsciously used as a calming strategy, just like stress eating and nail biting. Too bad that smoking and vaping exposes us to nervous system stimulants such as nicotine and other addictive chemicals (we'll come back to this).

For Level Two of threat and emotional pain, we have a surge of stress hormones to the point where we experience anxiety and agitation. If healthy coping strategies are not used regularly, it is common for teens and adults to overuse depressant drugs such as alcohol or marijuana as a way to cope. This numbing strategy has become so common in our society, but it comes with a big price for many. Drugs change the way we think and react to life. Obviously, there are very negative outcomes from misuse/overuse of these drugs.

For Level Three of emotional threat and emotional pain, we see the brain shut off the adrenaline tap altogether. Now the person is left with a numbness and is emotionally cold. At this stage, if the person seeks drugs, they are often stimulants in the form of hard drugs. They engage in risky behaviour to feel something, anything. This risky behaviour may include taking highly addictive substances, drug dealing, and other crimes. This stage is also a stage of emotional disconnection. The drugs become more important than any relationship. It truly is so sad.

Yes, drugs and emotional pain go hand in hand. This is yet another reason why those healthy strategies (towards strategies) are so important.

Red Flags

For the young people who seek drugs and alcohol not as a social event but as a means to escape from their daily lives or thoughts, it's very concerning. If you or someone you know is doing any of the following Red Flags, see these actions for what they really are, signs that the substance is in control of the individual.

- using during the school week,
- using during the day when you still have responsibilities,
- using alone,
- using as a sleep-aid,
- consuming way too much at parties, too often,
- using medication beyond the recommended dosage/frequency,
- searching through and/or stealing from medicine cabinets in homes,
- getting caught up in crime to support the drug/alcohol costs, (ie theft)
- putting others in harm to support the drug/alcohol use/costs (ie dealing/prostitution)

Whatever your drug of choice is, if it is an escape from the overwhelming aspects of life and thoughts and responsibilities, you know that when you are high or drunk, life seems less complicated. You are more relaxed and worry less, you forget your troubles. That's how it seems to you. But remember that is your high or drunk self talking – can you trust this mental state and believe that this is the best thing for you? Every time you sober up, things seem to get worse, more nagging, more work to catch up on, more people on you, more, more, more. Wait, I can sink back into my habit and make them go away even for a little while – yah that works.

I totally understand why drugs and alcohol are such an appealing escape. When I've had a rough day, going for a run or a walk calms me down, but so does a beer. Unfortunately, if you perceive life to be so hard that frequent escapes are necessary, they can spiral out of control very quickly. I have talked to too many teens who have come to a point where getting high or drunk is their main goal each day. Many will tell me, "It's not a problem," and that they are "not addicted." They say this because they want to do it. Only when they want to stop does it become a problem for them. Up until that point it is everyone else's problem.

The question of *how* you got started is only the tip of the iceberg. For some it is a matter of starting out drinking or doing drugs with friends or at parties and control just slowly slips away as the temptation takes over to use, whether it is to drown out boredom or daily troubles. For others, it's because they've watched their parents or older siblings do it. Some do it to get to sleep at night. For others, as in the case of many cigarette smokers in many societies, it is simply socially acceptable, and no real thought went into the decision to start. They believed it was just a part of growing up. There are countless ways to start and most appear harmless on the surface. Really it doesn't matter how, where or when you first chose to pick up the bottle or the joint or the bong or the needle or the pill. You've got to move past that question because if you think you've got a problem, then *how* you got started really doesn't matter. Instead ask the much deeper question which is why? *Why do you feel so low* about yourself that you feel the need to hurt yourself and those around you?

That is a tough question to face. It forces you to take a cold sober look at your life. The following chapters are dedicated to self-examination and healing. You must ask yourself, "Why I am so low?" Yes, all people with drug and alcohol problems are low. People who feel good about who they are and where they are going in life usually don't have trouble with drugs and alcohol. I say usually because there is always a risk of addiction in people who are genetically predisposed regardless of their strong sense of self. If your family members are addicted to anything whether it is recreational drugs or alcohol, or medications, or gambling, or eating, or sex, or electronic devices, or you name it, then you may have a genetic risk for addiction. Regardless of what you are addicted to, the predisposition to addiction can run in your family. If this sounds like your family tree and you get even a taste of strong medications, drugs or alcohol, you might not make it out without altering years or decades of your life.

The Myth of Strength in Numbers

The students who are regular users love it when we talk about drugs in class. They are "experts" on the topics of drug trips, crashes and how to cure hangovers. They often say, "Aw miss, it's no big deal –everyone is doing it." I can understand why this belief is so common. When you surround yourself with friends who use as often as you do, they become your world. You hang out in crowds of users and it reinforces the idea that everyone is doing it. When you go to a party on a weekend, you see more people doing it and you may even celebrate when you see someone new trying it.

In reality, you are seeing what you want to see and that becomes your view of the world. The truth is that most teens are not using or they are using in the socially acceptable ways described at the beginning of the chapter. They are still able to meet the demands of life and be successful. There are way more non-users out there, it's just that you don't know them personally. And if you stick with drugs, you probably won't hang out with them or get to know them. You have become part of the group that they want to avoid, not because of who you are, but because of what you use.

Don't take it personally. It's the drugs they don't want to be around. You may have felt this division. Have you ever felt judged by a look someone was giving you, or feel uncomfortable in a certain crowd? Do you get your back up? Do you feel like you can breathe again when you are back with your own friends and you can talk freely about drugs and laugh about it? That uncomfortable feeling forces you to seek your group and the drugs that you have in common. It's easy to feel angry in this situation. You feel like you don't fit in. You may go to extremes to be tough and show them that you don't care what others think of you. You can't let yourself care. You can't let yourself care what others think. If you cared, you might have to change what you are doing, and you don't want to do that. So, you are stuck on the outside. The response to being stuck on the outside is to create a circle around you so you are on the inside of something – misery loves company.

Be warned, in the beginning drugs and alcohol seem like fun, you can let loose. New friends will appear in a flash the moment you skip school to get high on a Tuesday afternoon. Socially you feel cool with a new crowd and you will reinforce for each other that it's ok. Others, like family and old friends, want you to stop but they don't matter to you. Nothing can stop you now – you feel good! Your loved ones might try to help you, but really it won't work. Understand this: you cannot stop, will not stop, until *you* really truly *want* to stop. It will never happen before that point.

If you are on the brink, or you are watching it unfold in friends and family members, it is critical that you begin to understand the slippery slope. To save yourself, you must open your eyes to the possibility of a much better life without your drug. Hopefully you will get to a point where you can admit to yourself that the way you are living is not what you want deep down, and then the journey begins. And it is a long journey. Will you clean up in the end? If you want it enough, I certainly have faith that you will. I believe in you. But I can't fix you. No one else can do this for you. You have to want to feel better. Help is critical. In many cases addiction counselling is necessary. Even though healing comes from within, outside help provides you with tools and strategies to be prepared for the challenges you will face.

If drugs and/or alcohol are still fun for you, you won't stop. But if you come to realize you are not in control of the drug, that the drug controls you, this scary understanding might mean you are ready to stop. Only when you want it to be over can you begin. Is there a better life out there for you, sober? Absolutely! No doubt about it! There is incredible strength inside of you. You can get through this! You've lost your way a little bit, learn from that. Now strengthen the realization that you are your own hero.

Life can be difficult, it's true, but I always ask the question, "Does your drug or alcohol habit make your life better?" Do not be short-sighted as you read this. I am not asking whether it makes this moment better, or this week better. I am asking, "Does it make your *life* better?" There is only one right answer to this question. People say life is hard – No. Life is challenging. Life throws curveballs at you and you can rise up or sink. Using drugs and alcohol to numb your pain is sinking. I want you to learn to rise up, to find the greatness inside of you. I want you to face your challenges, get through them and strengthen yourself from within.

Let's talk specifics. The three most common substances I talk with teens about are cigarettes (including e-cigarettes), cannabis (marijuana) and alcohol and, but we will also discuss harder drugs. Even if you think you know all there is to know about these, keep reading.

Cigarettes

Cigarettes and E-cigarettes (vaping) are a class by itself. Nicotine is a drug that you can use in broad daylight in between classes, on a work break, with anyone watching. You do not need to be at a party or hide it from mom and dad. (Ok, some of you do.) It will not get you drunk or high (but some vapes can.) It is incredibly addictive and extremely difficult to quit. So why use it?

If a person is very prone to stress overload, this drug is designed to trap you. It gives the illusion of all the things that can calm you down. Getting you outside for "fresh air," giving you a social outlet to vent your problems with friends, and putting something in your mouth (a subconscious attempt at engaging your brain's "Rest and Digest" stage.) There are many draws. Unfortunately, this strategy to relax backfires.

Manufacturers know the best time for a lifelong customer to begin is in the teenage years. It is when the vast majority of smokers start. And to keep you, they add an addictive chemical to what you are inhaling. When you are inhaling a stimulant such as nicotine, it kicks in after your smoke break, just as you are back inside dealing with the stressful conditions in your school or workplace. Now you feel more anxious and deeply desire for yet another smoke break to calm you down. Can you see the spiral?

Some E-cigarettes are designed to get a person OFF smoking. They will have little to no nicotine or other addictive substances. Obviously, these would be a safer alternative to ones that do contain nicotine or cannabis by-products.

When I see teens out on a smoke break at school, I can see the appeal. Honestly, school can be an alarming place. Especially if you would define yourself as "not good at school." If friends are with you when you are smoking, you can finally feel relaxed and you kind of feel cool. Yes, smoking makes kids feel cool. You can laugh or argue at that statement, but ask yourself, how did you feel when you first started smoking/vaping? Cool. Let's figure out if it really is cool.

I want you to think of a 45-year-old smoker or 75-year-old smoker – smelly and hacking away. Does that look cool? If you see younger kids say 10 or 12 smoking at a park, do they look cool to you? They feel pretty cool. But this is a joke. None of these people are cool because they smoke. Their addiction is their weakness. Each one of them lives with this little stick controlling them.

I feel very sad for people who choose to smoke, especially teens. When my children were young, they watched someone smoking and asked me, "Mommy why do people smoke?" My reply was raw. I didn't filter it at all. I replied, "Because they don't like themselves very much right now." It's a painful response but really, think about it. If you are already addicted to smoking or vaping, how are things going for you? How do you feel about yourself when you reach for yet another drag?

When I smoked as a young teenager, I was trying hard to be something that I was not. I didn't like myself. I see it in others all the time. We all know smoking is terrible for us. How can someone, who feels good about themselves, continually put something into their body that is so incredibly harmful for very little benefit? Smokers know it is addictive and that it is horrible for your lungs, the very organ that breathes life into every cell of your body. You can't possibly respect your amazing body and do this to it. Sorry, it's not cool. Now I ask you again, why are you so low?

Marijuana

Marijuana is one of the most commonly used drugs. We talk about it a lot in school. Here's a typical conversation I have in class.

I ask the students to tell me what they know about marijuana. First off, the students say, "It's harmless."

"Absolutely false," I say. "Keep describing it, I'll tell you when to stop, then I'll explain."

"It increases creativity," they say.

"True," I reply, "but so does meditation and being in nature."

"It is used medically so it can't be bad for us."

"Are you sick?" I ask.

"No."

These are perfectly healthy teenagers who say this. Chemotherapy drugs are used medically but they are not good for your body. Yes, the Cannabidiol (CBD) in Marijuana has some incredible potential for medical treatments, but do not lump yourself in with those who suffer from ill health, and make that your excuse to abuse it. Your health is good – cherish that, preserve that.

"It gives you the munchies."

"True."

"It helps me sleep."

"So does shutting off your screen, reading a book, drinking warm milk or camomile tea."

"Miss, it relaxes you."

"OK, Stop Right There. YES, this is true, I've been waiting for you to say this. Now we can talk about what marijuana does to teens and why it is not harmless. Now we can bring the conversation to a level of what you do care about, your day to day life, the quality of your life."

What does Marijuana do? It makes you relax. Well that's not so bad. Ok let me repeat that. It *really* makes you relax.

It makes you relax at the party, it makes you relax after your exam, and it makes you relax to go to sleep. How does it do that? The specific psychoactive component of marijuana, Tetrahydrocannabinol (THC), changes your nervous system. It changes how your brain responds to stressors/triggers. It numbs the stress response. The problem is that it continues to alter the brain even after the high is gone, actually it stays in your body for weeks. If you use it more often than it is metabolized, then your body constantly has the "relaxed" feel. The relaxing quality of marijuana becomes more appealing in this world where stress in increasing. Unfortunately, the reality is that not all stressors are bad. Some actually help us to function in society, in life. An alarm clock is a stressor, an assignment deadline is a stressor, a start time for school or a work shift or a team practise is a stressor. The natural process of the stress response is that your nervous system communicates to your glands and heart and muscles, it gets your blood flowing, gets your body moving so you accomplish your tasks. Your body is designed to respond to stressors. That is what keeps us functioning and productive.

If you use Marijuana enough, it makes you relax to the point that your body does not respond, and you ignore daily stressors in your life. It doesn't matter what time it is, who you are supposed to call, what assignment you are supposed to be doing, when your work shift started, when you wake up, if you go to class, if you make it to practice, if you go to your lesson. It simply doesn't matter. "I'll get to it later." Nothing matters. You are relaxed. Of course, eventually, the outside world starts to respond. Your parents, your teachers, your friends, your boss, your coaches say: "Why did you miss the assignment deadline?" "Why aren't your chores done?" "Why didn't you make it to practise on time?" "What is wrong with you?" Nag. Nag. Nag. And how will you respond to this nagging? This extra stress? Smoke up some more, then you can relax. The body doesn't necessarily crave it, but you rationalize further use in order to relax. Marijuana is not as physiologically addictive as it is psychologically addictive. It is called the "dropout drug" because you slowly let go of activities in your life that you used to enjoy. The nagging of others replaces the fun you once had in that activity and so you slowly one by one drop out of things that used to matter to you.

I had a student who was asking about marijuana because his Mom was a heavy user since her teenage years. He didn't live with her anymore, he lived with his dad and step mother. But he still visited his mom's house. The mom was very convincing about the idea that pot was harmless because it is a plant that grows naturally. He was worried about his Mom and the relaxed attitude she had about her habit. This student was trying to sort out the conflicting ideas about Pot/Marijuana. When I explained to him about the idea of it being a "drop-out drug," he was able to think back on his Mom's life and realized how true it was for her. She was unable to stick to anything. She had ended everything – she was a high school dropout, she couldn't keep her jobs, every relationship, whether it was with her own family or her boyfriends, became a failed relationship. The reality of how this drug had affected her life started to make sense to him.

It is important to recognize the common response from users. People who use pot often will say pot is harmless. That is the "relaxing drug" talking. As I have said before, I am not here to judge you. You can use what you want to use – it's your choice. But do not believe that marijuana is harmless. It isn't. Be aware of how you are responding to the responsibilities in your life. I have watched too many young people stop doing what they loved to do before, because of this drug. I have seen teens drop out of sports, lose jobs, let grades drop, fail courses, let good relationships end and put incredible strain on their family life. It seems very harmless at first, but if you do it enough it just might change the course of your life.

A Gr 12 student was not doing well in my class. His marks were sitting in the low 50's. Normally I wouldn't have thought much of it. As a teacher, every five months we start new classes. If I haven't taught a student before, they are new to me. Some students are high achievers and others are not. As much as we try we can't get to all the teens in time to figure out what is going on – it's a fact of teaching. But in this case, I had taught this guy before. I knew him back in grade nine. He was a star. Very smart and high marks came easily. He did well in everything he tried. He loved sports, was a star athlete, coaches and teachers knew this guy was going somewhere big. The girls loved him, and he was a genuinely nice guy. He came from a good family. And yet here he was four years later not handing in assignments and nearly failing. So, I asked him to stay afterschool one day and we chatted. I asked him how things were going. He went on to tell me that he wasn't playing sports anymore. I was shocked. He had quit everything that had meant so much to him. I asked him what he was doing with his time now. He said "nothing." I had my suspicions, so I asked him point blank, "Are you using Marijuana?" He was taken aback a little, but then said yes, and added that it was happening almost daily.

Now that you know it as the "dropout drug," I want to ask you a question. Can you recognize in one of your friends, or someone that you know who uses pot, that they have become very relaxed? Have they become too relaxed about priorities and responsibilities? Do you see that it is slowly changing their lives? When I ask this of my students, the answer is always, "Yes, I see it now. I know what you mean."

If you choose to use pot, then please be aware of its potential to change you. Marijuana is a stealth-like drug in that it causes you to let your life goals slip away while you are too relaxed to notice or too relaxed to care. But at some point, you wake up and look around at your life and ask, "What the hell happened?"

It is totally normal for you to be curious about marijuana. I've had students ask a lot of great questions. There are two excellent questions that come up often. The first is, "I've heard it can actually improve creativity and efficiency. Is this true?" They will often ask in reference to a singer/songwriter that they admire, that they think uses Marijuana. So, does Marijuana improve creativity and efficiency? Yes, it can, but let's figure out why.

Let's identify the enemy of Creativity. Over-thinking. We know that Marijuana relaxes you. It reduces your critical filter, it says "Relax." Without that critical filter on constantly, a person is left to explore and be in a state of peace. Think of this place as whispering, "There are no mistakes, only flow." (Sounds pretty good, right?) A person may even produce work quickly because there is no time spent assessing the messages of the critical filters. That could be seen as improving efficiency because the task was completed relatively quickly.

So, yes, we can say that marijuana can increase creativity and efficiency. However, is it possible that mistakes could be overlooked in this state? Most definitely.

Let's go back to the question and look at potential consequences. If they referred to a singer songwriter, I will ask them, "Are you planning to be a singer/songwriter?" (They always say no.) Why does it seem like it's OK for a singer/songwriter? How are people relying on them? If they mess up, what happens? The answer is, not much. We might not add one of their songs to our playlist, but life goes on.

Let's compare this to an electrician. Would you mind if an electrician was high while wiring your new home? Or if a bus driver was high while driving, or if a food inspector was high at work? Does it matter if they mess up? Yes. Will they notice or care if they mess up if they are high? If they don't, they may be endangering others, and they may lose their job and possibly their license to work.

Do singer/songwriters live perfect lives? No. We often hear about their failed relationships. Family members and partners constantly rely on each other. If one person is often living in a relaxed space induced by marijuana, another person who counts on them, is going to be disappointed too often.

The truth is we all rely on each other's brains, and accuracy, in our everyday lives. If you are planning to have a career and/or raise a healthy family, then being able to have a critical filter on is very important. We must be aware of our actions and be assessing/filtering them. There are other ways to enhance creativity.

Lots of Artists use meditation to create a space of mental peace where creativity can flourish, then when they are done, the filter returns and they carry on as responsible citizens. If they use marijuana to create that space, they are not in control of when that filter returns.

Another great question I hear is from students asking if it is harmless. They do so by referring to the 1970's when pot use was rampant. People that smoked pot then "turned out fine" the students say. This is a very important point of discussion. Earlier I mentioned two of the main components of marijuana, THC and CBD. It is important to know the differences between these chemicals.

THC is where the "high" comes from. CBD on the other hand seems to protect the brain. It calms the brain's activity. Medical scientists have found that isolated CBD has numerous medical uses with few side effects. Historically, naturally grown marijuana had balanced amounts of CBD and THC (approximately 4% each.) Over the past few decades, illegal cannabis growers have selectively grown the street drug to have much higher amounts of THC, giving users a higher high, while reducing the CBD that actually protects the brain from the THC. This combination increases the chance of dependency on the drug. In the 2016 documentary *What's in Today's Weed?* CBC Marketplace had chemical analysts determine the amounts of THC and CBD in street (illegal) marijuana. They found THC amounts in the 20-30% range, while CBD was 0-1%. The bottom line is this: the marijuana that is being sold illegally on the street today is very different from the marijuana of the 1970's.

It is also important to note that medical marijuana can be selectively grown to have the opposite ratio. There is medical marijuana that can be given to children with seizures that has 0-0.5% THC, while containing higher amounts of CBD. We can create many different strains of this plant. Legalization of marijuana could be helpful as it could lead to regulations and mandatory labelling of the amounts of THC and CBD in the products being sold. If you are going to use cannabis, it is safer to use legal substances that are regulated and labelled with THC and CBD amounts. And remember the lower the THC amount the better.

As we delve into this topic, it is also important to compare metabolism rates between pot and alcohol. When you drink alcohol, within 48 hours the alcohol is out of your system. Marijuana however can stay in your body for weeks, even months. So even though the high is gone, the drug is still in your body for days, weeks, months, affecting your nervous system, including your brain, and its response to stressors. If you are using pot regularly, then the drug never has a chance to fully leave your system before it is replaced again, and it is always affecting you whether you're high or not. After observing kids go from non-users to users to heavy users, and watching what is does to their lives, I see the same pattern over and over.

Alcohol

Alcohol is the most commonly used recreational drug, and it is one of the most common addictions in our society. It is an extremely tricky habit to control or quit because it is everywhere all around you. I am sure you have had direct experience with alcohol. Even if you have not used it, your parents or other adults in your life probably have and so you've seen the effects it has on people. If used responsibly it will relax you and take the edge off. It is very social and allows people to mingle and chat with ease. If used too often it can completely take over your life.

The Difference Between How Adults Drink and How Teens Drink

Adults drink to take the edge off and relax, teens drink to get drunk. Most adults can get a feel for how much they can drink and limit themselves responsibly. This takes experience and self-control. When you drink as a teen, you have no reference for how much your body can handle and how quickly, so getting drunk is very likely and for most teens it is the ultimate goal.

Consider what you drink. If you are getting drunk on beer or coolers, that is a safer way to do it. The alcohol content is low enough that you can get drunk, but you will become physically full before you will cause serious harm to your body. Bigger problems arise with hard liquors. As a teen, you will go for the easiest alcohol you can get your hands on and hide easily. Unfortunately, that often means hard liquor. Teens will over pour when mixing a drink and because you have no reference as to what a normal drink would taste like, you consume way more than an adult would. Even worse are those who drink hard liquor straight, i.e. right from the bottle. Unlike beer and coolers, alcohol is designed to be consumed in small quantities or one or two ounces (see equivalency pictures below). If you are consuming too much hard liquor, your stomach will not become full and so you could easily consume extremely dangerous amounts.

12 oz Lager Beer   1 Alcopop   4 oz Wine   1 oz Hard Liquor

There seems to be an endless debate between alcohol and marijuana. I have already outlined what I have observed in teens that regularly turn to pot. Marijuana is not harmless. However, I do think there is one advantage that pot has over alcohol. Alcohol can make you violent. Alcohol is a depressant – *getting* drunk can be fun, but once you *are* drunk, it will overexaggerate your sadness and anger and bring out tears and/or fists. If you get off easy, it will make you tired, but it has the potential to bring out the worst in people. Have you ever observed a friend overreact about a situation and spend the night in tears or get into a fight? Have you been on the receiving end of a violent or angry outburst from your drunken parent? Have you observed their short temper when they are hung-over? Or if your parent is an alcoholic and they haven't had their drink? Pay close attention to what alcohol does to them and to you. Make a decision now not to repeat that pattern in your life. Keep your alcohol consumption in check or don't drink at all.

My biggest concern is for those of you who are beginning to use alcohol as your coping strategy. As I mentioned in the chapter on stress and coping strategies, if this is what you turn to now, you are forming a habit and it will be what you continue to turn to as you get older. Life's responsibilities will increase and so will the stresses. Alcohol tears apart more families then you can imagine. The alcohol you turn to will keep you low and may lead you to take your exaggerated sadness and anger out on others – your friends, strangers, your spouse, and worst of all your children. It takes a huge toll on the individual in terms of strained relationships, difficulties at work, as well as the stress of hiding their problem from loved ones. Alcoholics are low and their drug keeps them down. If you are turning to alcohol outside of the socially acceptable times (at parties and celebrations) you are young enough to stop and change your habits now before it turns to an addiction. Take a close look at people whose lives are controlled by what they drink. This is not a place you want to be. Get help now.

Other Drugs

If you are drinking and using pot, there is a good chance you will go beyond and try other illicit drugs. But don't feel cool about this. Don't think that you have to go out looking for bigger drugs. The truth is, they are looking for you. Hard drugs are big money and the people behind the scenes are looking for users to get hooked so they can keep the money flowing. Dealers want users and they know where to find you. It used to be that you would have to go into a city center to get hard drugs, but no longer. More and more we are seeing suburban teens being drawn into dealing. The street drug industry knows that is where the start-up money is, teenagers spending mommy and daddy's money. I often hear about 'dealer' teens that show up at a party with cocaine and offer it out to their friends for free. "First ten times are free," they will say. What does that say to you? They are working for someone who knows what using cocaine ten times will do to you. It will turn you into an addict, an addict that will keep paying for more and more. The industry of hard drugs is one that traps its users. It knows the most addictive substances, (including medications) and keeps its users coming back for more. Their goal is to keep the cash flowing at the expense of the lives of their users. Do not feel cool and hip if you experiment. You are a sucker falling for a trap. You are inches away from being an addict. It will happen faster than you can possibly imagine. Being an addict is the farthest thing from cool.

I will repeat, you don't have to go looking for hard drugs, they are looking for you. You may think that you want to try new highs, but the truth is, the drug industry wants you more than you could possibly imagine.

The drug industry traps its users, but it also traps its dealers. Many students turn to dealing because of the temptation of big money, or because they need to support their own addiction. Far too many teenagers have had their lives threatened and have had to move cities to get away from the gang leaders they used to deal for. Even then they still never feel safe. When you buy street drugs, your money goes to support an industry of violence and destroying lives on every level. Is that where you want your money going? When your parents work all day, is this where they want their hard-earned money going, to support this industry?

I get so pissed off when I hear songs that glorify drugs. So many teens sing along and think it's cool when they really have no idea what kind of a Hell it really is. Why are drugs such a mainstream topic in music? Think about it. Drugs follow money. Wherever there is money, dealers will show up. So, any new celebrity will have *new friends* introducing them to the "cool clubs" and the "cool drugs." Those new friends are representing the drug industry and celebrities are their favourite clients. If a singer/songwriter gets in with them, they'll write about the drugs, and the dealers get free advertising.

New star/celebrity -> lots of new money -> new friends (dealers) arrive -> star's life intertwined with drugs -> musician starts to write songs about drugs -> teens listen, feel cool about drugs -> drug industry smiles.

The big picture is very interesting. Let's keep going and follow the star. The Star's relationship will crash (whether it is relationships with band members, a partner, spouse, their own kids.) We'll read about them going into rehab (maybe repeatedly.) Very sadly, we may read about their death from overdosing, or suicide with drugs in their system, or organ failure after years of drug use. Most people chalk it up to a tragic freak accident and move on. Tragic, yes. Freak accident? No.

Prescription medications are also a huge problem. A person can become addicted to prescription medication, and then feel like they constantly need more of it. Or a person consumes more then is prescribed, or a person takes medications that are not prescribed to them. Medications become street drugs for these reasons. This is an extremely common launch point for drugs controlling lives.

What is also so startling about hard drugs is how quickly a new one can appear. One day no one has heard of it, the next it seems to be the cool new drug. No one knows anything about it, hospitals are dealing with overdoses, and researchers are frantically trying to learn about it to try to protect people. It's just too new to know much about it. And yet many young people dive right it. They treat new drugs like they are the latest fashion item. Trying to keep up with the latest makes them feel cool. This is your body, your brain and your life you are playing with!!

Sadly, anyone can mix up a drug in their basement out of the most toxic of household substances and sell it to you. How low do you have to be to voluntarily put that in your body? If you are tempted, ask yourself, "Why do I hate myself so much that I put this inside of me?" If you are feeling that low, will this make your life better? Remember, I am not asking, "Will this make this moment better?" I am asking, "Will this make your life better?" How honest can you be with yourself right now?

Whether you are using a well-known street drug, or a new basement concoction, or a prescription medication, soon the decision will not be in your control. The desire to use will override any conscious thoughts you may have. You will do it because your body is screaming for it. You are addicted. The drug has altered the natural process of the way your nervous system experiences pleasure and pain. Without the drug, you feel less pleasure and more pain and the only way to feel relief is to use the drug. Sounds like great fun, doesn't it? Sounds so cool, right? Well on the bright side you are helping the drug dealers to make a living. At least you know your money, and your parents' hard-earned money, is going to a good cause.

Sorry, I cannot hide my sarcasm.

Don't Be a Fence Sitter

The fence sitter concept was introduced in the chapter on Sex, Love and Self-Esteem. A fence sitter is someone who isn't quite sure what they want to do. They can't quite make up their mind. When it comes to drugs and alcohol this is not a good place to be.

Let me explain. If there is a social gathering tonight and you are a fence sitter, it means that you have not really considered *if* or *what* you'll take tonight at the party. The dangerous part about being a fence sitter is that you are very easily swayed, and you have a pretty good chance of doing something that you did not really want to do. So, get off the fence! Decide *before* the party, when you are sober, what you will consume tonight. What consequences can you expect? Are you fine with those consequences?

Decide.

Decide what things you will NOT consume. Decide. Get off the fence.

Will you drink tonight?

If so will you drink hard liquor?

If so will you drink it straight?

Will you use cannabis/marijuana?

Will you figure out if it is legal or illegal weed?

Will you check the labels for lower THC amounts?

Will you use any other drugs going around at the party?

What will you do if a really close friend wants to try something and wants you to do it with them?

Will you permanently post pictures and comments to social media? Will you quickly press send?

How will you get home?

How will you react to a friend who tries to drive after drinking or smoking up?

Who will you leave with?

How will you know when you've had enough?

Who can you call if things get out of hand?

If you are currently a non-user, then I cannot stress enough the importance of taking a deep look at your emotional health before you head out to try these things. An overwhelmed mind makes poor decisions.

Considerations for Partying Safer

Things You May Want to Experience

- Having fun
- Relaxing
- Letting go of stress
- Laughing
- Hanging out with friends
- Meeting new people
- Meeting someone you'd like to date
- Hanging out with someone you like

Things You Do NOT Want to Experience

- Making a fool of yourself
- Puking
- Posting things on social media that you will regret later
- Seeking revenge on someone because your emotions are high and your judgement is low
- Getting into a fight
- Breaking the law
- Losing consciousness. We commonly call this passing out, but in reality, it is your brain shutting down from toxic overdose. Doesn't sound so fun when we put it that way does it?
- Going to the hospital
- Being arrested
- Cheating on your partner
- Getting pregnant/getting sexual partner pregnant
- Getting an STD
- Being raped
- Raping someone
- Becoming addicted to a hard drug
- Getting in a car accident
- Drowning

- Death
- Having yourself and your parents held legally responsible for the death of someone because they died after being at your party

Make decisions before you go out
"I will do this, I won't do that." You have a good chance of remembering the conversation you had with yourself beforehand and not getting into something that has bigger consequences then you are ready to deal with.

Alcohol and drugs reduce your good judgement
When you are using them, you do not want to put yourself into a situation where you need good judgement because it won't be there.

Decisions about transportation, decisions about trying a drug, decisions about having sex, decisions about cheating, decisions about elevating an argument or seeking revenge, decisions to post on social media, etc. These decisions have big consequences if you do not choose wisely. Make these decisions ahead of time when you are sober. You need good judgement to choose wisely.

Think of what you are consuming
People don't go in to hospitals for alcohol poisoning from drinking beer or coolers (see images.)

Can you get drunk from them? Yes. Can you have fun? Yes. Beer and coolers have far less alcohol than hard liquor. So you will feel physically full before you would put your life in danger.

If you are drinking hard liquor and you do not measure the amounts you are using, you will consume far more than your body can handle. Use a shot glass to measure. Aim for 1 shot per drink. Hard liquor is very powerful.

If you are mixing drugs and alcohol you will consume far more than your body and brain can handle.

Always eat before and with alcohol consumption.

Drink water before, during and after consuming alcohol.

Remember you want to be able to laugh on Monday morning at school. You do not want to dread going to school or dread checking the online comments because you are so embarrassed about your actions. In order to avoid social disasters, you need to retain some control over your actions. It is much better to have people laugh *with* you then laugh *at* you.

The Ultimate Home Wrecker

Drugs change everything in a family dynamic. If you have watched an adult in your life who is addicted (including alcoholism) then you know it affects everyone around them. Addictions in teens are just as, if not more, heart wrenching.

Tina came to me in tears one day at the start of class because she hadn't gotten her project done. The night before, her brother showed up, who she hadn't seen in weeks. He was kicked out of the house when he kept using drugs even after his parents begged him to stop. He got caught stealing from a neighbour to pay for his drugs, and he had already stolen from his own parents. When he came home, another huge fight started between him and the parents. Tina was so upset by this. She remembered when she and her brother used to get along so well. Everything changed so much when he started using. She couldn't understand how he could be so cruel to his own family.

When drugs take over, things *and people* that mattered to you before don't matter anymore. The drug becomes the most important thing. It makes you not care about others. Hearts are crushed by drugs, families are torn apart. Parents and siblings are left wounded and helpless until their addicted son or daughter wants to get help. Unfortunately, it often means the addicted individual has to hit rock bottom.

A Final Word on Addiction

To be addicted to anything is a weakness. I am sorry to be blunt, but it's the truth. Whether it is a physiological or psychological addiction, you have allowed something else to control you. That's the bad news.

The good news is that you have greatness inside of you. You have incredible inner strength that can help you get your life back under control.

If you have fears that you are addicted, reach out to someone you trust. Preferably a trustworthy adult, as most friends your age don't really know what to do with that kind of information. You can check out addictions services websites and contact them. A possible step may be talking to a professional (i.e. a counsellor). So many teens don't ask for help because they are afraid of this step. Do not avoid professional help. An addiction is a very strong thing. Yes, you may be coping, getting by, but the road from addiction to health is an incredibly difficult journey. These professionals can teach you tools and help to "fill your toolbox" so you will have greater success. Some addictions counsellors have personally been through this battle and have found their greatness. They found the inner strength to overcome one of the biggest challenges an individual can face. As a result, they can help sufferers in ways that few others can.

If you are thinking of quitting, there is one very important thing to consider. It is critical that you ask yourself if you are really ready to quit. Wise counsellors will be able to see through you in the first meeting. I've been told by counsellors that they can tell early on if a teen is ready to quit and they won't be able to do very much for them unless they are really ready. If the alcohol or drug is still fun for you, you are not ready to stop. Be brutally honest with yourself. If this is the choice you are going to make, to continue to abuse this substance, then do not be shocked and complain when you wake up at some point and realize that you are deeply unhappy and that your pain has followed you everywhere.

Another concern is that the longer you are using, the more difficult it will be to stop. Adults struggle for years, for decades, even their entire lives, over and over trying to quit. Teens can have a much easier time, so don't wait! I have heard so many teens say, "I can quit anytime I want." Ok, then do it for two or three months and try it out. Prove to yourself that you are not controlled by your substance. If you find that you are having a difficult time getting through a few months, you should take that as a big warning.

When you decide you want to live free of this drug, then make a commitment to yourself and seek help. Strength is in the support network you surround yourself with, and strength is within you. A better life is waiting for you. You can live free. You can live sober. You can create a wonderful, healthy life for yourself. You can make your life better.

Repeat this: "I can do this." Say it over and over until you know that it is true. Then act on this belief.

As Henry Ford said, "Whether you think you can or you think you can't, either way you are right."

You Can.

Big Picture Points

- *Partying is a fact of life for most teens.*

- *Accidents happen. Drugs and alcohol will forever be "Use at your own risk."*

- *The main concern, and the focus of this chapter, is for those of you for whom drinking and/or drugs have crept their way into less socially acceptable times. If you or someone you know is "using" during the week, or during the day, on their own, or as a sleep-aid, this is cause for concern.*

- *If you still enjoy your drug/alcohol habit, you will not view it as a problem.*

- *People with a strong sense of self, with true self-esteem, very rarely have problems with drug or alcohol addictions. People who gain a strong sense of self will kick their habit.*

- *You do not have to go looking for harder drugs, they are looking for you.*

- *Using drugs to escape from daily problems will always backfire.*

- *The most important question you can ask yourself is this: "Yes, life can be difficult, but does your drug or alcohol habit make your life better?" Do not be short-sighted as you read this. This question is not asking if it makes this moment better. It is asking, "Does it make your life better?" There is only one right answer to this question.*

- *If you have gotten into the drug/alcohol habit as a means of escaping problems, you must understand two things. 1, it never makes the original problems really go away, AND 2, it gives you a whole set of new problems.*

- *No one else can make you stop using, no matter how hard they try. Only when you decide that you want to stop can you begin the journey.*

- *Can you do it? Absolutely. Will your life improve? Absolutely. Will it be hard? Absolutely. Are you worth it? ABSOLUTELY!*

CHAPTER 8
Vice Grip

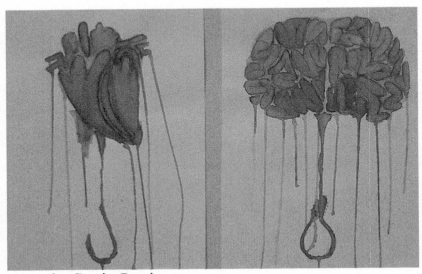

Art by Cassie Grenier

How Feeling Low Turns to Feeling Lost

You are a constant reflection of your esteem value. If you are low, then your thoughts, decisions and actions will keep providing you with circumstances that keep you low. This chapter examines how "low" turns to "lost." How low can you go?

Where are you now? Are you lost? It is easy to get lost at your stage of life. In fact, most of the cards are stacked against you finding your way through adolescence unscathed. This entire chapter is devoted to the lost souls. It is about the sneaky, mainly unconscious, ways we turn our A.S.A. (anxiety, sadness and/or anger) inward (internalizing stress) to harm ourselves, or outward (externalizing stress) to harm others. It should be noted, however, that it is impossible to hurt others without hurting ourselves. These vices that we will now discuss happen so easily and quickly that what you at first thought was "Ok" to dabble in, is now taking over your personal world. You are in the "vice grip."

First let's clear the air. As was mentioned in the chapter on Drugs and Alcohol, I do believe that a certain amount of partying and getting into trouble is a normal part of growing up. As you experiment in these behaviours, most of them we can simply chalk up as minor experiences. But for too many of you, you either already have, or you potentially will, go much deeper into one or more vices. What puts you at risk? Why do you continually engage in it over and over? How does it relate to self-esteem? And, most importantly, how do you get out?

Definitions of A Vice

Here are some definitions of vices taken from Wikipedia:
a. A moral weakness
b. An evil, degrading, or immoral practice or habit
c. A serious moral failing
d. Wicked or evil conduct or habits; corruption
e. A slight personal failing; a foible: the vice of untidiness
f. A flaw or imperfection; a defect

g. An undesirable habit

What Is Your Vice?

Drug abuse
Alcohol abuse
Multiple Body piercings
Multiple Tattoos
Sexual Promiscuity
Dieting
Eating disorders
Over eating
Over shopping
Gambling
Smoking
Cutting
Skipping curfews
Gossiping
Prescription Medications
Violent behaviour
Violent video games
Pornography
Vandalism
Theft
Crime
Lying
Cheating
Manipulative behaviour
Bullying
Suicidal thoughts or attempts
Any combination of the above

So, which ones do you identify with? Not everyone reading this currently has a vice, but do not mistake that for thinking you are in the clear. Learn to protect yourself so that you don't become trapped in a "vice grip." For many of you reading this, there is at least one item on the list that you can easily relate to. Why is that? On the surface, you might ask, "What's the big deal with that?" To you I say keep reading all the way to the end of the book.

Most of you, I am sure, are surprised that anyone thinks all of these items are actually problems. Really these don't seem like a big deal until we drown ourselves in them. For example, I can talk to students about drug use, in particular marijuana, and they may all say, "What's the big deal?" As we discussed in the chapter on drugs, if you are really using often, you must consider the effects on the important areas in your life that you stop being "present" for and you let slip away. Look at tattoos as another example. A little tattoo here or there is not a big deal, but if you continue to cover your body with them, you must at some point realize that you are harming your body's largest organ. An individual can rationalize covering their body with tattoos by saying their skin is their canvas for art. But really deep down, is the individual respecting their skin and how incredible it is? Do they have complete respect for their body? If the answer is no, I hope you can see that the tattoos are not the problem. The "why" is what we are after. The "what" are the vices, and they are just the surface; the symptoms of the real problem. We want to go deeper.

As you read the list of Vices, you might be thinking that these behaviours are everywhere and affect not only teens, but adults as well. Good observation. So, let's think about these adults who are trapped in their "vice grip." Are they happy? Give this question some serious consideration and it will soon become an obvious "no." How long have they been feeling this low? For the vast majority, it started in – you guessed it – the teenage years. They have lived their teen and adult lives with low self-esteem and have used these coping strategies to create temporary escapes from their anxiety, sadness and/or anger. Unfortunately, the longer they do it, the more permanent their vice becomes. Now let's get back to you and your vices. Do you still want to be doing this 20 or 30 years from now? You are not trapped – yet. The longer you have your vice, the harder it is to quit. You are still young, it is much easier for you to quit now. You can reset your path. First you need to take responsibility for where you are and then examine how you got there. Only after these have been accepted can you heal from the inside and strengthen yourself to get through the storm.

So, do you actually want to hurt yourself or is there something more to it? It may surprise you to know that I do not consider any of these vices listed above to be the problem. In my experience, the vices are simply the *symptoms* of the underlying issues that you are having difficulty with. They are the red flags that finally get noticed, when all the other flags that you've thrown at the world have been ignored. Unfortunately, many family members and friends want to treat the vice. They treat the drug addiction, the sexual promiscuity, the skipping school, the crime, but they never deal with what is really bothering you. This approach leaves you feeling misunderstood and now, on top of everything else, you feel like a burden and disappointment to those around you – now that's a recipe for success – NOT. Everyone really needs to take a big step backwards and ask, "How did it get to this point and how can we get back on track?"

One thing to also consider about vices is that so many of them are romanticized in the media. Think about how many movies, TV shows, or songs describe a very troubled teen who gets rescued by something or someone and then goes on to have a happy ending. This is a dangerous way to view a troubled teen with a harmful vice. Very few, if any, have a fairy tale ending. It downplays the harsh realities of the vice-victims. So here is your wake-up call. Do not wait around for someone else to save you. *You are your own hero.*

Important Note: There is a possibility that the cause of your troubles is actually an underlying Mental Health Illness. It is much more common than many people think. Seeking assessment and assistance is the best option here if you or a friend or family member suspects this might be the root cause. Do not try to handle this alone. Mental illnesses are true physiological conditions that require treatment. That being said, even if this is the case for you, I believe that everything I am writing still applies, and that, in addition to professional help and treatment, healing from the inside is critical.

Let's take another look at this original list and view it from the physiology and neuroscience of these Vices:

Why Do You Turn To Your Vice?

Group 1
Gossiping
Lying
Cheating
Manipulative behaviour
Dieting
Over eating (stress eating)
Eating disorders
Smoking
Over shopping
Drug abuse (calming drugs: Marijuana/Alcohol)

So many teens live here, where we are trying to seek safety in an unsafe place (the social world.) Our brain is trying to figure out how to get safe and secure. Dr. Gordon Neufeld explains that teenage brains revert back to a childhood survival tactic of following and obeying. Unfortunately, instead of following parents for survival, teens follow media and each other for social survival. Ideas will enter your mind of trying to change yourself to fit in, whether it is to change your look, your body, the way you talk, what you talk about, even choosing to put others down to boost your own ego, etc.

Strangely when we feel emotionally unsafe our brain also fixates on oral stimulation. Remember from Chapter 3, when we are in our alarm state (sympathetic nervous system) for too long, our brain tries to get us to the Parasympathetic system also known as the "rest and digest" stage. As we discussed, our brain thinks if we can kick start the digestive system (though oral stimulation) we can access our calm state. It is a very temporary fix. Eating and smoking won't make the problems go away, but our brain tries anyway. Also using nervous system depressant drugs temporarily slows the nervousness and the overwhelmed feelings. This is where vulnerable people seek and return to marijuana and alcohol too often.

Solutions for this stage include calming strategies and spending time in places that are emotionally safe. It may be in your bedroom, but if you are still on social media, your brain continues to be socially and emotionally on, so really you are not mentally at rest. Try drawing or reading a book instead. As for that oral stimulation brain trick, try chewing gum as a healthier alternative to nail biting, over eating, or smoking.

Group 2
Bullying
Skipping curfews
Alcohol and Cannabis misuse/overuse
Prescription Medications
Violent behaviour
Violent video games

This Second group of vices are more stimulating. Our brain knows that if we can over-stimulate the nervous system, it will shut off the alarm hormones, the adrenalin/cortisol taps. Then we can get some rest from the feelings of overwhelm. As a much healthier alternative, intense exercise would be a great substitute for any of these vices. The intense exercise does the same thing. It over-stimulates your stress adrenaline response, until it shuts off and you fall into a calmer state. Even if you think you are out of shape, get moving anyway and stick with it. In terms of becoming your own hero – regular exercise is Gold!

Group 3
Cutting
Multiple Body piercings
Multiple Tattoos
Sexual Promiscuity
Pornography
Vandalism
Gambling
Theft
Drug abuse (stimulants hard drugs ie meth, ecstasy, cocaine, etc)
Drug Dealing
Crime
Suicidal thoughts or attempts

This third group of vices is common for individuals who have experienced so much alarm/pain in their lives that the brain has shut off the adrenaline/cortisol taps simply to protect them from feeling so anxious all the time. Unfortunately, they are left with numbness. *It is important to note that Adrenaline is naturally also a wonderful rush that helps all of us to feel "alive." We feel it when we are having fun, when we are laughing, on rollercoasters, on dates, when we are working on something exciting, on vacations and during adventures.* When people don't have the adrenaline taps working properly, they do not feel anything at all. They then have to find really alarming things to do to create a sensation of aliveness.

When a person is numb to normal range of emotions, risky behaviours such as self-harm create small temporary rushes of adrenaline. Loving intimacy doesn't generate a sensation anymore, so they turn to promiscuous or risky sex. Sitting in the chair at the tattoo parlor gives a rush, but the rush is temporary, so they must go back for more tattoos. (Tattoos are commonly referred to as addictive. It is very rare to meet someone with only one tattoo.) Alcohol and Marijuana feed the numbness, so stimulant/hard drugs are sought to create a rushing sensation. All of this is temporary.

None of it is a long-term fix. All of these create *more* problems, more pain. It's a vicious cycle.

In his *Making Sense of Anxiety* course, Dr. Gordon Neufeld explains, when your brain is feeling overloaded and/or unsafe, the brain's natural release valve is in tears. Crying, even bawling, releases the pain that is built up. Unfortunately, we have a long held multi-generational belief that crying should be avoided, and as a result, now we also have an increase in anxiety, anger and numbness. These are the result of brains that have not been allowed to release. If you are at any of these vice stages, ask yourself, what is your opinion of/experience with crying? Could you allow yourself to cry without restraint? Do you have emotionally safe people and safe places to cry without restraint? Crying is the brain's reset switch.

If you re-read the chapter on Stress and Coping strategies, you'll see some deep connections to what you've just read as well as some more healthy coping strategies that you can use to support you as you get away from your vice grip.

False Causes

Vices evolve from unresolved pain. In what ways have you allowed your past experiences to shape who you are today? We can get deeply involved in vices, even addicted to them. People always wonder, what caused it? As you explore the reasons, I will be listing the most common root causes that I have observed in teens over the years. It doesn't necessarily mean they are your reasons. You are the expert of your life. No one knows your life story up to this point better then you do. The point of this is that if you are not happy with the way things are, you have to shake up your habitual thinking that caused you to get into trouble.

But before I can discuss the root causes, I must first discuss two common responses that are NOT root causes. When asked directly, "Why do you do this ____?" (fill in vice), there are two common quick responses.

I Don't Care

Many teens reply to questions about their vices with the response, "I don't care."

"I don't care what I do," and, "I don't care what happens to me," and, "I don't care what other people think." Well if you are telling the truth, that is so incredibly sad. I feel so sorry for you. What has happened in your life that has caused you not to care about yourself and what happens to you? Again, I am asking, why? Why do you not care? Saying I don't care is a defensive response, but it doesn't answer the bigger question, and this is why it is a false cause. You can convince yourself that you do not care, and in reality, you may feel that way now, but can you honestly say to yourself that you *never* will care? Many of these vices have serious long-term consequences to them. You might defend your actions with that kind of response, but at some point, you will care. Can you say honestly, "I don't care now, and I know I will never care." Go back to the image of the timeline shown in the introduction. Take a serious look at it.

The Rush

This is the second common response. Breaking rules gives you an adrenaline rush. This rush can be addictive and leaves you wanting more, just like a drug. There is a physiological reason for this adrenaline-seeking behaviour (as discussed in "group 3" above.) But although this is not why you *started* doing dangerous things in the first place, it is now one of the factors that keep you coming back for more. If you are doing it for the rush, then it is risky. Ask yourself the following questions:

- What's the risk?
- Is it extremely harmful to you?
- Is it harmful to others?
- If you continue to engage in it will you have respect for yourself or others?
- Do your actions scare you?

If you want to stop your vice there are healthier ways to get that adrenaline rush. Great alternatives are sports and exercise. There are so many, different kinds of sports out there, whether it is individual sports or team sports, there is truly something for everyone. Sports and exercise are wonderful energy outlets for every person. There are many healthy adrenaline rushes to try. Seek your adrenaline in a way that is not harmful for you or for others. Exercise is a great way to get your natural adrenaline tap flowing normally.

Root Causes

Now let's get to root causes. Try to explore your own. The following are the seven most common causes that I have observed in teens. And it can be common to have more than one root cause influencing you. Some of them are hard to swallow, tough to own up to. But if you want life to get better you have to release your vice's grip. And to really kick it, you have to own up to why it's there. Take your time with these, think through each one carefully, and put a star beside any that seem familiar to you. Take a deep breath. Stay open.

Coping

It is important to note that if your past experiences, such as school issues or pain from your family life, have weighed you down, and the stresses of daily life have piled up on top, you can easily turn to vices when life is overwhelming. If you don't learn positive coping strategies from your parents or others in your life, then you will learn negative ones. Everyone develops coping strategies to get them through rough times or even just to get them through the day. As discussed in Chapter 3, these strategies are either positive or negative. If you go back and look at Chapter 3 on stress and coping strategies, you can see how a negative coping strategy can spin out of control if it goes unchecked.

Control

For many it is a matter of control. We all want control over our lives and this is such a critical time for you, as you begin the phase of being in charge of your actions. So often our control is limited because of parental influences. We will exert control over whatever we can. For example, "Control over my body." We'll use drugs, starve ourselves, drink too much, have sex, eat unhealthy food, or get body piercings or tattoos. You can come up with so many reasons for engaging in these activities, but really it comes down to control. You are doing these actions against the will of your parents and even society. This is your secret. You are in control and the *power* (not necessarily the action itself) makes you feel good. You can continue to rationalize in your mind that it's Ok to continue. Really you can convince yourself of anything. If you try to explain it to others, you might even think you are convincing your listener. I doubt that you are, but you will feel that way.

Notice Me!

Don't be insulted by this phrase. It really does apply in many situations. Stay open. Negative attention is better than no attention at all. We all simply want love, but when love is not available, attention will work as a substitute. So many people have grown up without enough unconditional love and attention. We've talked about stage 3 vices. Well, some parents are living at that stage and they cannot connect deeply with their own children. Young children will "act out" if they aren't getting mom and dad's attention, every child does it, but sometimes it is because of an abundance of nervous energy. The attention seeking actions that get them into trouble can sometimes continue in the teen years except the ways to get in trouble are much more serious.

Maybe the only attention you drew to yourself, and therefore received, was negative. You may have been acting out as a coping mechanism for so long that you don't even think about it anymore, it becomes natural. But the older you get the more serious the games. It is the "You can't ignore me now" syndrome. Feeling emotionally neglected by your parents is a horrible way to grow up. So, acting out through negative means with extreme and/or harmful practises is a way of screaming, "Notice Me!" Most often it is friends who notice, and the friends become the attachment focus, but peer groups are never completely safe.

The classic "Bully" often falls into this category. We often see the bullies as monsters picking on smaller, weaker victims. In reality, they have very low self-esteem, usually due to the lack of positive attention at home. Their strange "self-help" strategy is to put others down, in an effort to make themselves feel higher. This "Power" concept was discussed in Chapter 2 on Distraction, Attention and Power.

Self-Punishment

Self-hatred. No self-worth. This one is often seen in victims of verbal, physical, emotional and sexual abuse. They were treated like dirt, so they believe that is who they are. If this is your root cause, you believe that you are not worthy of love from yourself or anyone else. The scars are deep for you and living a healthy life may seem impossible for you. I believe you are worth it. I believe one day you will know that you are worth it.

Sam has had a troubled past and his self-esteem is at an all-time low. His behaviour may cause him to be labelled negatively. He is different from others and he knows it. Cruelly, others call him a "freak." So, he gives in to that. He doesn't have the strength or esteem to fight it. He makes himself even more physically distinct, with piercings, hair colouring and dressing in a way that causes people to say, "What a freak." He totally takes on the persona. "This is who I am, this is where I belong." It is his self-punishment and his normal all at the same time.

We can also relate this to Jenny, from Chapter 5, a girl who has a horrible past of childhood sexual abuse. Because she was a child she had no control over the situation, and she had to give in to the abuse. Eventually she gets older and hears from the outside world that to have sex with many people is bad and makes you a slut, and attention from men makes you a tease. So, she looks at her past and sees herself as a tease and a slut. This may be difficult to comprehend, but if she tragically has experienced this worst form of attention, she may know it is wrong, but she doesn't know how to stop it, so part of her mind must give in, in order to cope. As she gets older, she associates herself with negative terms associated with sex, such as whore, tease, or slut. She may take on that persona living a very promiscuous life with many sexual partners. "This is who I am, this is where I belong." It is her *self-punishment* and her *normal* all at the same time.

Fear

a) <u>Fear of Change</u>. To some extent this is happening to *every* teen! There is so much change around each of you. Everyday brings something new to your life. Your brain seeks stability and predictability. But this stage of life is highly unpredictable. On top of basic alarms of learning new things and not fitting in to the ever-changing peer culture, many of you have other big changes going on: Moving homes, changing schools, family changes like divorce or new step parents, high school ending. Yes, changes happen to everyone, but if you were not shown how to properly deal with challenges in a productive way, then you begin to hate the circumstances that seem so out of your control. This root cause is often seen in combination with #1, "Control."

b) <u>Fear of not fitting in</u>. In peer groups, in school, in society, in your own family. Peer Pressure is real but not in the way you think it is. It is completely non-verbal and it is not discussed. The pressure comes in observing the actions of others and wanting to belong to something, to belong to anything. It comes because you do not want to be left out, or to feel different. Maybe it should be called self-pressure, instead of peer pressure.

c) <u>Fear of not being good enough</u>. This fear is incredibly common, and you can imagine why. When we are constantly bombarded with media messages telling us we are not attractive enough, not smart enough, don't have enough money, are not muscular enough, not skinny enough, not up with the latest clothes or electronic gadgets, etc., how the hell are we supposed to face the day with a smile?

This Is My Normal

All your life you have watched mom and/or dad cope with a tough life using cigarettes, or alcohol or drugs or being violent, or _____ (fill in their vice). So, this truly is "normal" for you. If your parents are currently caught in the grips of a vice and are addicted, this is a terrible thing to witness. Basically, the parents are modelling the thoughts and behaviours that life is so tough that this is the only way to get through it. What a sad lesson to be taught as a child or teen. Frequently, many of the teens I talk to who smoke, tell me of all the times they tried to quit and couldn't. I always ask, "Do your parents smoke?" If they say yes, I know this habit is more than a physiological addiction to nicotine. Smoking is a deeply entrenched family coping strategy that they learned long before they picked up a cigarette for the first time. Can you still stop for good? Absolutely! The next chapter is for you!

Speaking of how it affects children, don't you want to kick your vice long before you become a parent and pass it on?

Boredom

This root cause is relatively new in the history of teenagers. There has never been a time before this when teenagers as a group have had more money, less responsibility and more free time. This is a recipe for getting into trouble. At the very least it is a recipe for wasting your young life in front of electronic screens. Why do you have so much free time?

Having a part time job and/or volunteering are important parts of understanding your own value in the world, but many parents view work life so negatively that they want to protect you from it. They will work harder, and work overtime, to create more family money so you don't have to work. They will throw money and material possessions your way to compensate for the time they cannot spend with you because they are working. For you, a part time job will lessen the pressure on your parents and it will give you sense of responsibility. Just make sure it is a healthy and safe work environment and that school work always remains the priority.

How about extra-curricular activities? So often I talk to teens who feel like lost souls at school. After chatting for a while, I learn they are not connected to any school or community activity. Are you disconnected? Do you look around and see art clubs, sports teams, drama groups, music/band clubs, or others volunteering or working with community groups? Have you ever called people who are involved "lame," or called the activity lame? Have you falsely convinced yourself that this is true?

There are lots of great adults out there trying to create positive experiences for teens. Maybe it's a teacher or community member starting a team or a club, maybe they are organizing volunteer experiences, maybe it's a family member offering to teach a skill to you. Just because an adult is around doesn't mean it's lame. Life isn't meant to be a constant amusement park. There are down times, quiet times (you may refer to these times as "boring"), and there are times when adults are teaching you new things (you may also call these "boring"). But if you allowed yourself drop the hate for those experiences then you would see the value you are gaining and the interactions with others that will strengthen you.

There is so much more to do besides staring at a screen, or walking around with your friends complaining, or doing drugs and/or drinking, or harming your community and getting into trouble.

The truth is there is always something to do.

When you think you are bored

- Help someone
- Get out some tools and fix something that needs fixing
- Clean something that needs to be cleaned
- Watch a DIY video on something you are interested in
- Help with the cooking
- Do yard work or shovel snow
- Volunteer to help the local mechanic, hairstylist, gardener, etc., and learn new skills
- Practise a sport or instrument
- Start a project at home
- Get involved in a project at school though classes or clubs
- Read for pleasure or to learn about something new (Also try audio books)
- Watch a true-story movie about someone who had overcome a challenge
- Start a cause. What needs to be improved in your community? Is there anyone working on that? If so, join them. If not, get the ball rolling. Get passionate about improving your community.

Take pride in your actions. Notice how great you feel when you have accomplished something.

With every effort you make, you are expanding yourself.

Live each day on purpose, not by accident.

When Root Causes Overlap

Root causes can, of course, overlap. For example, "Notice Me!" and "Self-Punishment" and "This is My Normal" can be equally influencing in a household where parents are abusing themselves through addictions or cycles of bad relationships. Perhaps there is only one root cause in your life or maybe it is a bit of each of them. The list of root causes is by no means exhaustive. We haven't even touched on physiological addictions or genetics or diseases. I chose these seven because they are the most common root causes that I have observed as an educator and experienced myself as a teen. They are:

- Coping
- Control
- Notice Me!
- Self-Punishment
- Fear
- This is My Normal and
- Boredom

If any of these seven reasons sound familiar to you, then you and your loved ones need to be reminded that, as mentioned before, the vice itself is not the problem. It is a symptom of an underlying issue. Healing involves facing and understanding the underlying situations that cause self-esteem to fall. A healthy emotional state is the goal because that will lead to healthy life choices and an understanding of personal worth. From that point on, the *constant* decision NOT to engage in the addiction has some purpose.

So, what if you do not have a "vice" and yet can recognise yourself somewhere in the root causes? Well then, your timing is critical in order to prevent years, if not decades, of unnecessary self-induced pain and struggle. Being able to recognize the potential of falling is the first step to prevent the fall entirely. I invite you as well to begin your journey of self-healing. Chapter 9 begins with self-reflection questions to move you forward.

Motivation for Healing
You are sad and angry – I get that.

You don't care about what happens to you. That's sad, and for the most part, I don't believe you.

Your actions are yours to take, right? Why should anyone else care? Well, your loved ones care. Forcing them to watch *you* hurt yourself is rough on them. Maybe they are also physically or emotionally hurt by what you are doing. But perhaps you think punishing them isn't so bad? But here's the catch: hurting other people always ends up hurting you more. In terms of *how* the loved ones are hurt, it's by being forced to watch *you* hurt yourself. So what's painful for them is painful for you and vice versa.

There are also the consequences of your actions – oh yeah, those. But if your self-esteem is so low, these consequences, like long term health problems, probably won't scare you enough to make you stop. Sometimes you may *want* self-punishment.

So, if you don't care what happens to you then stop complaining, stop pretending you are a victim.

But here's the thing. Somewhere deep inside you there is a part of you that *does* care what happens. I call this the glimmer of hope. A small part of you wants to live. This part of you wants to feel good, to feel healthy, and it wants life to get better, and it wants to be happy. This small part of you wants the pain to stop. This is the part of you that is healthy.

So, I ask you one question. Are the independent actions you are taking making the world better? Are they making your life better? Are your vices improving your situation? I am not talking about in the short-term, I'm talking about your future life as well.

Consider your current relationships with others, and your vice. How are things with your parents, your siblings, your old "pre-vice" friends, your teachers, your coach, your boss? Now envision your future relationships, and remember your vice will still be there, with your wife/husband, your children (as babies, small children, teens) with your employer.

You know that silly question, "If you could have any power, what would it be?" Well, I wish I had the power to take teens into their future, but it would be two trips. One trip would be to see what happens if they don't drop their vice. They would see first-hand how it drags them down and holds them down even as adults, and how it creates a mess of every relationship they have. But then I would take them on another trip into a different future to show them how great life can be when they are living in a positive, healthy way without their vice. As an adult, I look around and I see both of these futures everywhere. I know where you will be heading if you drop your vice, and where you will be heading if you don't. Do you know?

If you can't envision your future, consider who you want to be like. Think of the adults around you. Do you have any adults in your life who you admire? Do you like the way they live and the way they approach life? Are there any that you respect? Do you admire the way they handle challenges in their lives? If so, are your actions moving you towards being like them, or away from being like them?

Edward was a student who got into a lot of trouble. He was always in detentions, he swore constantly, and smoked cigarettes and pot. To everyone around him he had an air of "I don't give a shit." One on one, he told me about how much he couldn't stand his dad. I asked if he had any respect for him. "Not a chance," was his reply. Over the next few chats (usually in detention) I learned that his dad yelled and argued a lot, swore constantly, and was a smoker. Eventually I challenged Edward by saying, "So you are turning yourself into a mirror image of someone you have no respect for. How do you feel about that?" His reply? Silence. Then, I asked if he could try to not swear in class. And he made a big effort to avoid swearing in class from that point on. He also told me a few weeks later that he was trying to quit smoking.

You can blame your parents, your siblings, your boyfriends/girlfriends, your friends, your teachers, or your boss.

You can blame their reactions to your "vice" for pushing you deeper into it. But the bottom line is this: you went out in search of self-control whether you knew it or not. Now it is your choice to better yourself. And guess what? You *are* in control.

Read the previous paragraph again, then close your eyes, and think about how you can apply it to your situation. Now I ask you, "Who do you want to become?" When you are living your life to the fullest, when you are making the world a better place, when you are acting out of compassion instead of jealousy, selfish desires, anger and self-hatred, who will you be? Now look at your life now and tell me, are you moving towards or away from who you want to be?

What are you going to have to do to get yourself on track? What healing will have to take place? What relationships in your life need tending to? We will examine all of this.

Remember it's all about you and YOU ARE IN CONTROL. Take responsibility for the unhappiness you've created in your life today. *Take responsibility for the happiness in your future.*

Reality Checks

Self-healing? How? The answer is in your hands. This book is dedicated to self-healing. Chapter 9 *Hero Training 101,* will provide you with very specific suggestions to assist you on your path towards positive change. Before we get to the Hero Training, however, the next area of "Reality Checks" is a crucial one. I have had many long talks with students who at first were convinced that they wanted to improve their lives, but after a while, they realized how much work was involved and they quit several times before they reached success. Some never made it very far and, to my knowledge, are still trapped by their vice. To help give you the motivation to escape your vice, I have listed below four key Reality Checks that you need to face. Keep in mind the importance of being open to tears. This journey will be a tough road, but crying releases your frustrations when they build up and then you can carry on with your quest. If you do this, it will ensure you will be one of the ones who make their lives better.

Be honest with yourself. Here goes...

Desire

You have to have the desire to change. It's simple. Change towards health and happiness cannot happen unless YOU want it to happen. Your parents can send you to therapy, your friends can try to help you quit, but until *you* seriously want to get better it is not going to happen. Professional help might be a crucial step in your recovery, but you have to be a key player in the plan, otherwise it simply won't work long term. Even professional help will only work when you are ready and really *want* to get better.

Remember at the beginning of the book when I asked, "Are you are unhappy?" And then I said, "Congratulations!" This is what it's all about. If you are unhappy with the way things are going, this gives you all the motivation you need to change your path. Your friends and family will be there to support you, but it is you who has to do the work. Think of a marathon runner. All along that gruelling 26-mile course they are pushing themselves on and on. Fans are standing on the side cheering, but they are not in the runner's shoes. This is *your* challenge, your race, fans or no fans. This is done *for* you, and *by* you.

Belief

Second, you have to believe that you can do it. Remember there have been countless people before you who have risen up against all odds to do the greatest things.

This is my favourite quote of all time:

"Whether you think you can or you think you can't, either way you are right." - Henry Ford.

What you believe comes true. If you think of yourself as a failure for the previous attempts at quitting your vice, then guess what? You will fail again and again. Talk to an adult smoker, one who has been smoking for many years, or even decades, and listen to the way they describe their attempts to quit. They will have many excuses, but if they think that quitting is too hard or that they are too weak, then they will never quit. The mind is incredibly powerful. As we will examine in the next chapters, you create your own reality with your thoughts. So, if you really want to quit, but you've tried and failed, then you may start to think of yourself as a failure.

"Oh, Great. One more thing to feel crappy about."

How's your self-esteem now? On top of everything else, now you are a failure. If this is the thought pattern in your head then, sorry, you will continue to fail. So, change it!

Can you quit? Stop. Look up at the wall and ask yourself.

Of course, you can. You can do anything that you set your mind to. Believe in where you want to go even when times are tough. Never lose faith in yourself.

Dis-identification

The third reality check is that you have to stop identifying with your vice. Thoughts like, "I am a Smoker," and, "I hang out with smokers," and so on, will forever trap you as a smoker. Look over the list of vices and think of what we say inside our heads: I am a cutter, I am fat, I am a slut, I am a criminal, I am a bully, I am known for my tattoos or my piercings or my black clothes, I am nothing else.

You are always telling the world not to judge you so stop judging yourself!

Changing your mind set is critical in order to improve your situation. We all want to fit in with something, whether it's playing sports, singing in a band, joining an art group, smoking up in the parking lot, or joining a street gang. Everyone will eventually find something to identify with. Then that becomes your label and, for the most part, you wear it with pride. If it is a shared vice, it's not so much what you do that you are proud of, it's that you belong to something. Is that really who you are? Is that what you will always be? Is that what you have always dreamed of becoming? Does it make you happy when you go to sleep at night? If the answers to these questions are, "No," then that is your true self telling you, "I want out." Break the cycle of your thoughts. Who are you? Really? It's time to find out.

Cut the Ties

Fourth, and very challenging, is to take a close look at your circle of friends. Do you all share the same vice? Do you do it together? Misery loves company. Engaging in these behaviours with someone else makes it not seem so bad – like you're not alone so it's OK to do it. It actually makes you feel better. I'll come back to that in a second. Let's say you overeat regularly, and you might be overweight. With your friends, you play video games and sit around and eat junk food. So, you are abusing your body and your friend is abusing his. If you don't care about your own health, you certainly can't care about your friend's health. I'll come back to this point too.

We join a group friends sometimes without choosing the quality of the friendship they provide. We pick friends because they live close to us, go to the same schools as us, or maybe because we share the same vice – that's a big one. If you start taking drugs, wow. Just watch the people appear in your life who want to share their misery with yet another lost soul. So, let's put this into perspective. This next part is so important, so crucial that I really want you to focus on it. Pause and think about your own friends as you read it.

Who are true friends? And this includes boyfriends/girlfriends. True friends will want to support you as you make your own life better. True friends want to trust and respect you. The other "friends" like you because your faults and unhealthy actions make THEM feel better about themselves.

Read that again. Now read it again. Now make a list in your mind or on paper of your friends. Next, categorize them into True Friends and "Other" Friends. If you don't know where they belong, then test it out. Tell them you want to stop doing X (whatever your common vice is.) Let's say it's drugs. Some will congratulate you. They might even join you if they wanted their own personal change, and they certainly will remain friends with you even when you don't hang out with them when they are getting high. Those are your True friends. The other friends will congratulate you at first but once you get serious about your actions, those friendships will dissolve. It's tough to hear this, but remind yourself that the only role you played was to make them feel better about themselves. Good riddance. Let them go find some other chump. You're on your way to much higher ground.

Self-Improvement - Dealing with Peers
You have two options here:
1. Fade
If you choose this route, you need to say no when your vice-friends want to hang out or are asking you to come and do the vice with them. Eventually they will get tired of asking and you can fade away from the group.
2. Talk to your vice friends
This path is a bit more challenging, but it is very telling and reinforces the kinds of friendships you have surrounded yourself with.

- *Sit down and tell your friends about your plans for change.*
- *Tell the ones closest to you first and individually. Ask them to be there with you when you tell your larger circle of friends.*
- *Be honest. Tell them that the vice isn't making your life any better. This might be a wakeup call for some of them too.*
- *Tell them it is the vice you are dropping, not them, and that you'll still be friends. But let them know you can't be around*

them while they are doing it. This is very important. If you want to be successful, you have to remove yourself from temptation.

- *Some may want to quit with you, but will not say so. They will just watch you closely to see if you succeed or fail. You decide if you succeed or fail. Are you going to show them there is a way out?*

- *Some will <u>want</u> to watch you fail. They'll be buddy, buddy with you. They'll tell you where and when everyone's meeting, they'll ask you if you want some, they will tempt you. They still want you to be their chump. They want to hold you back.*

- *Some may say, "You know what? I want to stop too." That's great, but if they are not as committed as you are, then they may cave and bring you down too. Whether you are doing this solo or with friends, your success is your success. Do not get caught up in their issues and weaknesses. If they can't do it, it is simply not their time.*

- *It's your time – forge on soldier.*

Understand this – it is absolute fact – you will find new friends. Healthier ones who want to make their lives better too. You will fuel each other's efforts and cheer each other on. They will be life-long friends and it won't matter how often you see them or what age they are or how far apart you are. They will magically appear in your life. They are like "shiny people" and are all about evolving, making their own life better, making the lives of others better, and making the world a better place. It's awesome!

Believe in where you are going. Eighty years from now on your death bed you will look back on your life and think about all that you have accomplished. The people you helped, the life you created and made better, the (self) love that fuelled you, the passion for life that you stirred in others, and most importantly how you turned your darkest hour into your greatest triumph.

Asking for Help

Getting help is an important part of healing. You might think that you are alone in your struggle, but help is out there. There are two things to consider when you are confessing your vice to someone.

What Are You Hoping to Get Out of This?

Many people tell people in their lives about their vice, but it is not in an effort to quit the vice. It may be under the disguise of wanting to quit, but in reality, they simply want attention and concern. They want to feel cared for. The vice keeps them vulnerable, in need of help, in need of others' attention. And so, in the end the confession and request for help is in vain and the vice will continue. In addition, the people who you repeatedly go to for "help," will get frustrated and lose faith in you, which furthers your downward spiral. I want to draw your attention back to reality check number one: desire. Don't ask for help until you truly want to stop, and you are ready to do 99% of the work to heal yourself.

Who Can You Trust?

In most cases, unless your home life is seriously unstable or dangerous, the best choice would be your parents. Deep down inside you know this. But if you are like every other teen I've dealt with, your parents are the last ones you want to go to. That is understandable, you are fearful of their reaction, the change to your home life and possible loss of freedom once your secret is out, and really you know you'll be letting them down. This is tough, but hopefully, eventually you can admit that the roller coaster of self-healing is going to require some understanding from the home front. Eventually having family on your side is important, but there are other people you may be more comfortable starting with if you are really scared of how your parents will react. Talk to an aunt or uncle, or grandparents, or a close adult family friend, or the parent of one of your friends, or a coach or teacher, or a counsellor at school. You can use their help to get to mom and dad through a side door in a way that it might be easier on everyone.

When my children were young my husband and I wrote a letter to them that they would receive in their early teenage years. It included this passage: Imagine, if you can, that it's coming from your own parents

We hope that you will go through your life knowing that whatever challenges you face, that you can come to us and talk openly. There will be times when you will think that we won't understand, or you will think that the issue is too big or too complicated. Do not give in to these false thoughts. There is no issue too big or too deep or too serious that we will not try to help you through. We have loved and cared for you since the day you were conceived, and we will do everything in our power to support you, guide you or just stand by you. You are never alone.

We love you more than you could possibly know.

Stay close to loved ones in mom and dad's generation, your Aunts and Uncles, or our friends that you have known your whole life. There may come a time when you are facing a difficult challenge and you might feel embarrassed or ashamed to talk to us (mom and dad) even though you shouldn't. Your own friends your age might be able to help, but their advice is limited to their life experiences and young age. This is when the adults in your life become so important. Use these wise adults, who know and love you, to talk to. It will be easier to bounce ideas off of them and they can help you, and/or help you to come to us. They love you so much. You never have to go through anything alone.

Love Mom and Dad

Now this letter, and its message, is more helpful if you come from a supportive family. If your parents are the source of your pain, or if they are dealing with their own addictions, poor coping strategies and vices, then they may not be much help for you. In this case, use the trusted adults I mentioned above in the form of teachers, coaches and school counsellors. They can help and become the support network you need, and can direct you to services in the community that will provide help as well. Schools are well equipped to deal with all kinds of issues that teens face. Support is always available.

Community Resources

There are doors that are open for you in the community in the form of kids help phone lines, counselling services, and health care professionals including addictions counsellors and mental health professionals. Your school guidance office should have contacts for them.

If you are not comfortable talking to your guidance counsellors first, the guidance office will have pamphlets for you pick up, take home and read on your own.

Just reach out.

Big Picture Points

- For many teens, it is easy for "low" to turn to "lost." Vices happen so easily and quickly. What you, at first, thought was ok to dabble in, is now taking over your personal world. You are in the "vice grip."

- Vices are the many ways we turn our A.S.A. (anxiety, sadness and/or anger) inward (internalizing stress) to harm ourselves, or outward (externalizing stress) to harm others. It is impossible to hurt others without hurting ourselves more.

- A Vice is an undesirable habit, a moral weakness, and it can turn into a negative coping strategy or even an addiction. Some examples are drug and alcohol abuse, sexual promiscuity, eating disorders, over eating, over shopping, cutting, skipping school, violent behaviour, violent video games, crime, lying, manipulative behaviour, bullying, and many more.

- Remember, vices are not the root problem. They are simply the symptoms of the underlying issues that you are having difficulty with. They are red flags that finally get noticed when all the other flags that you've thrown at the world have been ignored.

- Remember it's all about you and YOU ARE IN CONTROL. Take responsibility for the unhappiness you've created in your life today. Take responsibility for the happiness in your future.

- To heal you have to deal with the underlying situations that cause your self-esteem to fall. A healthy emotional state is the goal because that will lead to healthy life choices and an understanding of personal worth. From that point, the constant, conscious decision not to engage in the addiction has some purpose.

- Examine the four Reality Check questions to know if you are really ready to end your vice: The four are: Desire to quit, Belief that you can do it, Dis-identification with the vice, and Cutting the Ties of your vice social circle.

- Do not wait around for someone to save you. You are your own hero. Yes, you need help. Ask for it. Help is available, but only you can save you.

- You can turn your darkest hour into your greatest triumph.

CHAPTER 9
Hero Training 101

Photograph by Olivia Giroux

"Even if you are on the right track, you'll get run over if you just sit there."
-Will Rogers

I see teenagers every day who want to feel better, who want to be better. But they don't know how. I've been emphasizing in this book the importance of self-esteem and how it can be your greatest defence or your weakest link when pressure bombards you. You now know how important healthy self-esteem is. This Chapter gives you the tools to achieve and hold onto healthy self-esteem.

At the beginning of this book I told you that you have greatness inside of you. You do. Just like super powers. We have all the potential to be a Hero; our Own Hero. But we need some training. The powers you possess can be drained from you and you could lose your way again. It is critical that you are aware of the ways to refuel your energy, so you can heal yourself and stay strong. Step one of Hero Training is to take a close look at your starting point and focus on deep truths about you. Step two is to generate actions that refuel and maximize your powers. Step Three (in Chapter 10) is to change your habitual thought patterns so you live each day in the fullness of your own inner greatness and can appreciate the greatness in others.

Step One – Self-Examination

Your journey starts with self-examination: What? – Why? – How?

What is the problem?

Why is this problem there?

How do I regain control?

If you recall in the Chapter on Vices, we examined the "What" and we identified the surface problems. Now let's try to figure out why they are there. Only then can you start to regain control of your life. Healing is hard work. Are you ready? If so, then here is your first task. Get out some paper and a pen. Write each question down and spend some serious time being honest and detailed before you move onto the next question. Use the "Vices" chapter as a reference. Need motivation? Do you REALLY want life to get better? Then get to work!

Self-Healing Starter Kit

Pen and paper ready…

1. List your current vice(s) or potential (future risk) vices.
2. What is the likely Root Cause or combination of causes? (Some examples were provided in the previous chapter.)
   - Coping
   - Control
   - Notice Me
   - Self-Punishment
   - Boredom
   - Fear
   - Normal
   - Other (describe)
3. Expand on the above. What is your root cause story? Can you cry about this pain?
4. What are some problem situations that feed your vice? What are the triggers? Consider the people, events, times of day, and your emotional states when you turn to your vice.
5. Can you avoid some of these? Which ones?
6. List helpful people, places, situations that will support your healing, including professional help. Identify your safe spaces and go there as often as you can to calm yourself. Seek out your safe people and release with tears.
7. Confront the root cause. Ask yourself, what are the false beliefs that you have created in your mind, in your world? Correct them right now, here on this paper. For example: what are some excuses you have used to rationalize your vice?
8. What does the "inner doubter" – the voice inside your head – say to you that makes you lose faith in yourself? How can you confront that voice the next time it shows up?
9. Write out *Deep Truths* about who you are. Create your own or choose meaningful ones offered below.
10. List some strategies you can use. Create your own or choose meaningful ones offered below.

You might want to wait until the end of this chapter before listing out your "strategies" as some are given in more detail later on.

Deep Truths About You

Repeat these out loud to yourself:

- I deserve to be safe from harm.
- I can be happy in my life.
- I need to be positive more often.
- I can learn from my own mistakes.
- I can allow myself to cry when I need to
- I can let go of pain from the past.
- I can let go of bitterness and resentment.
- I am in control of my own happiness.
- My vice is not making my life any better. I am better off without it.
- Help and guidance is available to me.
- How I feel is my own response to situations.
- No one else can make me feel a certain way.
- I can change how I respond to triggers and stresses.
- Worrying only creates more worries.
- My body is a miracle and it is up to me to take care of it for my entire life.
- I am a wonderful, incredible being.
- I want to love myself on the inside and I believe one day I will.

All of these are true about you. There may be some you can connect to more easily today, but they are all true. Choose the ones that speak to you, and create some of your own.

Write them down, read them often, believe in them. You are worth it.

Actions

Now, reading and writing and believing can get the ball rolling, but only positive actions can keep you moving in the right direction. In addition to writing and reading these deep truths often, use the following strategies to create a healthy mindset that you can carry with you through life. We'll get into specific details on many of them and feel free to create some positive ones of your own.

Strategies

- Get outside – especially in nature.
- Get regular exercise.
- Focus on the positive – what have you got going for you – be grateful.
- Focus on solutions not problems.
- Keep a journal – use it to release your frustrations and to focus on solutions. Or use it as a gratitude journal and write things that you are grateful for. For example, write or read five things you are grateful for each night before you go to bed.
- Cry – really bawl – release your pent-up energy and then you'll have access to calm, clear thinking. Make sure you are in a safe place, with safe a person who will not judge you for this, they will simply let you let it out
- Keep busy – volunteer, join a club, play sports, learn to play an instrument.
- Social causes – learn about world issues and join a group to make a difference in the world.
- Practise time management.
- Be a self-advocate – speak up for yourself, ask for help, ask for guidance, ask for fair treatment.
- Seek help, reach out – talk to a guidance counsellor, coach, teacher, therapist, life coach.
- Do yoga, meditation, deep breathing.

- Adjust your "self-talk" – promote self-love, self-worth, self-esteem.
- Improve your communication skills to avoid confrontations.
- Become aware of "reminders" that will help you to notice when you are off track. Be thankful for them and heed them.
- Create and listen to your "happy mix." A music playlist that is positive and motivating.
- Less 'watching' more 'doing' – reset your free time so you are *really living* more often then you are on your screen/device watching others *really living*.
- Eat regularly and eat healthy foods.
- Read books that are inspirational.
- Explore your faith.
- Surround yourself with positive people, places and things, including music and activities.
- Get enough sleep.
- Write your *Deep Truths* in places where you will see them often.
- Take full responsibility for your actions and words and the consequences that follow.
- Learn to say, "I'm sorry" and "thank you" to the people in your life.

Let's take a closer look at some of these....

The Big Picture

When I look at the teenagers around me that seem to really be making the most of their existence and enjoying life, I see a group with similar characteristics. One key feature is that they are able to focus on the big picture.

Let me explain.

It is easy, too easy, to get caught up in what you don't have, what you don't look like, who you are not dating, what marks you are not getting, and whose attention you are not getting. Let's face it, every form of media, whether it's music, TV shows, videos, or magazines, they all make you feel like you need more stuff or that you need to look different in order to feel fulfilled. Throw in parental pressures, pressures from school, work and friends, and you have the perfect recipe for the "I'm not good enough syndrome." This happens when we give into the "Little Picture" which is essentially "all about me." ME ME me.

As a teen, you are at a dangerous time in life because it's a time when you can get lost in yourselves. While personal happiness and fulfillment is one of the ultimate goals, focusing on personal misery is, well, selfish. This might hurt to hear, but it's coming from someone who was selfish in my thoughts as a teenager. I used to think, "How can she/he/they do this to ME? Why is this happening to ME?" It is just like the history of astronomy where we used to believe that the sun, moon and all the planets revolved around the earth – an egocentric view. Then we discovered, shock of all shocks, that earth was not the center of the universe but instead part of a much larger cosmos. I too have evolved, I have matured and now as I look back I see that some teens do not fall into this trap of "me and my little world." Somehow, there are teenagers out there that do make it through these wild years with their head firmly on their shoulders and smiles on their faces. So how do they do it? I call it big picture vs little picture.

Teens who take interest in world issues such as human rights, animal rights, environmental issues, for example, are exposing themselves to the larger issues facing the world. They realize that their personal problems are incredibly small in comparison to these larger issues. You might ask, "How is taking on the world's problems going to make me feel better about my own life?" Well, it comes down to what you do with that information. We are all exposed to the world's problems, just pick up a newspaper and flip through some articles and you will get a dose of enough negativity to sink a ship. That is not where you want to get your information.

Ignore the papers, they bombard us with so much pain that we become numb to it. We turn off our emotions and then carry on in a ME, ME, me world.

Instead try to get involved with a school group or club that discusses specific world issues and then actually DO SOMETHING about it. Raise money for a specific cause, or simply raise awareness in others. Be part of the solution. Only then can you feel good about the craziness of the world. And as a side benefit, you are taking the focus off yourself. Your personal problems will pale in comparison as you focus your time and energy on making the world a better place. We are all passionate about something whether it is your hair style, your favourite sports team, your clothing, your body size, your addictions, your pain, or your cause. Ask yourself: What am I passionate about? What could you talk about for hours? What gets you going? What are you spending your waking hours focusing on? Really be honest.

Once you identify what you are passionate about, the next question is: Does my passion help to make the world a better place? If it is an egocentric or self-centered passion, then the answer is likely no. So, learn about something bigger and become passionate about that. You will be amazed at where it takes you. And you can take a more self-centered passion and make it bigger. For example, maybe your passion is fashion. You could translate that into human rights activism by making sure you only buy clothes that have been manufactured ethically, without the use of child labour, for example.

If you look around, you will see evidence of teens looking at the big picture all around you.

Do you know any teens at your school who volunteer? It could be at an animal shelter, or with people with special needs, or with elderly people or children.

Do you know of any teens who donate money for a cause they truly believe in?

Do you know any teens who are donating time or money for a local or international cause?

Do you have any clubs at your school who meet regularly to learn more about world issues and environmental solutions? If so go and check them out.

Don't give into the social divide between the "popular" teens and the ones who join the world issues clubs. The so called popular teens might snub the activists, but as a group the popular kids are all stuck in the egocentric world of "Little ME" and they all have really crappy self-esteem – although they might be good at hiding it. On the other hand, the activist kids, while they also have their issues, are exposed to things in their life that bring them fulfillment, so they are more stable and have a better chance at sailing instead of sinking.

Less Watching, More Doing
How do you spend your free time? With a constant world of entertainment at your fingertips, it is really easy to watch other people living life. How often are you an observer of the creations of others without actually taking any action in your own life? Do you love to watch sports but don't feel confident enough to play the sports yourself? Do you love movies, but don't create your own adventures in life? Do you love music but don't play any instruments? Do you adore superstars but don't think you have any talent? Observing can be relaxing and fun, whether it is movies, music, YouTube, etc. But if all that you do is observe and you don't live the adventures yourself, your sense of your abilities will diminish and so will your self-esteem.

Taking action and "really living" opens you up to challenges, resilience, adventure and a sense of accomplishment. The goal here is not for you to become famous, it is for you to take action – to really live – to see what you can do.

Play an instrument, enter a community run, play sports, create a game for your friends, build or fix something, go camping, write something, create art, try a new form of art, cook something new, help someone, organize something, go somewhere new, plan a vacation. REALLY LIVE LIFE. As often as you can. Spend your free time building your own life.

Stop Being Boring

"I'm bored." In my house, we have a saying: "Only boring people get bored." Get out there and try new things. A great way to get a new perspective on your life is to explore and find something new that you'd love to do. Whether it is in the form of art, music, dance, sports, or fixing things, seeing yourself grow and learn helps build your inner worth. There is a catch though. Do it as longs as you *feel good* while you are doing it. For example, while you are painting or playing guitar, are you thinking about your own misery, perhaps expressing your pain by painting it or singing about it? In the beginning that can help you to identify your pain and release it, but if you are stuck in a rut where all of your art or music is revolving around your pain then that is not helping your situation. Try to remember what it is about painting or guitar that you love so much, focus on the art itself, not the pain inside. Become passionate about something positive in your life. You don't need anyone else's approval to pursue this. Others in your life will probably not have the same passion for it, but that does not matter. Do it for you.

Some of you might find that working with children is rewarding. If you take this on, try to remember that children are like blank slates and become the product of their environment. Their self-esteem issues start at a very early age just as yours did. Many young people find helping children to be very rewarding and it can give a new perspective to their own childhood. Have you considered working or volunteering with children as a coach, volunteering in a classroom, babysitting, or volunteering to take foster kids for a walk? You might come to understand that we are a product of our surroundings, and that each of us is truly innocent inside. This understanding helps us forgive each other and forgive ourselves.

So, a final note. If there is a quiet moment in your day when nothing is going on, this doesn't mean it's boring. It's just a quiet moment. Relax. Be still, be quiet. It's ok. No one's going to judge you. Learn to appreciate those quiet times and feel peaceful. Life can and will get very busy. These moments that you call boring are actually an incredible gift of peace.

Avoid Nature Deficit Disorder – Get Outside

We, as a society, have enclosed ourselves indoors and created every imaginable convenience so that we do not have any need to connect with our natural surroundings. Researchers are now starting to understand the numerous negative impacts this is having on our population.

Richard Louv, in his 2005 book *Last Child in the Woods,* coined the phrase Nature Deficit Disorder (NDD) to describe what happens to people who rarely go outside for the sake of being outside in nature. Suffers of NDD experience depression, a disrupted sleep cycle and become so disconnected from their surroundings that they do not understand how intimately we fit into nature. This disconnect from nature not only harms them but also leads to an *absentminded* destruction of the natural world.

NDD sufferers experience depression because of a lack of sunlight and their natural sleep cycles are disrupted because they ignore the body's natural signals for sleep. The need for sleep doesn't fit into their "clock time" schedule, so they ignore it.

I'm going to pause here and explain a personal story. I am a nature lover. I run the environmental club at my school and many people know me as an environmentalist, but they don't know why. Here is my story: I was really depressed for a couple of years as a teenager. I went into counselling and I took antidepressants. These may have helped, but I know deep down that it was nature that saved me. My dad is a nature lover and he always took us camping and on canoe trips. During those dark times of sadness, I always felt amazing when I got out into nature. I felt healthy and free, no one was judging me, and I didn't judge myself when I was out there. I was able to just BE. The trips we'd go on were challenging but I never backed down. Meeting these challenges made me feel capable and strong. When I was not in nature and feeling down I'd start to think back about how I felt in nature and I started to seek nature to heal myself from the inside. To this day, I walk or run, snowshoe or bike in nature to reconnect and release sadness and anger. Camping trips will always be an important part of my life and the way I raise my family. I am a nature lover and an environmentalist because I owe a lot to nature. Living green is one of my ways of saying Thank You for helping me save myself.

You will never know how powerful this is until you try it. Make a goal to get outside regularly for sunshine, fresh air and exercise. Nature is incredibly healing. I truly believe that stress is an indoor illness. Throughout this book I have been talking about seeking safe spaces, so you can calm your brain down. Nature is the ultimate emotionally safe space. There is absolutely no judging, comparison, no fitting in, no right or wrong, no anger, no arguing. Being in nature is so incredibly freeing. Every single student I have ever brought on a nature excursion has felt calmer and more relaxed. Everyone feels better. To improve all areas of your life, get outside and into nature as often as possible.

Stop polluting/destroying nature - connect with it instead

All around us we see or hear or are told about the destruction of nature. Where do we get this idea that one life is worth more or less than another life? It can only happen in a mind that questions their own worth. Most people do not realize their own value, so the value of nature is almost incomprehensible to them. When you doubt your own value, it opens you up to doubt the value of others whether it is another person, an animal, a tree, it doesn't matter what you target, it is all the same – you are questioning the value of life.

Realize your connection to the world. Expose yourselves to nature. Look at a tree, a flower, a bird – really look at it until you can see its perfection. I always tell my students that I love myself.

Of course, at first, they look at me funny and think that I must be conceited. Then I go on to explain that I have learned to understand the incredible perfect life within me. I continue by saying that loving myself opens me up to see the incredible life in each of them – I tell them that I love them too. I can look at each and every one of my students and see perfection. Then I explain that I can also look at a tree or a squirrel or a bee and see perfection too. I can think of all of you reading this now and I know without any doubt that you are perfection too. Sure, your thoughts might be a little off track, but deep down you are life – incredible, perfect life.

With the brief encounters we have with nature, it is easy and all too common to say, "This is boring." Whether it is a family hike, a scenic drive or school field trip, at a quick glance it is boring. You can't change the channel, it isn't loud or fast paced and exciting and so in your mind it is *not worthy* of your attention. I see it all the time in students. The most rewarding times of my teaching career are when I have brought students into nature, especially on camping trips. Days in the natural world, with no contact with "civilization," and they all become transformed, because at some point they understand the importance of where they are. They also start to realize how "being" in nature releases them from their "little me" world.

You don't have to be deep in the forest to feel connected with nature. Try sitting at a local park and then close your eyes and listen to the birds and the wind in the trees, or lay down on your back on the grass and watch the clouds, or look up at the moon and stars at night. You are a part of something much bigger. Embrace that, connect with it.

Exercise

It has been brought up many times in this book that by facing challenges we find our greatness. Playing sports, whether it is team or individual, is an amazing avenue to find your inner strength. By pushing yourself and working harder to achieve something, you can't help but feel great. Every time you exercise, your body releases endorphins which are better than any high a drug could give you. On top of that, physical improvements come quickly, and you soon find that something you thought was hard to do is now easy. The benefits of exercise are enormous: you see improved health, decreased stress, improved relationships, brighter moods, better sleep, improved stamina, and overall positivity. It's amazing! But remember the quote back in Chapter 6 on Food and Body that says:

"Exercise for how it makes you feel on the inside, not for how it makes you look on the outside."

Challenge yourself. Sign up for a team or a community bike event or a charity run. This will give you the motivation you need to get off the couch. Do it with a friend or, if you don't have anyone else who is as motivated as you are, do it on your own. Once you get involved, you will attract healthy happier people into your life.

Unplug – Connect with Yourself

Let's talk about walking. When was the last time you went for a walk? Ok, I can just imagine your immediate response to this question. "I walk to school every day. I walk to the mall. I walk my dog." Or, "I walk to my friend's house." Alright, so you know how to put one foot in front of the other, but let me ask you this, when was the last time you walked alone without any electronic device? No music in your ears, no electronic communication with the internet or friends? When was the last time you walked for the purpose of walking without any form of electronic distraction? There is a wonderful quote by German Philosopher Friedrich Nietzsche:

"Great thoughts are conceived by walking"

I couldn't agree more, although I believe this to be true of running as well.

Wonderful, imaginative thoughts come into your mind or, if you are really lucky, your thoughts will slow down and become more focused and restful. People who meditate train their minds to do this in their quest for inner peace.

I have always chosen to search out nature wherever I lived and I walk quietly in nature almost daily. I can lose myself in nature and that is what I love about it. The "little me syndrome" has no place there. In many ways, it is therapy for me. I have used these walks to seek guidance in becoming a better partner, parent, and teacher. I ask for guidance in presenting lessons to my children and my students that will reach them and guide them toward their own inner strength. Ninety percent of the reflective lessons I have taught in the classroom came to me while I was walking or running. In fact, much of this book came to me through thoughts I had while out in nature. I would walk, relax, observe, listen, and thoughts would come, and I'd go home and write them down. In fact, this section you are reading is the result of today's walk.

Sometimes negative thoughts enter your mind and you may begin to focus on your problems. In times like this you must ask for positive solutions and then be still, be aware, and these solutions will present themselves to you. Afterwards, focus your energy and thoughts on the positive solutions. When you walk in peace and quiet, you are giving yourself an opportunity to become aware of your inner strength as well as your surroundings. When you allow yourself to "be" in the moment, you release yourself from thinking, or more accurately *over*-thinking. You begin to realize that your daily drama is not the most important thing in existence.

But why unplug? You might respond, "I listen to music and that helps me think." Yes, you have thoughts in your head, but your ideas are not your own, they belong to the person who wrote the song. Music may be OK sometimes, but you may want to try letting your own thoughts guide you.

Give yourself time each day to calm down, to remove yourself from your emotional drama, and let your soul guide you. Nothing happens by accident, everything happens for a reason, give your mind time to process the events and then consider the solutions or positive aspects of you and what you have learned. Let your thoughts show you your inner strength, your resilience. This cannot happen with your electronic distractions or devices.

If unplugging seems completely too crazy for you, try listening to instrumental music (no lyrics.) It comes in all types of music so you can still hear the beats that you like, but there's no voice filling your head with ideas and emotions. Music is a wonderful thing and it has been around almost as long as humans have, but we have filled our music with words that the writer or singer feels, and those feelings get absorbed into your head. When this is angry or negative music, this can end up keeping you down. If you give your brain a chance to rest you'd be surprised at what you might find out about yourself. You need peace to find peace.

There is a time when sad music may be helpful. If you have been holding onto pain and suppressing it, those bottled up emotions can truly destroy you from the inside out. If you can listen to sad music in a safe place, alone or with safe people, it can move you to tears. If you can let yourself really cry hard, that is an important release. It is very healthy and an important part of you moving through sad, complicated times and coming out stronger on the other side. Keep in mind, we've been telling people for centuries to stop crying, but recent brain science has confirmed it's one of the best things we can do to release our emotions. So yes, go ahead and put on the sad tunes too.

Tip: Create your own Happy Mix:

Can't let go of the Music for certain busy times of the day? Create a Happy Mix for yourself. Download and gather a huge list of songs that makes you feel good about yourself and the world. Let the positivity flow – let your thoughts and emotions run at a higher level. Listen to music that brings you up, not down.

For those of you who are in a place where you think you have nothing to offer the world, and you feel you have no worth, I would highly encourage you to get outside. With absolute certainly I can tell you that you have incredible potential and that you just need to open yourself up to the idea. Regardless of the perceived difficulties facing you, the answers lie within. All the great thinkers of all time have known that the answers were inside of them. The key is to understand that we need to slow down, remove the distractions, and just listen.

Energy is everywhere. Every minute of every day we make decisions to be working with positive energy or negative energy. Be conscious of your decisions.

When thoughts become overwhelming, go into nature where the energy is pure and positive.

Avoid Drainers

Energy flows towards what you are focusing on, so try to be aware of drainers. Drainers will draw energy out of you, and will leave you tired and weakened. They will draw you away from positivity and towards negativity. Drainers include certain friends or family members who complain all the time and want you to share in their misery. Everyone needs to vent at some point, but for many people all they do is vent. In any given conversation, they will find something frustrating, and will complain. Can you think of any drainers in your social circle or family? Is it possible that you have been a drainer to others?

Drainers can also include sad and angry music. I mentioned earlier, sad and angry music can guide us to an important release, but select a safe time and place so you really can release emotion. If you listen to this music throughout your day, you will train yourself NOT to fully release emotion. You'll be stifling it, and also not allowing yourself to enjoy enjoyable times. Yes, music is amazing, but you don't need to carry the sadness or anger with you all the time. Sometimes we like the song because we can relate to the lyrics, but remember that it keeps you stuck in your sad and angry mindset. Recognize the negative energy you feel. If you are not going to release your emotion at this moment, maybe, it's time to change your tune, or just turn it off.

Social media can be another drainer, changing your mood quickly by drawing your attention away from positive energy. How many times have you been stopped dead in your tracks after checking a status online? You were doing fine until you checked it, now you are thrown into A.S.A. (anxiety, sadness and/or anger). Whatever positive energy you were carrying was drained.

I have been around many of these drainers and I have learned to protect myself. If it is a person, I can put up a mental wall, I can hear them complain about life and I can sit with them and hear them out, and I visualize the wall protecting me from their negative energy. I still love them, but I am not going to let them drag me down to where they are. When they are done I say, "Do you need a hug?" I offer a positive spin on the situation if I can, but I try hard to not be affected by their misery. I try to reinforce to myself that this is their A.S.A. not mine. After talking to them, I wander off and think about things that I am grateful for in my life and I feel better right away. When it comes to electronic drainers like music or media, I simply control my exposure. I reduce it and use it only when I am strong, and I can keep it in perspective. If I see myself being drawn in I back out and shut it off. At these times, I can see through the shallowness of it all and smile that I don't belong to that space anymore.

Seek Relaxation

It is important to find relaxation on a regular basis. There are physiological benefits to slowing your mind and body down and there are also spiritual benefits. Some of these are an awareness of deeper levels of consciousness, which you can reach when you slow your body down. But if these seems airy-fairy to you I'll explain it another way.

Relaxation gives us perspective. If we know what it feels like to be truly relaxed (without drugs or alcohol by the way) then we can learn to recognize when we are starting to feel stressed and do something about it. So many people are walking around as stress balls and they don't even realize it because it feels normal to them. Yet inside, they are very unhealthy and emotionally unstable. If you feel all wound up all the time, a typical day for you may look something like this.

Wake up late. Argue with mom. Late for school. Catch a busy, loud bus. Get to school, crap didn't study for quiz. Talk to friends, "Oh my gawd! She did what?" Boring class, sneak rap music in my ear bud. Next class - test. Shit. Sit in silence. Try to concentrate. Try to remember. Try to think. Can't do it. Leave class pissed off. Fight with the ex in the hall. And on and on it goes.

There is no break. Stress, stress, stress, but it feels normal, normal, normal because it's all you've ever known. Your body and mind want to relax. They are tired. But it seems we've forgotten how. Maybe that is why so many people use drugs and alcohol to get the temporary rest they crave. Unfortunately, that just ends up making life harder in the end, adding more stress, and so the circle continues.

If you take the time to relax, alone in silence every once in a while, and focus your thoughts only on your breathing or the movement in the trees, then your body responds to you. So, does your mind. It opens up to deeper levels that can provide new perspective on the surface thoughts that fill up your brain during non-relaxed hours of the day. With new perspective, you can sift through the meaningless thoughts that get you all wound up and control your emotions. You can prevent the internalization and externalization of stress that we have discussed and then you can deal with the heart of the issue because you are not clouded by emotion. The bottom line is this. If you can teach yourself what it feels like to be relaxed while you are sober, you will be able to calm yourself down when the pressure is high. To do this you retrain your mind to know that a relaxed state is normal. Once in this state, you can recognize when your surface thoughts and emotions are getting out of control and then move quickly to get yourself out of the situation or use a natural technique – like focusing on your breath – to calm yourself down. It is easy to retrain your mind. All it takes about 10 minutes a day and it is well worth it.

Sharing Your Gifts

You are at a turning point in your life. You have pathways to steer towards and pathways to steer away from. The strategies described above combined with the deep truths about you are designed to help you steer towards a solid, confident you. Along the way you will learn a great deal about yourself and how you view your place in the world. The most obvious lessons will come when you look at others, see their pain, and recognize that you were once where they are. When these moments happen, you will realize how far you have come and how glad you are to be out of that place. Then you will be in a position to reach back and offer a hand to someone else in need.

Big Picture Points

- *"Opportunity is missed by most people because it is dressed in overalls and looks like work." – Thomas Edison*

- *Do you want to feel better? Are you really ready? Then get to work! Here is your first task. Get out some paper and a pen. Do the Self-Healing Starter Kit in this Chapter.*

- *It's time to realize some Deep Truths about you. You deserve to be safe from harm. You deserve to be happy in your life. You can let go of pain from the past. You can let go of bitterness and resentment. You are in control of your own happiness. Your vice is not making your life any better. And you are better off without it.*

- *There are many strategies you can use to heal yourself on the inside. Give them a try. You are worth it.*

- *Use strategies to lose the "I'm not good enough" syndrome. This syndrome happens when you lose sight of the big picture and give in to the little me. Personal happiness and fulfillment is the ultimate goal, but focusing on personal misery is just selfish.*

- *Get out there and try new things. A great way to get a new perspective is to explore and find something healthy that you love to do. Whether it is in the form of art, music, dance, sports, or fixing things, seeing yourself grow helps you to build your inner worth.*

- *Learn how shortcuts like connecting with nature, getting regular exercise, and unplugging can lift you immediately out of A.S.A.*

- *Along your journey, you will learn a great deal about yourself and how you view your place in the world. The most obvious lessons will come when you look at others, see their pain, and recognize that you were once where they are. When these moments happen, you'll realize how far you have come and how glad you are to be out of that place. This is a great time to reach back and offer a hand to someone else in need.*

CHAPTER 10
Finding Your Greatness

Photograph by Olivia Giroux

This final chapter is dedicated to your thought patterns; to the way you think and react to events and circumstances in your life. It's time to retrain your brain so you never fall back to the old self-defeating, self-sabotaging ways.

First let's see how far you have come.

You Are Aware Now

By now you know the importance of:

- Healing yourself from the inside.

- Having a positive sense of self-worth and true self-esteem and the impact that has on your decisions and actions.

- Appreciating the true value of yourself and others, and not hiding behind attention seeking, power seeking or distraction behaviours.

- Using healthy coping strategies to deal with your A.S.A. (Anxiety, Sadness and Anger)

- Allowing tears and crying to release pent-up emotions, so you can think clearly afterwards.

- Making better decisions with respect to family, friends, school, career, dating, relationships, drugs and alcohol, food, your body and health.

- Taking responsibility for your actions.

You are also aware that:

- You have the power and the strength within you to forgive, to love, and to heal yourself.

- You have many sources of support around you.

- While you may have some outer habits that need to change, on the inside you are capable and strong.

The Power of Thoughts

This first point for some of you may be difficult to comprehend so you may want to quickly dismiss it. Remain open. For others it might sound familiar, or make you smile because you not only understand this concept – you believe it, have used it, and have seen it in action.

Here it is: Your thoughts determine who you are.

You have read it many times in this book: you create your life. You create the good things that happen in your life and you create the bad. The amazing part is that you create it with your thoughts and actions. If you generate positive thoughts, positive results come back. If you put out negative thoughts, you get negative results back. Basically, you get back what you put out.

So, if you are going to complain, you will get more things to complain about. If you worry, you will get more things to worry about, if you live in fear, you'll get more things to be afraid of, and if you focus on negativity then more negative things will manifest in your life.

Great news! The opposite is also true. If you focus on being positive, then positive things will manifest in your life. If you can look on the bright side, see the glass half full, you will manifest more events to feel good about. If you focus on the small joys in life, then more joy will come to you. If you think "I can do this," then you will eventually succeed. If you focus on calm, you will experience peace regardless of where you are and what is going on around you. If you are open to planning and believing in a better life, then you will find wonderful opportunities and circumstances that will lead you up higher and higher.

More and more people around the world are coming into awareness of the power of positive thinking. When you come to this place you will realize how much fun life is, how amazing it is to be alive. And you will truly come alive. It is amazing. And every single one of you can make it to this place.

The hardest part is kicking the old habit and falling back into a negative mindset. But the good news is that every day is a new day and every thought is a chance for a new beginning. I've said it before and I'll say it again (my favourite saying.) "Whether you think you can or you think you can't, either way you are right." (Henry Ford.) Do you believe in your own power?

A Glimmer of Hope

I know many young people who have really tough lives. They are hardened by it, and they *believe* that life sucks and life is hard and that things won't get any better. Well if that's what you believe, then that is what you will experience.

Many teens feel hopeless at some point in their lives. They sometimes feel doomed, like there is no way out. I hear of so many tragic stories of teen suicide and it breaks my heart that these young people felt there was no way out of their sadness. I have learned that in life what you believe eventually manifests in your life. So my advice to someone in their darkest hour as you are hoping life will get better, is to give yourself a small glimmer of hope.

Even if the hope is only 1% of your thoughts, hold on to that glimmer. Instead of giving your attention to the other 99%, focus your attention on that 1% of hope. Use it as motivation to try the tips in this book or to take the positive advice of those around you. Do you know what will happen when you focus on that glimmer of hope? The 1% will grow. And you will see the results in your life. With each improvement, you will gain confidence that you can continue to improve your life. YOU ARE YOUR OWN HERO.

Consider the plight of Nelson Mandela, a black South African imprisoned for 27 years for opposing the apartheid movement. Even after 27 years in prison, he did not lose hope. He was inspired by the poem "Invictus." "I am the master of my fate, the captain of my soul." He went on to become the President of South Africa.

Forgiveness

Mistakes happen. They are a part of life. Making mistakes is how we learn. Mistakes are critical to our learning. They send us a consequence, so we remember to not make the same mistake twice. So, do not be afraid of making a mistake, and if you do make one, learn from it and move on. Forgive yourself. Do not judge yourself or others on their mistakes. I find people who are extremely judgemental of others are also extremely judgemental of themselves. They often make hurtful comments about the mistakes of others and at the same time are fearful of making their own mistakes. They have created a pain cycle and then live in it.

If someone has wronged you, hurt you, bothered you, do not hold that anger or sadness that it caused. Let it go. It is not beneficial to anyone to gossip or complain or bring it up over and over, or hold it over their head like a threat, or to bully them or tease them. Let it go. When you can forgive someone and look past their faults, it opens you up to see the wonderful sides of people you would not have seen before.

If someone wrongs you over and over, repeatedly hurts you, then don't dwell on it. Don't let their actions drag you down. If you need to, cry it out on your own, and then when you have released your frustrations, try to recognize *their* pain. Healthy individuals would not do that to you. You need to remove yourself from them. Distance yourself and move forward and leave them behind. Let it go. If you don't, it will eat you up inside so release it and move on.

Finding the Greatness in You

"A pessimist sees the difficulty in every opportunity; An optimist sees the opportunity in every difficulty." — Winston Churchill.

How do you face challenges? So many people avoid dealing with the challenges in their lives. This avoidance can surface in many ways:

- You could come up with excuses why you can't do it or can't try.
- You could blame the authority figures in your life (parents, teacher, bosses, coaches) for creating the challenges.

- You could say the challenge is stupid and not worth trying for – "This is stupid, this is boring."
- You could get down on yourself and give up – "I can't do this."
- You could become so busy doing insignificant things that you don't have time to do significant things that are challenging.

Facing Challenges Leads to Greatness

If you really want to feel better about yourself, then you have to feel capable in life,

In order for you to feel capable, you have to use your strengths.

In order to *see* your strengths, you have to try, again and again.

In order to *believe* in your strengths, you have to achieve something.

In order to achieve something, you have to face your challenges.

In order to face your challenges, you have to step outside your comfort zone.

So… to really feel better, you have to step outside of your comfort zone.

Only by doing this will you find your inner strength and capabilities.

Every time you do this, you will feel better and better. As other challenges arise you deal with them more easily because you truly know you can. Life gets easier and more wonderful. You end up living a life that you are amazed to live and able to look back on your accomplishments and be proud.

Yes, you have a challenge in front of you, Step outside of your comfort zone and face it.

You have greatness inside of you! Give yourself the opportunity to shine.

If you are unhappy, stressed, dealing with anxiety, sadness and/or anger, then one of your biggest challenges, which also means one of your greatest opportunities, is to feel better.

"We often miss opportunity because it is dressed in overalls and looks like work." — Thomas A. Edison.

Letting Go of Artificial Layers

We create identities for ourselves, and we define ourselves by those descriptions: I am a baseball player, I am Black, I am Muslim, I am a girl, I am a smoker, I am a cutter, I am stupid, and so on. All this builds layers on your identity. These layers create separation, because they make us focus on our differences with others. But these differences aren't real. We've just made them up. If we look at ourselves at a deeper level, as a human being or a living being, we can see our similarities with all other human beings and with other living beings too. We can feel a connection, a commonality, and it is a way to bridge gaps and a way to prevent arguments and fights. Focus on the similarities you share and you and those around you will be much happier.

I'll share a story of two boys who got into an argument in one of my Science classes. They were from very different backgrounds and knew nothing about each other. I made them stay after class, which was lunch hour, and made them sit together and eat lunch alone in the room. I gave them specific questions to ask each other, and they were to report back to me what they had learned about the other person including ten things they had in common. They talked quietly for the whole lunch and then reported back to me. In the end, they did not become great friends, but I did ask one of them years later if there had been any confrontations between them and he said nothing since that day.

Focus on the similarities not the differences. When I say focus on the similarities I don't mean for you to give up your individuality. When you can embrace the similarities you share with people, you can also begin to embrace and respect their uniqueness and your own uniqueness too. It is not about comparisons and judgement. It doesn't matter who is better because the truth is no one is better than anyone else, we all have equal value. Recognize the similarities, embrace and respect the differences.

Be Authentic, Be Real

When we talk about similarities, we do not mean joining the media trends in order to fit in. The similarities are the *deep truths in you* discussed in the previous chapter and these are the deep truths in everyone else too. You have to dig to find your own value and when you do recognize that value, you see the value in others too. Be authentic, be real. Authenticity will shine when you filter through the warped media pressures and be truly who you are. So often we give in and give up too easily to the values of the media. What media tells you is "cool" or is "in," what music to listen to, what clothes to wear, or what gadget to own. Many young people give up things they love because they don't want to be laughed at or excluded in any way, and in doing so they lose their authenticity. They become fearful of social embarrassment, of social failure. If this is where you are, then you won't take risks, and if you don't take risks then you won't push the boundary to explore your strengths and your passions. By following along with the media trends, you are in essence avoiding your own greatness. So, find strength in your own authenticity.

Take Risks, Step Out of Your Comfort Zone.

I am not talking about risk that could cause you physical harm, like diving into water when you don't know the depth. I'm talking about taking risks by trying new ways of looking at a situation. Step outside your conventional responses and try new things. If you think "Oh I can't do that!", then you are right. If you are scared to try something new such as a new sport, or a new course, a new activity, a new job, a new way to problem solve for a solution, then ask yourself, "What am I afraid of? Am I afraid of failure? How will I know what I am capable of if I don't try?"

Start with the possibility of improvement and use that to create a better life.

Letting Go of a Victim Mentality

Stop living like you are a victim in life.

Anyone can live their life like a victim. "This happened to me" or "this happens to me." They can re-live tragedies of their past over and over.

But what if you really were a victim? Your parents got divorced, your house was broken into, you were assaulted, and the list could go on. Ok, a very bad thing happened to you. You were a victim in a specific event. But if you hold onto that event and make it your excuse for your actions (or inactions), behaviors and failings then you are living with a victim mentality. I can't do well in school because mom and dad are divorced. I can't have a healthy relationship because I was cheated on.

I see victim mentality in many people. A horrible event dictates the actions for months and years to come. Yes, a bad thing happened to you, but now you are causing more bad things to happen and blaming them on your past.

"A victim mentality says that the past dictates who you are today." – Eckhart Tolle.

But you cannot change the past, you can only release it and connect with where you are right now. Let your thoughts and actions today dictate your future. If the past created how you feel this moment, then get busy creating your future the way you want it. Be a survivor.

Jack Canfield, author of the Chicken Soup for the Soul books, grew up in a dysfunctional family. He thought it made him different until he discovered that psychologists now believe that about 85% of families are dysfunctional. At that moment, he suddenly realized his situation was not so unique. The important thing to remember is, where are you going now? What are you going to do to make your life better? And what are you going to do to make the world a better place? How are you going to turn negative into positive?

What Do You Want

Look to the future – what do you want out of life?

On one level, you could ask for things like:

- Cars
- A house
- Clothes
- Money
- A good job
- A boyfriend or girlfriend
- Maybe you want to get married
- Some of you want to have children

But don't forget to also strive to reach the "big picture goals" such as:

- **Good health**
- **Time** to be with the ones you love
- **Patience** to treat yourself and loved ones with the respect you all deserve
- **Wisdom** to not repeat the errors of your past, or your parents' errors
- **Faith** to know there is more to life and more to you then you can see on the surface level
- **Inner peace** so you can calmly handle the twists and turns that life brings

Then, when you are thinking of these things, ask yourself, are my current actions bringing me closer to or farther away from these big picture goals?

Here and Now

Focus on the Present moment – it's the only thing that's real. The past is gone, and the future doesn't exist yet. But what you do in this moment determines your next moment. That's why the present is so important.

When we focus on the past we live in regret or longing.

When we focus on the future we live in anticipation, worry or fear.

When we can bring ourselves into the present moment – life is simple, you deal with the task at hand.

Here's an example:

I am in a fight with Nick and I have a test next class, but really all I have to do is walk down this hall and put one foot in front of the other and breath. Wow that simplifies things. I'll focus on the test when the paper is in front of me and I'll deal with Nick when I see him at the end of the day. One foot in front of the other, inhale, exhale.

The present moment is much easier to deal with. Try using triggers to bring yourself into the present moment and remind yourself to breath. For example, every time someone speaks on the PA system in your school or every time you see someone close a locker. At home, every time you touch a door handle, or drop something, or you hear your phone ringtone. Let these insignificant events remind you to be peaceful, and clear your mind of past memories and future projections. Neither of those are real. What do I need to do now? Breathe. Be.

Have you ever been so immersed in an assignment or a task that you entered a zone? Your entire focus was on what you were doing. It is a really, neat feeling and generally that state of presence produces very good results. That is one of my favourite reasons to play sports. When I am out on the field, I don't think about anything else except what I have to do right now. I feel the same when I am writing. When have you been truly present? What where you doing? Can you create that focus at other times of the day? It may take a bit of practise, but you can learn to be present at any time. This is true inner peace.

Peace.
It does not mean to be in a place where there is
no noise, trouble or hard work.
It means to be in the midst of all those things
and still be calm in your heart.
-unknown author

Using the "here and now" strategy is perhaps most important when you are going to sleep. How many times have you laid in your bed and painfully relived the negative events of your past or worried yourself sick over fears of tomorrow. What is real? The Here and Now – your comfy bed, your warm blankets, the breeze from your window, your breathing. Inhale, exhale. This is reality. Here and Now. A new day begins tomorrow, let it be.

Focus on Solutions

Solutions are all around you. The trouble is that when you focus on the problems in your life, the solutions fall to the background. If you focus on what is wrong that is all you will see. You will find yourself saying, "I don't know what to do," or, "this feeling will never go away." If you can shift your thinking from closed (problem focused) to open (solution focused) the answers you need will magically present themselves. The reason for this is that they were always there, but your mind was too closed, too negative, to see them.

So how do you open yourself to solutions?

Peace.

Quiet.

Calm your mind.

If you find yourself spinning, focusing on a problem, going in circles reliving feelings of anger, pain, fear, nervousness, sadness, anxiety then:

- Pause.
- Breathe.
- Silently ask for guidance in seeing the solutions.
- Remain peaceful for as long as you can.

Then ask yourself, "Is there anything I can do about this right now?" If the answer is no, then put it out of your mind. As you move through the day, be aware of people, places, things, suggestions, and ideas that present themselves to you. At night when you lay in your bed, think of how this challenge (don't call it a problem) is allowing you to learn something or is strengthening you in some way. Be aware of positive solutions that present themselves and follow that path to see where it leads you.

Everything will be OK in the end,
If it's not OK, it's not the End
-Unknown author

Surround Yourself with Inspiration

For inspiration, read biographies of the many people who have overcome incredible challenges to find their greatness. Watch documentaries or read about Nelson Mandela, Martin Luther King Jr, Terry Fox, Helen Keller, Ben Carson, Malala Yousafzai, Spenser West and so many more.

Choose to surround yourself with positive, inspiring people, people who live in hope. Surround yourself with positive music, positive events, and positive books.

Wonder

Take time to live in awe and amazement of the world around you. It is too easy to skip over the miracles of life and become too busy. Stop. Breathe. Consider your breath, the air in your lungs, complexity of your brain, the intricate movements of your hands, the stability of your feet, the fragrance of a flower, the seeds inside a fruit, the feathers of a bird's wings. Pause. Wonder, be amazed, be grateful. There are miracles around you and inside of you every second of every day.

Imagine how you would feel sitting beside someone famous. Think of how you would smile and be in awe of them, and feel grateful to be in their presence. The truth is you are in the presence of greatness all the time. Slow down long enough to notice, to be aware. Take time to wonder.

Explore your Faith

Take time to nurture your soul, your spirit. Explore the possibility that there is more to life then what you can see with your eyes. Examine your relationship with the concept of a higher power. Talk to people about their own faith, these discussions can be fascinating. There are so many mysteries to life, how can you not be curious about something bigger then what we can see? When it comes to exploring faith, there is no specific direction, but you may find yourself developing a set of beliefs. Just remember this, everyone has a right to their own beliefs. There is no right or wrong in this area.

Recognize the Value in Others

In the previous chapter, you learned about the *deep truths in you.* It is critical that you understand these are the deep truths for everyone else too. As you learn to rise up and uncover the greatness inside of yourself, it is incredibly important that you acknowledge the greatness inside of everyone else as well, even if they themselves do not yet see it.

Everyone has value, every one of us is important. Every one of us has a journey to make that will reveal to ourselves and to the rest of the world our amazing skills and talents and strengths. Respect yourself and respect all others. Imagine the kind of world we can create when we understand and take action from this place of awareness.

Final Hero Advice: Use Your Powers for Good

The world needs you. I have long believed that we are all here to make the world a better place. By reaching inside and discovering the greatness inside you, you can heal your own pain; you can rise up to overcome your challenges. You Are Your Own Hero.

Once you prove your powers to yourself, then you are in a special position to share your powers with the world. Use your powers for good. Heal yourself, and then help others to learn to heal themselves too. Help others to find their own greatness. Make the world a better place.

I believe this book found its way to you for a reason. You are ready to come alive. You have amazing strengths and powers to overcome obstacles. Bring your perseverance, your determination, your grit. Challenges are presented to you to show you your greatness. Set your goals, and get your work boots on, you now have your toolbox full of strategies. Your journey begins now!

- Believe in yourself
- Believe that life is incredible
- Believe that you can create your own happiness
- Believe in your own journey

Your incredible life lies ahead.
Create it.
You are capable. You are wonderful.
Trust.
Believe.
Be Amazing.

Big Picture Points

- *Your thoughts are powerful. The more you complain, the more things you get to complain about. If you worry, you'll get more things to worry about. If you live in fear, you'll get more things to be afraid of. If you focus on negativity, then negative things will manifest in your life.*

- *If you look on the bright side, at the glass half full, you will manifest more things in your life to feel good about. If you focus on the small joys in life, then more joy will come to you. If you focus on "I can do this," then you will succeed. If you are open to believing in a better life for you, then you will find wonderful opportunities and circumstances that will lead you up higher and higher.*

- *More and more people around the world are coming into awareness of the power of positive thinking. When you come to this place you will realize how much fun life is, how amazing it is to be alive. And you will truly come alive. It is amazing. And every single one of you can make it to this place.*

- *Advice to someone in their darkest hour: Is there a chance that life could get better? Is there a small glimmer of hope somewhere inside that this horrible feeling is temporary? Hold on to that glimmer of hope. Focus your attention on it. If you give your attention to it, it will grow and grow.*

- *Facing Challenges leads to Greatness. If you really want to feel better about yourself, then you have to feel capable in life. In order for you to feel capable, you have to use your strengths. In order to see your strengths, you have to try, again and again. In order to believe in your strengths, you have to achieve something. In order to achieve something, you have to face your challenges. In order to face your challenges, you have to step outside your comfort zone.*

- *Surround yourself with positive, inspiring people, people who live in hope. Surround yourself with positive music, positive movies, positive events, and positive books.*

- *Believe in yourself. Believe that life is incredible. Believe that you can create your own happiness. Believe in your own journey. You have the strength and the power to overcome obstacles. Challenges are presented to you to show you your greatness.*

- *Life is amazing! You are amazing!*

THE END

– or rather,

Your Beginning…

Works Cited

Gray, John. *Men Are from Mars: Women Are from Venus: a Practical Guide for Improving Communication and Getting What You Want in Your Relationships.* HarperCollins Publishers, 1992.

Neufeld, Gordon, and Maté Gabor. *Hold on to Your Kids: Why Parents Need to Matter More than Peers.* Vintage Canada, 2013.

Tolle, Eckhart, and Russell E. DiCarlo. *The Power of Now: A Guide to Spiritual Enlightenment.* Yellow Kite, 2016.

Coming soon from A. Reid-Larade:

Bring Your Own Hope
The Young Citizen's Guide to Building Hope for the Future

The first book in the *BYOH* series, *How to Be Your Own Hero*, is about finding inner strength, inner power. The second book inspires and motivates young citizens to use their powers for good.

Bring Your Own Hope, The Young Citizen's Guide to Building Hope for the Future (BYOH for the Future) was inspired by years of conversations with teens and young citizens in their 20's as they tried to navigate the frustrating aspects of the world they were, and are, inheriting.

It is easy to lose faith in Humanity. It is easy to not care. We want to have hope, but sometimes it can be hard to hold onto it, hard to care, when it seems like the world continually lets you down. *Bring Your Own Hope* will restore your faith in Humanity and raise you up to a point where you will live your life with purpose, coming from a place of Hope.

Many young citizens worry about the future. They worry about the future of humanity, the future of our planet, our future safety, the future of our world economies, the future of jobs, and where we all fit in.

The only thing that can challenge our worries is Hope.
Hope can dismantle our fears and keep our worries in check.
Hope directs our actions towards a brighter collective future.

What do we have to be hopeful about, you may ask? *Bring Your Own Hope* answers that question for young citizens with tangible examples. *BYOH for the Future* takes a big picture look at modern society, looking back at where we've been and looking forward to where we are going. Looking back and acknowledging our ancestors' resilience, we gain deeper faith in our own resilience and we can better appreciate our current civilized lives. This has an immediate effect of calming our worries. From there, we look to the future, following the examples of great changemakers in areas of human rights, environment, energy production, business policies, and many more.

Bring Your Own Hope focuses on the power of everyday people to create positive change. It highlights the value of diversity and each citizens' contributions of their strengths, talents and skills. Along the way, you will also read about some amazing things going on around the world that are not directly visible in our daily lives, but are improving our world, right now. *Bring Your Own Hope* also examines the potential of the human mind, how we can choose and find hope, and how that can shape our future.

This book comes at a critical time in Humanity's story. If most of our citizens remain in a self-limiting mindset of no-hope, then they will continue to carry an "I don't care" attitude. This is extremely dangerous for all of us. *BYOH for the future* builds hope for young citizens in their Teens, 20's, 30's and beyond so we can care enough to purposely pursue positive progress.

You are only as young as the last time
you changed your mind.
This good news book is for young minds of all ages.

Bring Your Own Hope will take you on a journey that will leave you hopeful for the future of humanity and for the world. It will inspire you to use your powers for good.

For more information, visit www.byoh.ca.

Made in the USA
Coppell, TX
19 January 2021

48444475R10198